PENGUIN BOOKS

QUIET

Our lives are driven by a fact that most of us can't name and don't understand. It defines who our friends and lovers are, which careers we choose, and whether we blush when we're embarrassed.

That fact is whether we're an introvert or an extrovert.

The introvert/extrovert divide is the most fundamental dimension of personality. And at least a third of us are on the introverted side. Without introverts we wouldn't have the Apple computer, the theory of relativity or Van Gogh's sunflowers. Yet recently extroverts have taken over. Sensitivity and seriousness are seen as undesirable.

In the international bestseller *Quiet*, Susan Cain shows how the brain chemistry of introverts and extroverts differs, and how society undervalues introverts. She gives introverts the tools to take full advantage of their strengths.

Passionately argued, superbly researched and filled with real stories, *Quiet* will permanently change how you see yourself.

'A vigorous, brainy and highly engaging defence of introversion'
Bookpage

'Cain's intelligence, respect for research and vibrant prose put *Quiet* in an elite class with the best books from Malcolm Gladwell, Daniel Pink and other masters of psychological non-fiction'
Teresa Amabile, Harvard Business School

'*Quiet* legitimizes and even celebrates the "niche" that represents half the people in the world. Think Malcolm Gladwell for people who don't take themselves too seriously'
Guy Kawasaki, author of *Enchantment*

'Superb. Based on meticulous research, *Quiet* is a compelling reflection on how the Extrovert Ideal shapes our lives and why this is deeply unsettling. Cain has written an elegant and powerful plea for introversion. It will open up a new and different conversation on how we need to empower the legions of people who are disposed to be quiet, reflective and sensitive'
Brian Little, Department of Social and Developmental Psychology, Cambridge University

'An intelligent and often surprising look at what makes us who we are' *Booklist*

'An introvert's manifesto – an eloquent call for a new social order. Like the powerful introverts that fill its pages, this book is brilliant, profound, full of feeling and brimming with insights. Those who are quiet, Cain makes clear, have much to say. Read this book and listen'
Sheri Fink, Pulitzer Prize-winning author and journalist

'Brilliant, illuminating, empowering'
Jonathan Fields, author of *Uncertainty: Turning Fear and Doubt Into Fuel for Brilliance*

'Cain gives excellent portraits of a number of introverts and shatters misconceptions. She holds the reader's interest by presenting individual profiles, looking at places dominated by extroverts (Harvard Business School) and introverts (a West Coast retreat), and reporting on the latest studies. Her diligence, research and passion for this important topic has richly paid off' *Publishers Weekly*

'A brilliant, important and personally affecting book'
Christine Kenneally, author of *The First Word*

Quiet

THE POWER OF INTROVERTS
IN A WORLD THAT CAN'T
STOP TALKING

SUSAN CAIN

PENGUIN BOOKS

PENGUIN BOOKS

Published by the Penguin Group
Penguin Books Ltd, 80 Strand, London WC2R ORL, England
Penguin Group (USA), Inc., 375 Hudson Street, New York, New York 10014, USA
Penguin Group (Canada), 90 Eglinton Avenue East, Suite 700, Toronto, Ontario, Canada M4P 2Y3
(a division of Pearson Penguin Canada Inc.)
Penguin Ireland, 25 St Stephen's Green, Dublin 2, Ireland (a division of Penguin Books Ltd)
Penguin Group (Australia), 707 Collins Street, Melbourne, Victoria 3008, Australia
(a division of Pearson Australia Group Pty Ltd)
Penguin Books India Pvt Ltd, 11 Community Centre, Panchsheel Park, New Delhi – 110 017, India
Penguin Group (NZ), 67 Apollo Drive, Rosedale, Auckland 0632, New Zealand
(a division of Pearson New Zealand Ltd)
Penguin Books (South Africa) (Pty) Ltd, Block D, Rosebank Office Park, 181 Jan Smuts Avenue,
Parktown North, Gauteng 2193, South Africa
Penguin Books Ltd, Registered Offices: 80 Strand, London WC2R ORL, England

www.penguin.com

First published in the USA by Crown Publishers, an imprint of the Crown Publishing Group,
a division of Random House, Inc., New York 2012
First published in Great Britain by Viking 2012
Published in Penguin Books 2013

009

Copyright © Susan Cain, 2012

The BIS/BAS Scales on pages 171–2 copyright © 1994 by the American
Psychological Association. Adapted with permission. From 'Behavioral Inhibition,
Behavioral Activation, and Affective Responses to Impending Reward and
Punishment: The BIS/BAS Scales.' *Journal of Personality and Social Psychology* 67(2):
319–33. The use of APA information does not imply endorsement by APA.

Printed in Great Britain by Clays Ltd, St Ives plc

A CIP catalogue record for this book is available from the British Library

ISBN: 978-0-141-02919-1

www.greenpenguin.co.uk

Penguin Books is committed to a sustainable
future for our business, our readers and our planet.
This book is made from Forest Stewardship
Council™ certified paper.

ALWAYS LEARNING   **PEARSON**

To my childhood family

to Grandad   12/18

Merry Christmas, I could imagine you telling me about the subject matter of this book so hopefully you will enjoy reading it too. Also being cheeky because I feel like you can be a fan of the charismatic extrovert when maybe this book will show is not always the best way - let me know! Lots of love,
               Thalia

A species in which everyone was General Patton would not succeed, any more than would a race in which everyone was Vincent van Gogh. I prefer to think that the planet needs athletes, philosophers, sex symbols, painters, scientists; it needs the warmhearted, the hardhearted, the coldhearted, and the weakhearted. It needs those who can devote their lives to studying how many droplets of water are secreted by the salivary glands of dogs under which circumstances, and it needs those who can capture the passing impression of cherry blossoms in a fourteen-syllable poem or devote twenty-five pages to the dissection of a small boy's feelings as he lies in bed in the dark waiting for his mother to kiss him goodnight. . . . Indeed the presence of outstanding strengths presupposes that energy needed in other areas has been channeled away from them.

—ALLEN SHAWN

Contents

Author's Note

I have been working on this book officially since 2005, and unofficially for my entire adult life. I have spoken and written to hundreds, perhaps thousands, of people about the topics covered inside, and have read as many books, scholarly papers, magazine articles, chat-room discussions, and blog posts. Some of these I mention in the book; others informed almost every sentence I wrote. *Quiet* stands on many shoulders, especially the scholars and researchers whose work taught me so much. In a perfect world, I would have named every one of my sources, mentors, and interviewees. But for the sake of readability, some names appear only in the Notes or Acknowledgments.

For similar reasons, I did not use ellipses or brackets in certain quotations but made sure that the extra or missing words did not change the speaker's or writer's meaning. If you would like to quote these written sources from the original, the citations directing you to the full quotations appear in the Notes.

I've changed the names and identifying details of some of the people whose stories I tell, and in the stories of my own work as a lawyer and consultant. To protect the privacy of the participants in Charles di Cagno's public speaking workshop, who did not plan to be included in a book when they signed up for the class, the story of my first evening in class is a composite based on several sessions; so is the story of Greg and Emily, which is based on many interviews with similar couples. Subject to the limitations of memory, all other stories are recounted as they happened or were told to me. I did not fact-check the stories people told me about themselves, but only included those I believed to be true.

Quiet

INTRODUCTION

The North and South of Temperament

Montgomery, Alabama. December 1, 1955. Early evening. A public bus pulls to a stop and a sensibly dressed woman in her forties gets on. She carries herself erectly, despite having spent the day bent over an ironing board in a dingy basement tailor shop at the Montgomery Fair department store. Her feet are swollen, her shoulders ache. She sits in the first row of the Colored section and watches quietly as the bus fills with riders. Until the driver orders her to give her seat to a white passenger.

The woman utters a single word that ignites one of the most important civil rights protests of the twentieth century, one word that helps America find its better self.

The word is "No."

The driver threatens to have her arrested.

"You may do that," says Rosa Parks.

A police officer arrives. He asks Parks why she won't move.

"Why do you all push us around?" she answers simply.

"I don't know," he says. "But the law is the law, and you're under arrest."

On the afternoon of her trial and conviction for disorderly conduct, the Montgomery Improvement Association holds a rally for Parks at the

Holt Street Baptist Church, in the poorest section of town. Five thousand gather to support Parks's lonely act of courage. They squeeze inside the church until its pews can hold no more. The rest wait patiently outside, listening through loudspeakers. The Reverend Martin Luther King Jr. addresses the crowd. "There comes a time that people get tired of being trampled over by the iron feet of oppression," he tells them. "There comes a time when people get tired of being pushed out of the glittering sunlight of life's July and left standing amidst the piercing chill of an Alpine November."

He praises Parks's bravery and hugs her. She stands silently, her mere presence enough to galvanize the crowd. The association launches a citywide bus boycott that lasts 381 days. The people trudge miles to work. They carpool with strangers. They change the course of American history.

I had always imagined Rosa Parks as a stately woman with a bold temperament, someone who could easily stand up to a busload of glowering passengers. But when she died in 2005 at the age of ninety-two, the flood of obituaries recalled her as soft-spoken, sweet, and small in stature. They said she was "timid and shy" but had "the courage of a lion." They were full of phrases like "radical humility" and "quiet fortitude." What does it mean to be quiet *and* have fortitude? these descriptions asked implicitly. How could you be shy *and* courageous?

Parks herself seemed aware of this paradox, calling her autobiography *Quiet Strength*—a title that challenges us to question our assumptions. Why *shouldn't* quiet be strong? And what else can quiet do that we don't give it credit for?

~

Our lives are shaped as profoundly by personality as by gender or race. And the single most important aspect of personality—the "north and south of temperament," as one scientist puts it—is where we fall on the introvert-extrovert spectrum. Our place on this continuum influences our choice of friends and mates, and how we make conversation, resolve differences, and show love. It affects the careers we choose and whether or not we succeed at them. It governs how likely we are to exercise, commit adultery, function well without sleep, learn from our mistakes, place big bets in the stock market, delay gratification, be a good leader, and ask "what if."* It's reflected in our brain pathways, neurotransmitters, and remote corners of our nervous systems. Today introversion and extroversion are two of the most exhaustively researched subjects in personality psychology, arousing the curiosity of hundreds of scientists.

These researchers have made exciting discoveries aided by the latest technology, but they're part of a long and storied tradition. Poets and philosophers have been thinking about introverts and extroverts since the dawn of recorded time. Both personality types appear in the Bible and in the writings of Greek and Roman physicians, and some evolutionary psychologists say that the history of these types reaches back even farther than that: the animal kingdom also boasts "introverts" and "extroverts," as we'll see, from fruit flies to pumpkinseed fish to rhesus monkeys. As with other complementary pairings—masculinity and femininity, East and West, liberal and conservative—humanity would be unrecognizable, and vastly diminished, without both personality styles.

Take the partnership of Rosa Parks and Martin Luther King Jr.: a formidable orator refusing to give up his seat on a segregated bus wouldn't have had the same effect as a modest woman who'd clearly prefer to keep silent but for the exigencies of the situation. And Parks didn't have the stuff to thrill a crowd if she'd tried to stand up and announce that she had a dream. But with King's help, she didn't have to.

Yet today we make room for a remarkably narrow range of personality styles. We're told that to be great is to be bold, to be happy is to be sociable. We see ourselves as a nation of extroverts—which means that we've lost sight of who we really are. Depending on which study you consult, one third to one half of Americans are introverts—in other words,

---

*Answer key: exercise: extroverts; commit adultery: extroverts; function well without sleep: introverts; learn from our mistakes: introverts; place big bets: extroverts; delay gratification: introverts; be a good leader: in some cases introverts, in other cases extroverts, depending on the type of leadership called for; ask "what if": introverts.

one out of every two or three people you know. (Given that the United States is among the most extroverted of nations, the number must be at least as high in other parts of the world.) If you're not an introvert yourself, you are surely raising, managing, married to, or coupled with one.

If these statistics surprise you, that's probably because so many people pretend to be extroverts. Closet introverts pass undetected on playgrounds, in high school locker rooms, and in the corridors of corporate America. Some fool even themselves, until some life event—a layoff, an empty nest, an inheritance that frees them to spend time as they like—jolts them into taking stock of their true natures. You have only to raise the subject of this book with your friends and acquaintances to find that the most unlikely people consider themselves introverts.

It makes sense that so many introverts hide even from themselves. We live with a value system that I call the Extrovert Ideal—the omnipresent belief that the ideal self is gregarious, alpha, and comfortable in the spotlight. The archetypal extrovert prefers action to contemplation, risk-taking to heed-taking, certainty to doubt. He favors quick decisions, even at the risk of being wrong. She works well in teams and socializes in groups. We like to think that we value individuality, but all too often we admire one *type* of individual—the kind who's comfortable "putting himself out there." Sure, we allow technologically gifted loners who launch companies in garages to have any personality they please, but they are the exceptions, not the rule, and our tolerance extends mainly to those who get fabulously wealthy or hold the promise of doing so.

Introversion—along with its cousins sensitivity, seriousness, and shyness—is now a second-class personality trait, somewhere between a disappointment and a pathology. Introverts living under the Extrovert Ideal are like women in a man's world, discounted because of a trait that goes to the core of who they are. Extroversion is an enormously appealing personality style, but we've turned it into an oppressive standard to which most of us feel we must conform.

The Extrovert Ideal has been documented in many studies, though this research has never been grouped under a single name. Talkative people, for example, are rated as smarter, better-looking, more interesting, and more desirable as friends. Velocity of speech counts as well as volume: we rank fast talkers as more competent and likable than slow

1 T 10 F
2 F 11 T
3 F 12 F
4 F 13 T
5 T 14 F   19 F
6 F 15 F   20 T
7 F 16 F   ___
8 F 17 F   7 T
9 T 18 T   13 F

ones. The same dynamics apply in groups, where research shows that the voluble are considered smarter than the reticent—even though there's zero correlation between the gift of gab and good ideas. Even the word *introvert* is stigmatized—one informal study, by psychologist Laurie Helgoe, found that introverts described their own physical appearance in vivid language ("green-blue eyes," "exotic," "high cheekbones"), but when asked to describe generic introverts they drew a bland and distasteful picture ("ungainly," "neutral colors," "skin problems").

But we make a grave mistake to embrace the Extrovert Ideal so unthinkingly. Some of our greatest ideas, art, and inventions—from the theory of evolution to van Gogh's sunflowers to the personal computer—came from quiet and cerebral people who knew how to tune in to their inner worlds and the treasures to be found there. Without introverts, the world would be devoid of:

> the theory of gravity
> the theory of relativity
> W. B. Yeats's "The Second Coming"
> Chopin's nocturnes
> Proust's *In Search of Lost Time*
> Peter Pan
> Orwell's *Nineteen Eighty-Four* and *Animal Farm*
> The Cat in the Hat
> Charlie Brown
> *Schindler's List*, *E.T.*, and *Close Encounters of the Third Kind*
> Google
> Harry Potter*

As the science journalist Winifred Gallagher writes: "The glory of the disposition that stops to consider stimuli rather than rushing to engage with them is its long association with intellectual and artistic achievement. Neither $E=mc^2$ nor *Paradise Lost* was dashed off by a party

* Sir Isaac Newton, Albert Einstein, W. B. Yeats, Frédéric Chopin, Marcel Proust, J. M. Barrie, George Orwell, Theodor Geisel (Dr. Seuss), Charles Schulz, Steven Spielberg, Larry Page, J. K. Rowling.

animal." Even in less obviously introverted occupations, like finance, politics, and activism, some of the greatest leaps forward were made by introverts. In this book we'll see how figures like Eleanor Roosevelt, Al Gore, Warren Buffett, Gandhi—and Rosa Parks—achieved what they did not in spite of but *because of* their introversion.

Yet, as *Quiet* will explore, many of the most important institutions of contemporary life are designed for those who enjoy group projects and high levels of stimulation. As children, our classroom desks are increasingly arranged in pods, the better to foster group learning, and research suggests that the vast majority of teachers believe that the ideal student is an extrovert. We watch TV shows whose protagonists are not the "children next door," like the Cindy Bradys and Beaver Cleavers of yesteryear, but rock stars and webcast hostesses with outsized personalities, like Hannah Montana and Carly Shay of *iCarly*. Even Sid the Science Kid, a PBS-sponsored role model for the preschool set, kicks off each school day by performing dance moves with his pals. ("Check out my moves! I'm a rock star!")

As adults, many of us work for organizations that insist we work in teams, in offices without walls, for supervisors who value "people skills" above all. To advance our careers, we're expected to promote ourselves unabashedly. The scientists whose research gets funded often have confident, perhaps overconfident, personalities. The artists whose work adorns the walls of contemporary museums strike impressive poses at gallery openings. The authors whose books get published—once accepted as a reclusive breed—are now vetted by publicists to make sure they're talk-show ready. (You wouldn't be reading this book if I hadn't convinced my publisher that I was enough of a pseudo-extrovert to promote it.)

If you're an introvert, you also know that the bias against quiet can cause deep psychic pain. As a child you might have overheard your parents apologize for your shyness. ("Why can't you be more like the Kennedy boys?" the Camelot-besotted parents of one man I interviewed repeatedly asked him.) Or at school you might have been prodded to come "out of your shell"—that noxious expression which fails to appreciate that some animals naturally carry shelter everywhere they go, and that some humans are just the same. "All the comments from childhood still ring in my ears, that I was lazy, stupid, slow, boring," writes a member of an e-mail list called Introvert Retreat. "By the time I was old enough to figure out that I was simply introverted, it was a part of my being, the assumption that there is something inherently wrong with me. I wish I could find that little vestige of doubt and remove it."

Now that you're an adult, you might still feel a pang of guilt when you decline a dinner invitation in favor of a good book. Or maybe you like to eat alone in restaurants and could do without the pitying looks from fellow diners. Or you're told that you're "in your head too much," a phrase that's often deployed against the quiet and cerebral.

Of course, there's another word for such people: thinkers.

~

I have seen firsthand how difficult it is for introverts to take stock of their own talents, and how powerful it is when finally they do. For more than ten years I trained people of all stripes—corporate lawyers and college students, hedge-fund managers and married couples—in negotiation skills. Of course, we covered the basics: how to prepare for a negotiation, when to make the first offer, and what to do when the other person says "take it or leave it." But I also helped clients figure out their natural personalities and how to make the most of them.

My very first client was a young woman named Laura. She was a Wall Street lawyer, but a quiet and daydreamy one who dreaded the spotlight and disliked aggression. She had managed somehow to make it through the crucible of Harvard Law School—a place where classes are conducted in huge, gladiatorial amphitheaters, and where she once got so nervous that she threw up on the way to class. Now that she was in the real world, she wasn't sure she could represent her clients as forcefully as they expected.

For the first three years on the job, Laura was so junior that she never had to test this premise. But one day the senior lawyer she'd been working with went on vacation, leaving her in charge of an important negotiation. The client was a South American manufacturing company that was about to default on a bank loan and hoped to renegotiate its terms;

a syndicate of bankers that owned the endangered loan sat on the other side of the negotiating table.

Laura would have preferred to hide under said table, but she was accustomed to fighting such impulses. Gamely but nervously, she took her spot in the lead chair, flanked by her clients: general counsel on one side and senior financial officer on the other. These happened to be Laura's favorite clients: gracious and soft-spoken, very different from the master-of-the-universe types her firm usually represented. In the past, Laura had taken the general counsel to a Yankees game and the financial officer shopping for a handbag for her sister. But now these cozy outings—just the kind of socializing Laura enjoyed—seemed a world away. Across the table sat nine disgruntled investment bankers in tailored suits and expensive shoes, accompanied by their lawyer, a square-jawed woman with a hearty manner. Clearly not the self-doubting type, this woman launched into an impressive speech on how Laura's clients would be lucky simply to accept the bankers' terms. It was, she said, a very magnanimous offer.

Everyone waited for Laura to reply, but she couldn't think of anything to say. So she just sat there. Blinking. All eyes on her. Her clients shifting uneasily in their seats. Her thoughts running in a familiar loop: *I'm too quiet for this kind of thing, too unassuming, too cerebral.* She imagined the person who would be better equipped to save the day: someone bold, smooth, ready to pound the table. In middle school this person, unlike Laura, would have been called "outgoing," the highest accolade her seventh-grade classmates knew, higher even than "pretty," for a girl, or "athletic," for a guy. Laura promised herself that she only had to make it through the day. Tomorrow she would go look for another career.

Then she remembered what I'd told her again and again: she was an introvert, and as such she had unique powers in negotiation—perhaps less obvious but no less formidable. She'd probably prepared more than everyone else. She had a quiet but firm speaking style. She rarely spoke without thinking. Being mild-mannered, she could take strong, even aggressive, positions while coming across as perfectly reasonable. And she tended to ask questions—lots of them—and actually listen to the answers, which, no matter what your personality, is crucial to strong negotiation.

So Laura finally started doing what came naturally.

"Let's go back a step. What are your numbers based on?" she asked.

"What if we structured the loan this way, do you think it might work?"

"That way?"

"Some other way?"

At first her questions were tentative. She picked up steam as she went along, posing them more forcefully and making it clear that she'd done her homework and wouldn't concede the facts. But she also stayed true to her own style, never raising her voice or losing her decorum. Every time the bankers made an assertion that seemed unbudgeable, Laura tried to be constructive. "Are you saying that's the only way to go? What if we took a different approach?"

Eventually her simple queries shifted the mood in the room, just as the negotiation textbooks say they will. The bankers stopped speechifying and dominance-posing, activities for which Laura felt hopelessly ill-equipped, and they started having an actual conversation.

More discussion. Still no agreement. One of the bankers revved up again, throwing his papers down and storming out of the room. Laura ignored this display, mostly because she didn't know what else to do. Later on someone told her that at that pivotal moment she'd played a good game of something called "negotiation jujitsu"; but she knew that she was just doing what you learn to do naturally as a quiet person in a loudmouth world.

Finally the two sides struck a deal. The bankers left the building, Laura's favorite clients headed for the airport, and Laura went home, curled up with a book, and tried to forget the day's tensions.

But the next morning, the lead lawyer for the bankers—the vigorous woman with the strong jaw—called to offer her a job. "I've never seen anyone so nice and so tough at the same time," she said. And the day after that, the lead banker called Laura, asking if *her* law firm would represent *his* company in the future. "We need someone who can help us put deals together without letting ego get in the way," he said.

By sticking to her own gentle way of doing things, Laura had reeled in new business for her firm and a job offer for herself. Raising her voice and pounding the table was unnecessary.

Today Laura understands that her introversion is an essential part of who she is, and she embraces her reflective nature. The loop inside her head that accused her of being too quiet and unassuming plays much less often. Laura knows that she can hold her own when she needs to.

~

What exactly do I mean when I say that Laura is an *introvert*? When I started writing this book, the first thing I wanted to find out was precisely how researchers define introversion and extroversion. I knew that in 1921 the influential psychologist Carl Jung had published a bombshell of a book, *Psychological Types*, popularizing the terms *introvert* and *extrovert* as the central building blocks of personality. Introverts are drawn to the inner world of thought and feeling, said Jung, extroverts to the external life of people and activities. Introverts focus on the meaning they make of the events swirling around them; extroverts plunge into the events themselves. Introverts recharge their batteries by being alone; extroverts need to recharge when they don't socialize enough. If you've ever taken a Myers-Briggs personality test, which is based on Jung's thinking and used by the majority of universities and Fortune 100 companies, then you may already be familiar with these ideas.

But what do contemporary researchers have to say? I soon discovered that there is no all-purpose definition of introversion or extroversion; these are not unitary categories, like "curly-haired" or "sixteen-year-old," in which everyone can agree on who qualifies for inclusion. For example, adherents of the Big Five school of personality psychology (which argues that human personality can be boiled down to five primary traits) define introversion not in terms of a rich inner life but as a lack of qualities such as assertiveness and sociability. There are almost as many definitions of *introvert* and *extrovert* as there are personality psychologists, who spend a great deal of time arguing over which meaning is most accurate. Some think that Jung's ideas are outdated; others swear that he's the only one who got it right.

Still, today's psychologists tend to agree on several important points:

for example, that introverts and extroverts differ in the level of outside stimulation that they need to function well. Introverts feel "just right" with less stimulation, as when they sip wine with a close friend, solve a crossword puzzle, or read a book. Extroverts enjoy the extra bang that comes from activities like meeting new people, skiing slippery slopes, and cranking up the stereo. "Other people are very arousing," says the personality psychologist David Winter, explaining why your typical introvert would rather spend her vacation reading on the beach than partying on a cruise ship. "They arouse threat, fear, flight, and love. A hundred people are very stimulating compared to a hundred books or a hundred grains of sand."

Many psychologists would also agree that introverts and extroverts work differently. Extroverts tend to tackle assignments quickly. They make fast (sometimes rash) decisions, and are comfortable multitasking and risk-taking. They enjoy "the thrill of the chase" for rewards like money and status.

Introverts often work more slowly and deliberately. They like to focus on one task at a time and can have mighty powers of concentration. They're relatively immune to the lures of wealth and fame.

Our personalities also shape our social styles. Extroverts are the people who will add life to your dinner party and laugh generously at your jokes. They tend to be assertive, dominant, and in great need of company. Extroverts think out loud and on their feet; they prefer talking to listening, rarely find themselves at a loss for words, and occasionally blurt out things they never meant to say. They're comfortable with conflict, but not with solitude.

Introverts, in contrast, may have strong social skills and enjoy parties and business meetings, but after a while wish they were home in their pajamas. They prefer to devote their social energies to close friends, colleagues, and family. They listen more than they talk, think before they speak, and often feel as if they express themselves better in writing than in conversation. They tend to dislike conflict. Many have a horror of small talk, but enjoy deep discussions.

A few things introverts are not: The word *introvert* is not a synonym for hermit or misanthrope. Introverts *can* be these things, but most are perfectly friendly. One of the most humane phrases in the English language—"Only connect!"—was written by the distinctly introverted E. M. Forster in a novel exploring the question of how to achieve "human love at its height."

Nor are introverts necessarily shy. Shyness is the fear of social disapproval or humiliation, while introversion is a preference for environments that are not overstimulating. Shyness is inherently painful; introversion is not. One reason that people confuse the two concepts is that they sometimes overlap (though psychologists debate to what degree). Some psychologists map the two tendencies on vertical and horizontal axes, with the introvert-extrovert spectrum on the horizontal axis, and the anxious-stable spectrum on the vertical. With this model, you end up with four quadrants of personality types: calm extroverts, anxious (or impulsive) extroverts, calm introverts, and anxious introverts. In other words, you can be a shy extrovert, like Barbra Streisand, who has a larger-than-life personality and paralyzing stage fright; or a non-shy introvert, like Bill Gates, who by all accounts keeps to himself but is unfazed by the opinions of others.

You can also, of course, be both shy *and* an introvert: T. S. Eliot was a famously private soul who wrote in "The Waste Land" that he could "show you fear in a handful of dust." Many shy people turn inward, partly as a refuge from the socializing that causes them such anxiety. And many introverts are shy, partly as a result of receiving the message that there's something wrong with their preference for reflection, and partly because their physiologies, as we'll see, compel them to withdraw from high-stimulation environments.

But for all their differences, shyness and introversion have in common something profound. The mental state of a shy extrovert sitting quietly in a business meeting may be very different from that of a calm introvert—the shy person is afraid to speak up, while the introvert is simply overstimulated—but to the outside world, the two appear to be the same. This can give both types insight into how our reverence for alpha status blinds us to things that are good and smart and wise. For very different reasons, shy and introverted people might choose to spend their days in behind-the-scenes pursuits like inventing, or researching, or holding the hands of the gravely ill—or in leadership positions they execute with quiet competence. These are not alpha roles, but the people who play them are role models all the same.

~

If you're still not sure where you fall on the introvert-extrovert spectrum, you can assess yourself here. Answer each question "true" or "false," choosing the answer that applies to you more often than not.*

1. _____ I prefer one-on-one conversations to group activities.
2. _____ I often prefer to express myself in writing.
3. _____ I enjoy solitude.
4. _____ I seem to care less than my peers about wealth, fame, and status.
5. _____ I dislike small talk, but I enjoy talking in depth about topics that matter to me.
6. _____ People tell me that I'm a good listener.
7. _____ I'm not a big risk-taker.
8. _____ I enjoy work that allows me to "dive in" with few interruptions.
9. _____ I like to celebrate birthdays on a small scale, with only one or two close friends or family members.
10. _____ People describe me as "soft-spoken" or "mellow."
11. _____ I prefer not to show or discuss my work with others until it's finished.
12. _____ I dislike conflict.
13. _____ I do my best work on my own.
14. _____ I tend to think before I speak.
15. _____ I feel drained after being out and about, even if I've enjoyed myself.
16. _____ I often let calls go through to voice mail.

* This is an informal quiz, not a scientifically validated personality test. The questions were formulated based on characteristics of introversion often accepted by contemporary researchers.

17. _____ If I had to choose, I'd prefer a weekend with absolutely nothing to do to one with too many things scheduled.

18. _____ I don't enjoy multitasking.

19. _____ I can concentrate easily.

20. _____ In classroom situations, I prefer lectures to seminars.

The more often you answered "true," the more introverted you probably are. If you found yourself with a roughly equal number of "true" and "false" answers, then you may be an ambivert—yes, there really is such a word.

But even if you answered every single question as an introvert or extrovert, that doesn't mean that your behavior is predictable across all circumstances. We can't say that every introvert is a bookworm or every extrovert wears lampshades at parties any more than we can say that every woman is a natural consensus-builder and every man loves contact sports. As Jung felicitously put it, "There is no such thing as a pure extrovert or a pure introvert. Such a man would be in the lunatic asylum."

This is partly because we are all gloriously complex individuals, but also because there are so many different *kinds* of introverts and extroverts. Introversion and extroversion interact with our other personality traits and personal histories, producing wildly different kinds of people. So if you're an artistic American guy whose father wished you'd try out for the football team like your rough-and-tumble brothers, you'll be a very different kind of introvert from, say, a Finnish businesswoman whose parents were lighthouse keepers. (Finland is a famously introverted nation. Finnish joke: How can you tell if a Finn likes you? He's staring at your shoes instead of his own.)

Many introverts are also "highly sensitive," which sounds poetic, but is actually a technical term in psychology. If you are a sensitive sort, then you're more apt than the average person to feel pleasantly overwhelmed by Beethoven's "Moonlight Sonata" or a well-turned phrase or an act of extraordinary kindness. You may be quicker than others to feel sickened by violence and ugliness, and you likely have a very strong conscience. When you were a child you were probably called "shy," and to this day feel nervous when you're being evaluated, for example when giving a speech or on a first date. Later we'll examine why this seemingly unrelated collection of attributes tends to belong to the same person and why this person is often introverted. (No one knows exactly how many introverts are highly sensitive, but we know that 70 percent of sensitives are introverts, and the other 30 percent tend to report needing a lot of "down time.")

All of this complexity means that not everything you read in *Quiet* will apply to you, even if you consider yourself a true-blue introvert. For one thing, we'll spend some time talking about shyness and sensitivity, while you might have neither of these traits. That's OK. Take what applies to you, and use the rest to improve your relationships with others.

Having said all this, in *Quiet* we'll try not to get too hung up on definitions. Strictly defining terms is vital for researchers whose studies depend on pinpointing exactly where introversion stops and other traits, like shyness, start. But in *Quiet* we'll concern ourselves more with the *fruit* of that research. Today's psychologists, joined by neuroscientists with their brain-scanning machines, have unearthed illuminating insights that are changing the way we see the world—and ourselves. They are answering questions such as: Why are some people talkative while others measure their words? Why do some people burrow into their work and others organize office birthday parties? Why are some people comfortable wielding authority while others prefer neither to lead nor to be led? *Can* introverts be leaders? Is our cultural preference for extroversion in the natural order of things, or is it socially determined? From an evolutionary perspective, introversion must have survived as a personality trait for a reason—so what might the reason be? If you're an introvert, should you devote your energies to activities that come naturally, or should you stretch yourself, as Laura did that day at the negotiation table?

The answers might surprise you.

If there is only one insight you take away from this book, though, I hope it's a newfound sense of entitlement to be yourself. I can vouch personally for the life-transforming effects of this outlook. Remember that first client I told you about, the one I called Laura in order to protect her identity?

That was a story about me. I was my own first client.

Part

One

THE EXTROVERT IDEAL

1

THE RISE OF THE "MIGHTY LIKEABLE FELLOW"

How Extroversion Became the Cultural Ideal

Strangers' eyes, keen and critical.
Can you meet them proudly—confidently—without fear?
—PRINT ADVERTISEMENT FOR WOODBURY'S SOAP, 1922

The date: 1902. The place: Harmony Church, Missouri, a tiny, dot-on-the-map town located on a floodplain a hundred miles from Kansas City. Our young protagonist: a good-natured but insecure high school student named Dale.

Skinny, unathletic, and fretful, Dale is the son of a morally upright but perpetually bankrupt pig farmer. He respects his parents but dreads following in their poverty-stricken footsteps. Dale worries about other things, too: thunder and lightning, going to hell, and being tongue-tied at crucial moments. He even fears his wedding day: What if he can't think of anything to say to his future bride?

One day a Chautauqua speaker comes to town. The Chautauqua movement, born in 1873 and based in upstate New York, sends gifted speakers across the country to lecture on literature, science, and religion. Rural Americans prize these presenters for the whiff of glamour they bring from the outside world—and their power to mesmerize an audience. This particular speaker captivates the young Dale with his own rags-to-riches tale: once he'd been a lowly farm boy with a bleak future, but he developed a charismatic speaking style and took the stage at Chautauqua. Dale hangs on his every word.

A few years later, Dale is again impressed by the value of public speaking. His family moves to a farm three miles outside of Warrensburg, Missouri, so he can attend college there without paying room and board. Dale observes that the students who win campus speaking contests are seen as leaders, and he resolves to be one of them. He signs up for every contest and rushes home at night to practice. Again and again he loses; Dale is dogged, but not much of an orator. Eventually, though, his efforts begin to pay off. He transforms himself into a speaking champion and campus hero. Other students turn to him for speech lessons; he trains them and they start winning, too.

By the time Dale leaves college in 1908, his parents are still poor, but corporate America is booming. Henry Ford is selling Model Ts like griddle cakes, using the slogan "for business and for pleasure." J.C. Penney, Woolworth, and Sears Roebuck have become household names. Electricity lights up the homes of the middle class; indoor plumbing spares them midnight trips to the outhouse.

The new economy calls for a new kind of man—a salesman, a social operator, someone with a ready smile, a masterful handshake, and the ability to get along with colleagues while simultaneously outshining them. Dale joins the swelling ranks of salesmen, heading out on the road with few possessions but his silver tongue.

Dale's last name is Carnegie (Carnagey, actually; he changes the spelling later, likely to evoke Andrew, the great industrialist). After a few grueling years selling beef for Armour and Company, he sets up shop as a public-speaking teacher. Carnegie holds his first class at a YMCA night school on 125th Street in New York City. He asks for the usual two-dollars-per-session salary for night school teachers. The Y's director, doubting that a public-speaking class will generate much interest, refuses to pay that kind of money.

But the class is an overnight sensation, and Carnegie goes on to found the Dale Carnegie Institute, dedicated to helping businessmen root out the very insecurities that had held him back as a young man. In 1913 he publishes his first book, *Public Speaking and Influencing Men in Business*. "In the days when pianos and bathrooms were luxuries," Carnegie writes, "men regarded ability in speaking as a peculiar gift, needed only by the lawyer, clergyman, or statesman. Today we have come to realize that it is the indispensable weapon of those who would forge ahead in the keen competition of business."

~

Carnegie's metamorphosis from farmboy to salesman to public-speaking icon is also the story of the rise of the Extrovert Ideal. Carnegie's journey reflected a cultural evolution that reached a tipping point around the turn of the twentieth century, changing forever who we are and whom we admire, how we act at job interviews and what we look for in an employee, how we court our mates and raise our children. America had shifted from what the influential cultural historian Warren Susman called a Culture of Character to a Culture of Personality—and opened up a Pandora's Box of personal anxieties from which we would never quite recover.

In the Culture of Character, the ideal self was serious, disciplined, and honorable. What counted was not so much the impression one made in public as how one behaved in private. The word *personality* didn't exist in English until the eighteenth century, and the idea of "having a good personality" was not widespread until the twentieth.

But when they embraced the Culture of Personality, Americans started to focus on how others perceived them. They became captivated by people who were bold and entertaining. "The social role demanded of all in the new Culture of Personality was that of a performer," Susman famously wrote. "Every American was to become a performing self."

The rise of industrial America was a major force behind this cultural evolution. The nation quickly developed from an agricultural society of little houses on the prairie to an urbanized, "the business of America is business" powerhouse. In the country's early days, most Americans lived like Dale Carnegie's family, on farms or in small towns, interacting with people they'd known since childhood. But when the twentieth century arrived, a perfect storm of big business, urbanization, and mass immigration blew the population into the cities. In 1790, only 3 percent of Americans lived in cities; in 1840, only 8 percent did; by 1920, more than a third of the country were urbanites. "We cannot all live in cities," wrote the news editor Horace Greeley in 1867, "yet nearly all seem determined to do so."

Americans found themselves working no longer with neighbors but with strangers. "Citizens" morphed into "employees," facing the question of how to make a good impression on people to whom they had no civic or family ties. "The reasons why one man gained a promotion or one woman suffered a social snub," writes the historian Roland Marchand, "had become less explicable on grounds of long-standing favoritism or old family feuds. In the increasingly anonymous business and social relationships of the age, one might suspect that anything—including a first impression—had made the crucial difference." Americans responded to these pressures by trying to become salesmen who could sell not only their company's latest gizmo but also themselves.

One of the most powerful lenses through which to view the transformation from Character to Personality is the self-help tradition in which Dale Carnegie played such a prominent role. Self-help books have always loomed large in the American psyche. Many of the earliest conduct guides were religious parables, like *The Pilgrim's Progress*, published in 1678, which warned readers to behave with restraint if they wanted to make it into heaven. The advice manuals of the nineteenth century were less religious but still preached the value of a noble character. They featured case studies of historical heroes like Abraham Lincoln, revered not only as a gifted communicator but also as a modest man who did not, as Ralph Waldo Emerson put it, "offend by superiority." They also celebrated regular people who lived highly moral lives. A popular 1899 manual called *Character: The Grandest Thing in the World* featured a timid shop girl who gave away her meager earnings to a freezing beggar, then rushed off before anyone could see what she'd done. Her virtue, the reader understood, derived not only from her generosity but also from her wish to remain anonymous.

But by 1920, popular self-help guides had changed their focus from inner virtue to outer charm—"to know *what* to say and *how* to say it," as one manual put it. "To create a personality is power," advised another.

"Try in every way to have a ready command of the manners which make people think 'he's a mighty likeable fellow,'" said a third. "That is the beginning of a reputation for personality." *Success* magazine and *The Saturday Evening Post* introduced departments instructing readers on the art of conversation. The same author, Orison Swett Marden, who wrote *Character: The Grandest Thing in the World* in 1899, produced another popular title in 1921. It was called *Masterful Personality*.

Many of these guides were written for businessmen, but women were also urged to work on a mysterious quality called "fascination." Coming of age in the 1920s was such a competitive business compared to what their grandmothers had experienced, warned one beauty guide, that they had to be visibly charismatic: "People who pass us on the street can't know that we're clever and charming unless we look it."

Such advice—ostensibly meant to improve people's lives—must have made even reasonably confident people uneasy. Susman counted the words that appeared most frequently in the personality-driven advice manuals of the early twentieth century and compared them to the character guides of the nineteenth century. The earlier guides emphasized attributes that anyone could work on improving, described by words like

> Citizenship
> Duty
> Work
> Golden deeds
> Honor
> Reputation
> Morals
> Manners
> Integrity

But the new guides celebrated qualities that were—no matter how easy Dale Carnegie made it sound—trickier to acquire. Either you embodied these qualities or you didn't:

> Magnetic
> Fascinating

Stunning

Attractive

Glowing

Dominant

Forceful

Energetic

It was no coincidence that in the 1920s and the 1930s, Americans became obsessed with movie stars. Who better than a matinee idol to model personal magnetism?

~

Americans also received advice on self-presentation—whether they liked it or not—from the advertising industry. While early print ads were straightforward product announcements ("EATON'S HIGHLAND LINEN: THE FRESHEST AND CLEANEST WRITING PAPER"), the new personality-driven ads cast consumers as performers with stage fright from which only the advertiser's product might rescue them. These ads focused obsessively on the hostile glare of the public spotlight. "ALL AROUND YOU PEOPLE ARE JUDGING YOU SILENTLY," warned a 1922 ad for Woodbury's soap. "CRITICAL EYES ARE SIZING YOU UP RIGHT NOW," advised the Williams Shaving Cream company.

Madison Avenue spoke directly to the anxieties of male salesmen and middle managers. In one ad for Dr. West's toothbrushes, a prosperous-looking fellow sat behind a desk, his arm cocked confidently behind his hip, asking whether you've "EVER TRIED SELLING *YOURSELF* TO *YOU? A* FAVORABLE FIRST IMPRESSION IS THE GREATEST SINGLE FACTOR IN BUSINESS OR SOCIAL SUCCESS." The Williams Shaving Cream ad featured a slick-haired, mustachioed man urging readers to "LET YOUR FACE REFLECT CONFIDENCE, NOT WORRY! IT'S THE 'LOOK' OF YOU BY WHICH YOU ARE JUDGED MOST OFTEN."

Other ads reminded women that their success in the dating game

depended not only on looks but also on personality. In 1921 a Woodbury's soap ad showed a crestfallen young woman, home alone after a
disappointing evening out. She had "longed to be successful, gay, triumphant," the text sympathized. But without the help of the right soap, the
woman was a social failure.

Ten years later, Lux laundry detergent ran a print ad featuring a
plaintive letter written to Dorothy Dix, the Dear Abby of her day. "Dear
Miss Dix," read the letter, "How can I make myself more popular? I am
fairly pretty and not a dumbbell, but I am so timid and self-conscious
with people. I'm always sure they're not going to like me. . . . —Joan G."

Miss Dix's answer came back clear and firm. If only Joan would use
Lux detergent on her lingerie, curtains, and sofa cushions, she would
soon gain a "deep, sure, inner conviction of being charming."

This portrayal of courtship as a high-stakes performance reflected the
bold new mores of the Culture of Personality. Under the restrictive (in
some cases repressive) social codes of the Culture of Character, both genders displayed some reserve when it came to the mating dance. Women
who were too loud or made inappropriate eye contact with strangers
were considered brazen. Upper-class women had more license to speak
than did their lower-class counterparts, and indeed were judged partly
on their talent for witty repartee, but even they were advised to display
blushes and downcast eyes. They were warned by conduct manuals that
"the coldest reserve" was "more admirable in a woman a man wishe[d] to
make his wife than the least approach to undue familiarity." Men could
adopt a quiet demeanor that implied self-possession and a power that
didn't need to flaunt itself. Though shyness per se was unacceptable, reserve was a mark of good breeding.

But with the advent of the Culture of Personality, the value of for-
mality began to crumble, for women and men alike. Instead of paying
ceremonial calls on women and making serious declarations of intention, men were now expected to launch verbally sophisticated courtships
in which they threw women "a line" of elaborate flirtatiousness. Men
who were too quiet around women risked being thought gay; as a popular
1926 sex guide observed, "homosexuals are invariably timid, shy, retiring." Women, too, were expected to walk a fine line between propriety

and boldness. If they responded too shyly to romantic overtures, they were sometimes called "frigid."

The field of psychology also began to grapple with the pressure to project confidence. In the 1920s an influential psychologist named Gordon Allport created a diagnostic test of "Ascendance-Submission" to measure social dominance. "Our current civilization," observed Allport, who was himself shy and reserved, "seems to place a premium upon the aggressive person, the 'go-getter.'" In 1921, Carl Jung noted the newly precarious status of introversion. Jung himself saw introverts as "educators and promoters of culture" who showed the value of "the interior life which is so painfully wanting in our civilization." But he acknowledged that their "reserve and apparently groundless embarrassment naturally arouse all the current prejudices against this type."

But nowhere was the need to appear self-assured more apparent than in a new concept in psychology called the inferiority complex. The IC, as it became known in the popular press, was developed in the 1920s by a Viennese psychologist named Alfred Adler to describe feelings of inadequacy and their consequences. "Do you feel insecure?" inquired the cover of Adler's best-selling book, *Understanding Human Nature*. "Are you fainthearted? Are you submissive?" Adler explained that all infants and small children feel inferior, living as they do in a world of adults and older siblings. In the normal process of growing up they learn to direct these feelings into pursuing their goals. But if things go awry as they mature, they might be saddled with the dreaded IC—a grave liability in an increasingly competitive society.

The idea of wrapping their social anxieties in the neat package of a psychological complex appealed to many Americans. The Inferiority Complex became an all-purpose explanation for problems in many areas of life, ranging from love to parenting to career. In 1924, *Collier's* ran a story about a woman who was afraid to marry the man she loved for fear that he had an IC and would never amount to anything. Another popular magazine ran an article called "Your Child and That Fashionable Complex," explaining to moms what could cause an IC in kids and how to prevent or cure one. *Everyone* had an IC, it seemed; to some it was, paradoxically enough, a mark of distinction. Lincoln, Napoleon, Teddy Roosevelt, Edison, and Shakespeare—all had suffered from ICs, according to a 1939 *Collier's* article. "So," concluded the magazine, "if you have a big, husky, in-growing inferiority complex you're about as lucky as you could hope to be, provided you have the backbone along with it."

Despite the hopeful tone of this piece, child guidance experts of the 1920s set about helping children to develop winning personalities. Until then, these professionals had worried mainly about sexually precocious girls and delinquent boys, but now psychologists, social workers, and doctors focused on the everyday child with the "maladjusted personality"—particularly shy children. Shyness could lead to dire outcomes, they warned, from alcoholism to suicide, while an outgoing personality would bring social and financial success. The experts advised parents to socialize their children well and schools to change their emphasis from book-learning to "assisting and guiding the developing personality." Educators took up this mantle enthusiastically. By 1950 the slogan of the Mid-Century White House Conference on Children and Youth was "A healthy personality for every child."

Well-meaning parents of the midcentury agreed that quiet was unacceptable and gregariousness ideal for both girls and boys. Some discouraged their children from solitary and serious hobbies, like classical music, that could make them unpopular. They sent their kids to school at increasingly young ages, where the main assignment was learning to socialize. Introverted children were often singled out as problem cases (a situation familiar to anyone with an introverted child today).

William Whyte's *The Organization Man*, a 1956 best-seller, describes how parents and teachers conspired to overhaul the personalities of quiet children. "Johnny wasn't doing so well at school," Whyte recalls a mother telling him. "The teacher explained to me that he was doing fine on his lessons but that his social adjustment was not as good as it might be. He would pick just one or two friends to play with, and sometimes he was happy to remain by himself." Parents welcomed such interventions, said Whyte. "Save for a few odd parents, most are grateful that the schools work so hard to offset tendencies to introversion and other suburban abnormalities."

Parents caught up in this value system were not unkind, or even obtuse; they were only preparing their kids for the "real world." When these children grew older and applied to college and later for their first jobs, they faced the same standards of gregariousness. University admissions officers looked not for the most exceptional candidates, but for the most extroverted. Harvard's provost Paul Buck declared in the late 1940s that Harvard should reject the "sensitive, neurotic" type and the "intellectually over-stimulated" in favor of boys of the "healthy extrovert kind." In 1950, Yale's president, Alfred Whitney Griswold, declared that the ideal Yalie was not a "beetle-browed, highly specialized intellectual, but a well-rounded man." Another dean told Whyte that "in screening applications from secondary schools he felt it was only common sense to take into account not only what the college wanted, but what, four years later, corporations' recruiters would want. 'They like a pretty gregarious, active type,' he said. 'So we find that the best man is the one who's had an 80 or 85 average in school and plenty of extracurricular activity. We see little use for the "brilliant" introvert.'"

This college dean grasped very well that the model employee of the midcentury—even one whose job rarely involved dealing with the public, like a research scientist in a corporate lab—was not a deep thinker but a hearty extrovert with a salesman's personality. "Customarily, whenever the word brilliant is used," explains Whyte, "it either precedes the word 'but' (e.g., 'We are all for brilliance, but . . .') or is coupled with such words as erratic, eccentric, introvert, screwball, etc." "These fellows will be having contact with other people in the organization," said one 1950s executive about the hapless scientists in his employ, "and it helps if they make a good impression."

The scientist's job was not only to do the research but also to help sell it, and that required a hail-fellow-well-met demeanor. At IBM, a corporation that embodied the ideal of the company man, the sales force gathered each morning to belt out the company anthem, "Ever Onward," and to harmonize on the "Selling IBM" song, set to the tune of "Singin' in the Rain." "Selling IBM," it began, "we're selling IBM. What a glorious feeling, the world is our friend." The ditty built to a stirring close: "We're always in trim, we work with a vim. We're selling, just selling, IBM."

Then they went off to pay their sales calls, proving that the admissions people at Harvard and Yale were probably right: only a certain type of fellow could possibly have been interested in kicking off his mornings this way.

The rest of the organization men would have to manage as best they could. And if the history of pharmaceutical consumption is any indication, many buckled under such pressures. In 1955 a drug company named Carter-Wallace released the anti-anxiety drug Miltown, reframing anxiety as the natural product of a society that was both dog-eat-dog and relentlessly social. Miltown was marketed to men and immediately became the fastest-selling pharmaceutical in American history, according to the social historian Andrea Tone. By 1956 one of every twenty Americans had tried it; by 1960 a third of all prescriptions from U.S. doctors were for Miltown or a similar drug called Equanil. "ANXIETY AND TENSION ARE THE COMMONPLACE OF THE AGE," read the Equanil ad. The 1960s tranquilizer Serentil followed with an ad campaign even more direct in its appeal to improve social performance. "FOR THE ANXIETY THAT COMES FROM NOT FITTING IN," it empathized.

~

Of course, the Extrovert Ideal is not a modern invention. Extroversion is in our DNA—literally, according to some psychologists. The trait has been found to be less prevalent in Asia and Africa than in Europe and America, whose populations descend largely from the migrants of the world. It makes sense, say these researchers, that world travelers were more extroverted than those who stayed home—and that they passed on their traits to their children and their children's children. "As personality traits are genetically transmitted," writes the psychologist Kenneth Olson, "each succeeding wave of emigrants to a new continent would give rise over time to a population of more engaged individuals than reside in the emigrants' continent of origin."

We can also trace our admiration of extroverts to the Greeks, for whom oratory was an exalted skill, and to the Romans, for whom the worst possible punishment was banishment from the city, with its teeming social life. Similarly, we revere our founding fathers precisely because they were loudmouths on the subject of freedom: *Give me liberty or give me death!* Even the Christianity of early American religious revivals, dating back to the First Great Awakening of the eighteenth century, depended on the showmanship of ministers who were considered successful if they caused crowds of normally reserved people to weep and shout and generally lose their decorum. "Nothing gives me more pain and distress than to see a minister standing almost motionless, coldly plodding on as a mathematician would calculate the distance of the Moon from the Earth," complained a religious newspaper in 1837.

As this disdain suggests, early Americans revered action and were suspicious of intellect, associating the life of the mind with the languid, ineffectual European aristocracy they had left behind. The 1828 presidential campaign pitted a former Harvard professor, John Quincy Adams, against Andrew Jackson, a forceful military hero. A Jackson campaign slogan tellingly distinguished the two: "John Quincy Adams who can write / And Andrew Jackson who can fight."

The victor of that campaign? The fighter beat the writer, as the cultural historian Neal Gabler puts it. (John Quincy Adams, incidentally, is considered by political psychologists to be one of the few introverts in presidential history.)

But the rise of the Culture of Personality intensified such biases, and applied them not only to political and religious leaders, but also to regular people. And though soap manufacturers may have profited from the new emphasis on charm and charisma, not everyone was pleased with this development. "Respect for individual human personality has with us reached its lowest point," observed one intellectual in 1921, "and it is delightfully ironical that no nation is so constantly talking about personality as we are. We actually have schools for 'self-expression' and 'self-development,' although we seem usually to mean the expression and development of the personality of a successful real estate agent."

Another critic bemoaned the slavish attention Americans were starting to pay to entertainers: "It is remarkable how much attention the stage and things pertaining to it are receiving nowadays from the magazines," he grumbled. Only twenty years earlier—during the Culture of Character, that is—such topics would have been considered indecorous;

now they had become "such a large part of the life of society that it has become a topic of conversation among all classes."

Even T. S. Eliot's famous 1915 poem *The Love Song of J. Alfred Prufrock*—in which he laments the need to "prepare a face to meet the faces that you meet"—seems a *cri de coeur* about the new demands of self-presentation. While poets of the previous century had wandered lonely as a cloud through the countryside (Wordsworth, in 1802) or repaired in solitude to Walden Pond (Thoreau, in 1845), Eliot's Prufrock mostly worries about being looked at by "eyes that fix you in a formulated phrase" and pin you, wriggling, to a wall.

~

Fast-forward nearly a hundred years, and Prufrock's protest is enshrined in high school syllabi, where it's dutifully memorized, then quickly forgotten, by teens increasingly skilled at shaping their own online and offline personae. These students inhabit a world in which status, income, and self-esteem depend more than ever on the ability to meet the demands of the Culture of Personality. The pressure to entertain, to sell ourselves, and never to be visibly anxious keeps ratcheting up. The number of Americans who considered themselves shy increased from 40 percent in the 1970s to 50 percent in the 1990s, probably because we measured ourselves against ever higher standards of fearless self-presentation. "Social anxiety disorder"—which essentially means pathological shyness—is now thought to afflict nearly one in five of us. The most recent version of the *Diagnostic and Statistical Manual (DSM-IV)*, the psychiatrist's bible of mental disorders, considers the fear of public speaking to be a pathology—not an annoyance, not a disadvantage, but a *disease*—if it interferes with the sufferer's job performance. "It's not enough," one senior manager at Eastman Kodak told the author Daniel Goleman, "to be able to sit at your computer excited about a fantastic regression analysis if you're squeamish about presenting those results to an executive group." (Apparently it's OK to be squeamish about doing a regression analysis if you're excited about giving speeches.)

But perhaps the best way to take the measure of the twenty-first-century Culture of Personality is to return to the self-help arena. Today, a full century after Dale Carnegie launched that first public-speaking workshop at the YMCA, his best-selling book *How to Win Friends and Influence People* is a staple of airport bookshelves and business best-seller lists. The Dale Carnegie Institute still offers updated versions of Carnegie's original classes, and the ability to communicate fluidly remains a core feature of the curriculum. Toastmasters, the nonprofit organization established in 1924 whose members meet weekly to practice public speaking and whose founder declared that "all talking is selling and all selling involves talking," is still thriving, with more than 12,500 chapters in 113 countries.

The promotional video on Toastmasters' website features a skit in which two colleagues, Eduardo and Sheila, sit in the audience at the "Sixth Annual Global Business Conference" as a nervous speaker stumbles through a pitiful presentation.

"I'm so glad I'm not him," whispers Eduardo.

"You're joking, right?" replies Sheila with a satisfied smile. "Don't you remember last month's sales presentation to those new clients? I thought you were going to faint."

"I wasn't that bad, was I?"

"Oh, you were that bad. Really bad. Worse, even."

Eduardo looks suitably ashamed, while the rather insensitive Sheila seems oblivious.

"But," says Sheila, "you can fix it. You can do better. . . . Have you ever heard of Toastmasters?"

Sheila, a young and attractive brunette, hauls Eduardo to a Toastmasters meeting. There she volunteers to perform an exercise called "Truth or Lie," in which she's supposed to tell the group of fifteen-odd participants a story about her life, after which they decide whether or not to believe her.

"I bet I can fool everyone," she whispers to Eduardo sotto voce as she marches to the podium. She spins an elaborate tale about her years as an opera singer, concluding with her poignant decision to give it all up to spend more time with her family. When she's finished, the toastmaster of the evening asks the group whether they believe Sheila's story. All hands in the room go up. The toastmaster turns to Sheila and asks whether it was true.

"I can't even carry a tune!" she beams triumphantly.

Sheila comes across as disingenuous, but also oddly sympathetic. Like the anxious readers of the 1920s personality guides, she's only trying to get ahead at the office. "There's so much competition in my work environment," she confides to the camera, "that it makes it more important than ever to keep my skills sharp."

But what do "sharp skills" look like? Should we become so proficient at self-presentation that we can dissemble without anyone suspecting? Must we learn to stage-manage our voices, gestures, and body language until we can tell—sell—any story we want? These seem venal aspirations, a marker of how far we've come—and not in a good way—since the days of Dale Carnegie's childhood.

Dale's parents had high moral standards; they wanted their son to pursue a career in religion or education, not sales. It seems unlikely that they would have approved of a self-improvement technique called "Truth or Lie." Or, for that matter, of Carnegie's best-selling advice on how to get people to admire you and do your bidding. *How to Win Friends and Influence People* is full of chapter titles like "Making People Glad to Do What You Want" and "How to Make People Like You Instantly."

All of which raises the question, how did we go from Character to Personality without realizing that we had sacrificed something meaningful along the way?

THE MYTH OF CHARISMATIC LEADERSHIP

The Culture of Personality, a Hundred Years Later

Society is itself an education in the extrovert values, and rarely has there been a society that has preached them so hard. No man is an island, but how John Donne would writhe to hear how often, and for what reasons, the thought is so tiresomely repeated.

— WILLIAM WHYTE

Salesmanship as a Virtue: Live with Tony Robbins

"Are you excited?" cries a young woman named Stacy as I hand her my registration forms. Her honeyed voice rises into one big exclamation point. I nod and smile as brightly as I can. Across the lobby of the Atlanta Convention Center, I hear people shrieking.

"What's that noise?" I ask.

"They're getting everyone pumped up to go inside!" Stacy enthuses. "That's part of the whole UPW experience." She hands me a purple spiral binder and a laminated nametag to wear around my neck. UNLEASH THE POWER WITHIN, proclaims the binder in big block letters. Welcome to Tony Robbins's entry-level seminar.

I've paid $895 in exchange, according to the promotional materials, for learning how to be more energetic, gain momentum in my life, and conquer my fears. But the truth is that I'm not here to unleash the power within me (though I'm always happy to pick up a few pointers); I'm here because this seminar is the first stop on my journey to understand the Extrovert Ideal.

I've seen Tony Robbins's infomercials—he claims that there's always one airing at any given moment—and he strikes me as one of the more extroverted people on earth. But he's not just any extrovert. He's the king of self-help, with a client roster that has included President Clinton, Tiger Woods, Nelson Mandela, Margaret Thatcher, Princess Diana, Mikhail Gorbachev, Mother Teresa, Serena Williams, Donna Karan— and 50 million other people. And the self-help industry, into which hundreds of thousands of Americans pour their hearts, souls, and some $11 billion a year, by definition reveals our conception of the ideal self, the one we aspire to become if only we follow the seven principles of this and the three laws of that. I want to know what this ideal self looks like.

Stacy asks if I've brought my meals with me. It seems a strange question: Who carries supper with them from New York City to Atlanta? She explains that I'll want to refuel at my seat; for the next four days, Friday through Monday, we'll be working fifteen hours a day, 8:00 a.m. to 11:00 p.m., with only one short afternoon break. Tony will be onstage *the entire time* and I won't want to miss a moment.

I look around the lobby. Other people seem to have come prepared— they're strolling toward the hall, cheerfully lugging grocery bags stuffed with PowerBars, bananas, and corn chips. I pick up a couple of bruised apples from the snack bar and make my way to the auditorium. Greeters wearing UPW T-shirts and ecstatic smiles line the entrance, springing up and down, fists pumping. You can't get inside without slapping them five. I know, because I try.

Inside the vast hall, a phalanx of dancers is warming up the crowd to the Billy Idol song "Mony Mony," amplified by a world-class sound system, magnified on giant Megatron screens flanking the stage. They move in sync like backup dancers in a Britney Spears video, but are dressed like middle managers. The lead performer is a fortysomething balding fellow wearing a white button-down shirt, conservative tie, rolled-up sleeves, and a great-to-meet-you smile. The message seems to be that we can all learn to be this exuberant when we get to work every morning.

Indeed, the dance moves are simple enough for us to imitate at our seats: jump and clap twice; clap to the left; clap to the right. When the song changes to "Gimme Some Lovin'," many in the audience climb atop their metal folding chairs, where they continue to whoop and clap. I stand somewhat peevishly with arms crossed until I decide that there's nothing to be done but join in and hop up and down along with my seatmates.

Eventually the moment we've all been waiting for arrives: Tony Robbins bounds onstage. Already gigantic at six feet seven inches, he looks a hundred feet tall on the Megatron screen. He's movie-star handsome, with a head of thick brown hair, a Pepsodent smile, and impossibly defined cheekbones. EXPERIENCE TONY ROBBINS LIVE! the seminar advertisement had promised, and now here he is, dancing with the euphoric crowd.

It's about fifty degrees in the hall, but Tony is wearing a short-sleeved polo shirt and shorts. Many in the audience have brought blankets with them, having somehow known that the auditorium would be kept refrigerator-cold, presumably to accommodate Tony's high-octane metabolism. It would take another Ice Age to cool this man off. He's leaping and beaming and managing, somehow, to make eye contact with all 3,800 of us. The greeters jump rapturously in the aisles. Tony opens his arms wide, embracing us all. If Jesus returned to Earth and made his first stop at the Atlanta Convention Center, it would be hard to imagine a more jubilant reception.

This is true even in the back row where I'm sitting with others who spent only $895 for "general admission," as opposed to $2,500 for a "Diamond Premiere Membership," which gets you a seat up front, as close to Tony as possible. When I bought my ticket over the phone, the account rep advised me that the people in the front rows—where "you're looking directly at Tony for sure" instead of relying on the Megatron— are generally "more successful in life." "Those are the people who have more energy," she advised. "Those are the people who are screaming." I have no way of judging how successful the people next to me are, but they certainly seem thrilled to be here. At the sight of Tony, exquisitely stage-lit to set off his expressive face, they cry out and pour into the aisles rock-concert style.

Soon enough, I join them. I've always loved to dance, and I have to admit that gyrating en masse to Top 40 classics is an excellent way to pass the time. Unleashed power comes from high energy, according to Tony, and I can see his point. No wonder people travel from far and wide to see him in person (there's a lovely young woman from Ukraine sitting—no, leaping—next to me with a delighted smile). I really must start doing aerobics again when I get back to New York, I decide.

~

When the music finally stops, Tony addresses us in a raspy voice, half Muppet, half bedroom-sexy, introducing his theory of "Practical Psychology." The gist of it is that knowledge is useless until it's coupled with action. He has a seductive, fast-talking delivery that Willy Loman would have sighed over. Demonstrating practical psychology in action, Tony instructs us to find a partner and to greet each other as if we feel inferior and scared of social rejection. I team up with a construction worker from downtown Atlanta, and we extend tentative handshakes, looking bashfully at the ground as the song "I Want You to Want Me" plays in the background.

Then Tony calls out a series of artfully phrased questions:

"Was your breath full or shallow?"

"SHALLOW!" yells the audience in unison.

"Did you hesitate or go straight toward them?"

"HESITATE!"

"Was there tension in your body or were you relaxed?"

"TENSION!"

Tony asks us to repeat the exercise, but this time to greet our partners as if the impression we make in the first three to five seconds determines whether they'll do business with us. If they don't, "everyone you care about will die like pigs in hell."

I'm startled by Tony's emphasis on business success—this is a seminar about personal power, not sales. Then I remember that Tony is not only a life coach but also a businessman extraordinaire; he started his career in sales and today serves as chairman of seven privately held companies.

BusinessWeek once estimated his income at $80 million a year. Now he seems to be trying, with all the force of his mighty personality, to impart his salesman's touch. He wants us not only to feel great but to radiate waves of energy, not just to be liked, but to be *well* liked; he wants us to know how to sell ourselves. I've already been advised by the Anthony Robbins Companies, via a personalized forty-five-page report generated by an online personality test that I took in preparation for this weekend, that "Susan" should work on her tendency to tell, not sell, her ideas. (The report was written in the third person, as if it was to be reviewed by some imaginary manager evaluating my people skills.)

The audience divides into pairs again, enthusiastically introducing themselves and pumping their partners' hands. When we're finished, the questions repeat.

"Did that feel better, yes or no?"

"YES!"

"Did you use your body differently, yes or no?"

"YES!"

"Did you use more muscles in your face, yes or no?"

"YES!"

"Did you move straight toward them, yes or no?"

"YES!"

This exercise seems designed to show how our physiological state influences our behavior and emotions, but it also suggests that salesmanship governs even the most neutral interactions. It implies that every encounter is a high-stakes game in which we win or lose the other person's favor. It urges us to meet social fear in as extroverted a manner as possible. We must be vibrant and confident, we must not seem hesitant, we must smile so that our interlocutors will smile upon us. Taking these steps will make us feel good—and the better we feel, the better we can sell ourselves.

Tony seems the perfect person to demonstrate such skills. He strikes me as having a "hyperthymic" temperament—a kind of extroversion-on-steroids characterized, in the words of one psychiatrist, by "exuberant, upbeat, overenergetic, and overconfident lifelong traits" that have been recognized as an asset in business, especially sales. People with these traits often make wonderful company, as Tony does onstage.

But what if you admire the hyperthymic among us, but also like your calm and thoughtful self? What if you love knowledge for its own sake, not necessarily as a blueprint to action? What if you wish there were more, not fewer, reflective types in the world?

Tony seems to have anticipated such questions. "But I'm not an extrovert, you say!" he told us at the start of the seminar. "So? You don't have to be an extrovert to feel alive!"

True enough. But it seems, according to Tony, that you'd better act like one if you don't want to flub the sales call and watch your family die like pigs in hell.

~

The evening culminates with the Firewalk, one of the flagship moments of the UPW seminar, in which we're challenged to walk across a ten-foot bed of coals without burning our feet. Many people attend UPW because they've heard about the Firewalk and want to try it themselves. The idea is to propel yourself into such a fearless state of mind that you can withstand even 1,200-degree heat.

Leading up to that moment, we spend hours practicing Tony's techniques—exercises, dance moves, visualizations. I notice that people in the audience are starting to mimic Tony's every movement and facial expression, including his signature gesture of pumping his arm as if he were pitching a baseball. The evening crescendoes until finally, just before midnight, we march to the parking lot in a torchlit procession, nearly four thousand strong, chanting YES! YES! YES! to the thump of a tribal beat. This seems to electrify my fellow UPWers, but to me this drum-accompanied chant—YES! Ba-da-da-da, YES! Dum-dum-dum-DUM, YES! Ba-da-da-*da*—sounds like the sort of thing a Roman general would stage to announce his arrival in the city he's about to sack. The greeters who manned the gates to the auditorium earlier in the day with high fives and bright smiles have morphed into gatekeepers of the Firewalk, arms beckoning toward the bridge of flames.

As best I can tell, a successful Firewalk depends not so much on your state of mind as on how thick the soles of your feet happen to be, so I watch from a safe distance. But I seem to be the only one hanging back. Most of the UPWers make it across, whooping as they go.

"I did it!" they cry when they get to the other side of the firepit. "I did it!"

They've entered a Tony Robbins state of mind. But what exactly does this consist of?

It is, first and foremost, a superior mind—the antidote to Alfred Adler's inferiority complex. Tony uses the word *power* rather than *superior* (we're too sophisticated nowadays to frame our quests for self-improvement in terms of naked social positioning, the way we did at the dawn of the Culture of Personality), but everything about him is an exercise in superiority, from the way he occasionally addresses the audience as "girls and boys," to the stories he tells about his big houses and powerful friends, to the way he towers—literally—over the crowd. His superhuman physical size is an important part of his brand; the title of his best-selling book, *Awaken the Giant Within*, says it all.

His intellect is impressive, too. Though he believes university educations are overrated (because they don't teach you about your emotions and your body, he says) and has been slow to write his next book (because no one reads anymore, according to Tony), he's managed to assimilate the work of academic psychologists and package it into one hell of a show, with genuine insights the audience can make their own.

Part of Tony's genius lies in the unstated promise that he'll let the audience share his own journey from inferiority to superiority. He wasn't always so grand, he tells us. As a kid, he was a shrimp. Before he got in shape, he was overweight. And before he lived in a castle in Del Mar, California, he rented an apartment so small that he kept his dishes in the bathtub. The implication is that we can *all* get over whatever's keeping us down, that even introverts can learn to walk on coals while belting out a lusty YES.

The second part of the Tony state of mind is good-heartedness. He wouldn't inspire so many people if he didn't make them feel that he truly cared about unleashing the power within each of them. When Tony's onstage, you get the sense that he's singing, dancing, and emoting with every ounce of his energy and heart. There are moments, when the crowd is on its feet, singing and dancing in unison, that you can't help but love him, the way many people loved Barack Obama with a kind of shocked delight when they first heard him talk about transcending red and blue. At one point, Tony talks about the different needs people have—for love, certainty, variety, and so on. He is motivated by love, he tells us, and we believe him.

But there's also this: throughout the seminar, he constantly tries to "upsell" us. He and his sales team use the UPW event, whose attendees have already paid a goodly sum, to market multi-day seminars with even more alluring names and stiffer price tags: Date with Destiny, about $5,000; Mastery University, about $10,000; and the Platinum Partnership, which, for a cool $45,000 a year, buys you and eleven other Platinum Partners the right to go on exotic vacations with Tony.

During the afternoon break, Tony lingers onstage with his blond and sweetly beautiful wife, Sage, gazing into her eyes, caressing her hair, murmuring into her ear. I'm happily married, but right now Ken is in New York and I'm here in Atlanta, and even I feel lonely as I watch this spectacle. What would it be like if I were single or unhappily partnered? It would "arouse an eager want" in me, just as Dale Carnegie advised salesmen to do with their prospects so many years ago. And sure enough, when the break is over, a lengthy video comes on the mega-screen, pitching Tony's relationship-building seminar.

In another brilliantly conceived segment, Tony devotes part of the seminar to explaining the financial and emotional benefits of surrounding oneself with the right "peer group"—after which a staffer begins a sales pitch for the $45,000 Platinum program. Those who purchase one of the twelve spots will join the "ultimate peer group," we are told—the "cream of the crop," the "elite of the elite of the elite."

I can't help but wonder why none of the other UPWers seem to mind, or even to notice, these upselling techniques. By now many of them have shopping bags at their feet, full of stuff they bought out in the lobby—DVDs, books, even eight-by-ten glossies of Tony himself, ready for framing.

But the thing about Tony—and what draws people to buy his products—is that like any good salesman, he *believes* in what he's pitching. He apparently sees no contradiction between wanting the best for people and wanting to live in a mansion. He persuades us that he's using his sales skills not only for personal gain but also to help as many of us as he can reach. Indeed, one very thoughtful introvert I know, a successful salesman who gives sales training seminars of his own, swears that Tony Robbins not only improved his business but also made him a better person. When he started attending events like UPW, he says, he focused on who he wanted to become, and now, when he delivers his own seminars, he *is* that person. "Tony gives me energy," he says, "and now I can create energy for other people when I'm onstage."

~

At the onset of the Culture of Personality, we were urged to develop an extroverted personality for frankly selfish reasons—as a way of outshining the crowd in a newly anonymous and competitive society. But nowadays we tend to think that becoming more extroverted not only makes us more successful, but also makes us better people. We see salesmanship as a way of sharing one's gifts with the world.

This is why Tony's zeal to sell to and be adulated by thousands of people at once is seen not as narcissism or hucksterism, but as leadership of the highest order. If Abraham Lincoln was the embodiment of virtue during the Culture of Character, then Tony Robbins is his counterpart during the Culture of Personality. Indeed, when Tony mentions that he once thought of running for president of the United States, the audience erupts in loud cheers.

But does it always make sense to equate leadership with hyperextroversion? To find out, I visited Harvard Business School, an institution that prides itself on its ability to identify and train some of the most prominent business and political leaders of our time.

The Myth of Charismatic Leadership: Harvard Business School and Beyond

The first thing I notice about the Harvard Business School campus is the way people walk. No one ambles, strolls, or lingers. They stride, full of forward momentum. It's crisp and autumnal the week I visit, and the students' bodies seem to vibrate with September electricity as they advance across campus. When they cross each other's paths they don't merely nod—they exchange animated greetings, inquiring about this one's summer with J. P. Morgan or that one's trek in the Himalayas.

They behave the same way inside the social hothouse of the Spangler Center, the sumptuously decorated student center. Spangler has floor-to-ceiling silk curtains in sea-foam green, rich leather sofas, giant Samsung high-definition TVs silently broadcasting campus news, and soaring ceilings festooned with high-wattage chandeliers. The tables and sofas are clustered mostly on the perimeter of the room, forming a brightly lit center catwalk down which the students breezily parade, seemingly unaware that all eyes are on them. I admire their nonchalance.

The students are even better turned out than their surroundings, if such a thing is possible. No one is more than five pounds overweight or has bad skin or wears odd accessories. The women are a cross between Head Cheerleader and Most Likely to Succeed. They wear fitted jeans, filmy blouses, and high-heeled peekaboo-toed shoes that make a pleasing clickety–clack on Spangler's polished wood floors. Some parade like fashion models, except that they're social and beaming instead of aloof and impassive. The men are clean-cut and athletic; they look like people who expect to be in charge, but in a friendly, Eagle Scout sort of way. I have the feeling that if you asked one of them for driving directions, he'd greet you with a can-do smile and throw himself into the task of helping you to your destination—whether or not he knew the way.

I sit down next to a couple of students who are in the middle of planning a road trip—HBS students are forever coordinating pub crawls and parties, or describing an extreme-travel junket they've just come back from. When they ask what brings me to campus, I say that I'm conducting interviews for a book about introversion and extroversion. I don't tell them that a friend of mine, himself an HBS grad, once called the place the "Spiritual Capital of Extroversion." But it turns out that I don't *have* to tell them.

"Good luck finding an introvert around here," says one.

"This school is predicated on extroversion," adds the other. "Your grades and social status depend on it. It's just the norm here. Everyone around you is speaking up and being social and going out."

"Isn't there anyone on the quieter side?" I ask.

They look at me curiously.

"I couldn't tell you," says the first student dismissively.

~

Harvard Business School is not, by any measure, an ordinary place. Founded in 1908, just when Dale Carnegie hit the road as a traveling salesman and only three years before he taught his first class in public speaking, the school sees itself as "educating leaders who make a difference in the world." President George W. Bush is a graduate, as are an impressive collection of World Bank presidents, U.S. Treasury secretaries, New York City mayors, CEOs of companies like General Electric, Goldman Sachs, Procter & Gamble, and, more notoriously, Jeffrey Skilling, the villain of the Enron scandal. Between 2004 and 2006, 20 percent of the top three executives at the Fortune 500 companies were HBS grads.

HBS grads likely have influenced your life in ways you're not aware of. They have decided who should go to war and when; they have resolved the fate of Detroit's auto industry; they play leading roles in just about every crisis to shake Wall Street, Main Street, and Pennsylvania Avenue. If you work in corporate America, there's a good chance that Harvard Business School grads have shaped your everyday life, too, weighing in on how much privacy you need in your workspace, how many team-building sessions you need to attend per year, and whether creativity is best achieved through brainstorming or solitude. Given the scope of their influence, it's worth taking a look at who enrolls here— and what they value by the time they graduate.

The student who wishes me luck in finding an introvert at HBS no doubt believes that there are none to be found. But clearly he doesn't know his first-year classmate Don Chen. I first meet Don in Spangler, where he's seated only a few couches away from the road-trip planners. He comes across as a typical HBS student, tall, with gracious manners, prominent cheekbones, a winsome smile, and a fashionably choppy, surfer-dude haircut. He'd like to find a job in private equity when he graduates. But talk to Don for a while and you'll notice that his voice is softer than those of his classmates, his head ever so slightly cocked, his grin a little tentative. Don is "a bitter introvert," as he cheerfully puts it—bitter because the more time he spends at HBS, the more convinced he becomes that he'd better change his ways.

Don likes having a lot of time to himself, but that's not much of an option at HBS. His day begins early in the morning, when he meets for an hour and a half with his "Learning Team"—a pre-assigned study group in which participation is mandatory (students at HBS practically go to the bathroom in teams). He spends the rest of the morning in class, where ninety students sit together in a wood-paneled, U-shaped amphitheater with stadium seating. The professor usually kicks off by directing a student to describe the case study of the day, which is based on a real-life business scenario—say, a CEO who's considering changing her company's salary structure. The figure at the heart of the case study, in this case the CEO, is referred to as the "protagonist." *If you were the protagonist*, the professor asks—and soon you will be, is the implication—*what would you do?*

The essence of the HBS education is that leaders have to act confidently and make decisions in the face of incomplete information. The teaching method plays with an age-old question: If you don't have all the facts—and often you won't—should you wait to act until you've collected as much data as possible? Or, by hesitating, do you risk losing others' trust and your own momentum? The answer isn't obvious. If you speak firmly on the basis of bad information, you can lead your people into disaster. But if you exude uncertainty, then morale suffers, funders won't invest, and your organization can collapse.

The HBS teaching method implicitly comes down on the side of certainty. The CEO may not know the best way forward, but she has to act anyway. The HBS students, in turn, are expected to opine. Ideally, the student who was just cold-called has already discussed the case study with his Learning Team, so he's ready to hold forth on the protagonist's best moves. After he finishes, the professor encourages other students to offer their own views. Half of the students' grade, and a much larger percentage of their social status, is based on whether they throw themselves into this fray. If a student talks often and forcefully, then he's a player; if he doesn't, he's on the margins.

Many of the students adapt easily to this system. But not Don. He has trouble elbowing his way into class discussions; in some classes he barely speaks at all. He prefers to contribute only when he believes he has something insightful to add, or honest-to-God disagrees with someone. This sounds reasonable, but Don feels as if he should be more comfortable talking just so he can fill up his share of available airtime.

Don's HBS friends, who tend to be thoughtful, reflective types like him, spend a lot of time talking about talking in class. How much class participation is too much? How little is too little? When does publicly disagreeing with a classmate constitute healthy debate, and when does it seem competitive and judgmental? One of Don's friends is worried because her professor sent around an e-mail saying that anyone with real-world experience on the day's case study should let him know in advance. She's sure that the professor's announcement was an effort to limit stupid remarks like the one she made in class last week. Another worries that he's not loud enough. "I just have a naturally soft voice," he says, "so when my voice sounds normal to others, I feel like I'm shouting. I have to work on it."

The school also tries hard to turn quiet students into talkers. The professors have their own "Learning Teams," in which they egg each other on with techniques to draw out reticent students. When students fail to speak up in class, it's seen not only as their own deficit but also as their professor's. "If someone doesn't speak by the end of the semester, it's problematic," Professor Michel Anteby told me. "It means I didn't do a good job."

The school even hosts live informational sessions and web pages on how to be a good class participator. Don's friends earnestly reel off the tips they remember best.

"Speak with conviction. Even if you believe something only fifty-five percent, say it as if you believe it a hundred percent."

"If you're preparing alone for class, then you're doing it wrong. Nothing at HBS is intended to be done alone."

"Don't think about the perfect answer. It's better to get out there and say something than to never get your voice in."

The school newspaper, *The Harbus*, also dispenses advice, featuring articles with titles like "How to Think and Speak Well—On the Spot!," "Developing Your Stage Presence," and "Arrogant or Simply Confident?"

These imperatives extend beyond the classroom. After class, most people eat lunch at the Spangler dining hall, which one grad describes as "more like high school than high school." And every day, Don wrestles with himself. Should he go back to his apartment and recharge over a quiet lunch, as he longs to do, or join his classmates? Even if he forces himself to go to Spangler, it's not as if the social pressure will end there. As the day wears on, there will be more such dilemmas. Attend the late-afternoon happy hours? Head out for a late, rowdy evening? Students at HBS go out in big groups several nights a week, says Don. Participation isn't mandatory, but it feels as if it is to those who don't thrive on group activities.

"Socializing here is an extreme sport," one of Don's friends tells me. "People go out *all the time*. If you don't go out one night, the next day people will ask, 'Where were you?' I go out at night like it's my job." Don has noticed that the people who organize social events—happy hours, dinners, drinking fests—are at the top of the social hierarchy. "The professors tell us that our classmates are the people who will go to our weddings," says Don. "If you leave HBS without having built an extensive social network, it's like you failed your HBS experience."

By the time Don falls into bed at night, he's exhausted. And sometimes he wonders why, exactly, he should have to work so hard at being outgoing. Don is Chinese-American, and recently he worked a summer job in China. He was struck by how different the social norms were, and how much more comfortable he felt. In China there was more emphasis on listening, on asking questions rather than holding forth, on putting others' needs first. In the United States, he feels, conversation is about how effective you are at turning your experiences into stories, whereas a Chinese person might be concerned with taking up too much of the other person's time with inconsequential information.

"That summer, I said to myself, 'Now I know why these are my people,'" he says.

But that was China, this is Cambridge, Massachusetts. And if one judges HBS by how well it prepares students for the "real world," it seems to be doing an excellent job. After all, Don Chen will graduate into a business culture in which verbal fluency and sociability are the two most important predictors of success, according to a Stanford Business School study. It's a world in which a middle manager at GE once told me that "people here don't even want to meet with you if you don't have a PowerPoint and a 'pitch' for them. Even if you're just making a recommendation to your colleague, you can't sit down in someone's office and tell them what you think. You have to make a presentation, with pros and cons and a 'takeaway box.'"

Unless they're self-employed or able to telecommute, many adults work in offices where they must take care to glide down the corridors greeting their colleagues warmly and confidently. "The business world," says a 2006 article from the Wharton Program for Working Professionals, "is filled with office environments similar to one described by an Atlanta area corporate trainer: 'Here everyone knows that it's important to be an extrovert and troublesome to be an introvert. So people work real hard at looking like extroverts, whether that's comfortable or not. It's like making sure you drink the same single-malt scotch the CEO drinks and that you work out at the right health club.'"

Even businesses that employ many artists, designers, and other imaginative types often display a preference for extroversion. "We want to attract creative people," the director of human resources at a major media company told me. When I asked what she meant by "creative," she answered without missing a beat. "You have to be outgoing, fun, and jazzed up to work here."

Contemporary ads aimed at businesspeople would give the Williams

Luxury Shaving Cream ads of yesteryear a run for their money. One line of TV commercials that ran on CNBC, the cable business channel, featured an office worker losing out on a plum assignment.

> BOSS TO TED AND ALICE. Ted, I'm sending Alice to the sales
> conference because she thinks faster on her feet than you.
> TED. (speechless) . . .
> BOSS. So, Alice, we'll send you on Thursday—
> TED. She does not!

Other ads explicitly sell their products as extroversion-enhancers. In 2000, Amtrak encouraged travelers to "DEPART FROM YOUR INHIBITIONS." Nike became a prominent brand partly on the strength of its "Just Do It" campaign. And in 1999 and 2000, a series of ads for the psychotropic drug Paxil promised to cure the extreme shyness known as "social anxiety disorder" by offering Cinderella stories of personality transformation. One Paxil ad showed a well-dressed executive shaking hands over a business deal. "I can taste success," read the caption. Another showed what happens without the drug: a businessman alone in his office, his forehead resting dejectedly on a clenched fist. "I should have joined in more often," it read.

~

Yet even at Harvard Business School there are signs that something might be wrong with a leadership style that values quick and assertive answers over quiet, slow decision-making.

Every autumn the incoming class participates in an elaborate role-playing game called the Subarctic Survival Situation. "It is approximately 2:30 p.m., October 5," the students are told, "and you have just crash-landed in a float plane on the east shore of Laura Lake in the subarctic region of the northern Quebec-Newfoundland border." The students are divided into small groups and asked to imagine that their group has salvaged fifteen items from the plane—a compass, sleeping bag, axe, and so on. Then they're told to rank them in order of importance to the group's survival. First the students rank the items individually; then they do so as a team. Next they score those rankings against an expert's to see how well they did. Finally they watch a videotape of their team's discussions to see what went right—or wrong.

The point of the exercise is to teach group synergy. Successful synergy means a higher ranking for the team than for its individual members. The group fails when any of its members has a better ranking than the overall team. And failure is exactly what can happen when students prize assertiveness too highly.

One of Don's classmates was in a group lucky to include a young man with extensive experience in the northern backwoods. He had a lot of good ideas about how to rank the fifteen salvaged items. But his group didn't listen, because he expressed his views too quietly.

"Our action plan hinged on what the most vocal people suggested," recalls the classmate. "When the less vocal people put out ideas, those ideas were discarded. The ideas that were rejected would have kept us alive and out of trouble, but they were dismissed because of the conviction with which the more vocal people suggested their ideas. Afterwards they played us back the videotape, and it was so embarrassing."

The Subarctic Survival Situation may sound like a harmless game played inside the ivory tower, but if you think of meetings you've attended, you can probably recall a time—plenty of times—when the opinion of the most dynamic or talkative person prevailed to the detriment of all. Perhaps it was a low-stakes situation—your PTA, say, deciding whether to meet on Monday or Tuesday nights. But maybe it was important: an emergency meeting of Enron's top brass, considering whether or not to disclose questionable accounting practices. (See chapter 7 for more on Enron.) Or a jury deliberating whether or not to send a single mother to jail.

I discussed the Subarctic Survival Situation with HBS professor Quinn Mills, an expert on leadership styles. Mills is a courteous man dressed, on the day we met, in a pinstriped suit and yellow polka-dot tie. He has a sonorous voice, and uses it skillfully. The HBS method "presumes that leaders should be vocal," he told me flat out, "and in my view that's part of reality."

But Mills also pointed to the common phenomenon known as the "winner's curse," in which two companies bid competitively to acquire a third, until the price climbs so high that it becomes less an economic activity than a war of egos. The winning bidders will be damned if they'll let their opponents get the prize, so they buy the target company at an inflated price. "It tends to be the assertive people who carry the day in these kinds of things," says Mills. "You see this all the time. People ask, 'How did this happen, how did we pay so much?' Usually it's said that they were carried away by the situation, but that's not right. Usually they're carried away by people who are assertive and domineering. The risk with our students is that they're very good at getting their way. But that doesn't mean they're going the *right* way."

If we assume that quiet and loud people have roughly the same number of good (and bad) ideas, then we should worry if the louder and more forceful people always carry the day. This would mean that an awful lot of bad ideas prevail while good ones get squashed. Yet studies in group dynamics suggest that this is exactly what happens. We perceive talkers as smarter than quiet types—even though grade-point averages and SAT and intelligence test scores reveal this perception to be inaccurate. In one experiment in which two strangers met over the phone, those who spoke more were considered more intelligent, better looking, and more likable. We also see talkers as leaders. The more a person talks, the more other group members direct their attention to him, which means that he becomes increasingly powerful as a meeting goes on. It also helps to speak fast; we rate quick talkers as more capable and appealing than slow talkers.

All of this would be fine if more talking were correlated with greater insight, but research suggests that there's no such link. In one study, groups of college students were asked to solve math problems together and then to rate one another's intelligence and judgment. The students who spoke first and most often were consistently given the highest ratings, even though their suggestions (and math SAT scores) were no better than those of the less talkative students. These same students were given similarly high ratings for their creativity and analytical powers during a separate exercise to develop a business strategy for a start-up company.

A well-known study out of UC Berkeley by organizational behavior professor Philip Tetlock found that television pundits—that is, people who earn their livings by holding forth confidently on the basis of limited information—make worse predictions about political and economic trends than they would by random chance. And the very worst prognosticators tend to be the most famous and the most confident—the very ones who would be considered natural leaders in an HBS classroom.

The U.S. Army has a name for a similar phenomenon: "the Bus to Abilene." "Any army officer can tell you what that means," Colonel (Ret.) Stephen J. Gerras, a professor of behavioral sciences at the U.S. Army War College, told *Yale Alumni Magazine* in 2008. "It's about a family sitting on a porch in Texas on a hot summer day, and somebody says, 'I'm bored. Why don't we go to Abilene?' When they get to Abilene, somebody says, 'You know, I didn't really want to go.' And the next person says, 'I didn't want to go—I thought you wanted to go,' and so on. Whenever you're in an army group and somebody says, 'I think we're all getting on the bus to Abilene here,' that is a red flag. You can stop a conversation with it. It is a very powerful artifact of our culture."

The "Bus to Abilene" anecdote reveals our tendency to follow those who initiate action—any action. We are similarly inclined to empower dynamic speakers. One highly successful venture capitalist who is regularly pitched by young entrepreneurs told me how frustrated he is by his colleagues' failure to distinguish between good presentation skills and true leadership ability. "I worry that there are people who are put in positions of authority because they're good talkers, but they don't have good ideas," he said. "It's so easy to confuse schmoozing ability with talent. Someone seems like a good presenter, easy to get along with, and those traits are rewarded. Well, why is that? They're valuable traits, but we put too much of a premium on presenting and not enough on substance and critical thinking."

In his book *Iconoclast*, the neuroeconomist Gregory Berns explores what happens when companies rely too heavily on presentation skills to weed out good ideas from nonstarters. He describes a software company called Rite-Solutions that successfully asks employees to share ideas through an online "idea market," as a way of focusing on substance rather than style. Joe Marino, president of Rite-Solutions, and Jim Lavoie, CEO of the company, created this system as a reaction to problems they'd experienced elsewhere. "In my old company," Lavoie told Berns, "if you had a great idea, we would tell you, 'OK, we'll make an appointment for you to address the murder board'"—a group of people charged with vetting new ideas. Marino described what happened next:

> Some technical guy comes in with a good idea. Of course questions are asked of that person that they don't know. Like, "How big's the market? What's your marketing approach? What's your business plan for this? What's the product going to cost?" It's embarrassing. Most people can't answer those kinds of questions. The people who made it through these boards were not the people with the best ideas. *They were the best presenters.*

Contrary to the Harvard Business School model of vocal leadership, the ranks of effective CEOs turn out to be filled with introverts, including Charles Schwab; Bill Gates; Brenda Barnes, CEO of Sara Lee; and James Copeland, former CEO of Deloitte Touche Tohmatsu. "Among the most effective leaders I have encountered and worked with in half a century," the management guru Peter Drucker has written, "some locked themselves into their office and others were ultra-gregarious. Some were quick and impulsive, while others studied the situation and took forever to come to a decision. . . . The one and only personality trait the effective ones I have encountered did have in common was something they did *not* have: they had little or no 'charisma' and little use either for the term or what it signifies." Supporting Drucker's claim, Brigham Young University management professor Bradley Agle studied the CEOs of 128 major companies and found that those considered charismatic by their top executives had bigger salaries but not better corporate performance.

We tend to overestimate how outgoing leaders need to be. "Most leading in a corporation is done in small meetings and it's done at a distance, through written and video communications," Professor Mills told me. "It's not done in front of big groups. You have to be able to do some of that; you can't be a leader of a corporation and walk into a room full of analysts and turn white with fear and leave. But you don't have to do a whole lot of it. I've known a lot of leaders of corporations who are highly introspective and who really have to make themselves work to do the public stuff."

Mills points to Lou Gerstner, the legendary chairman of IBM. "He went to school here," he says. "I don't know how he'd characterize himself. He has to give big speeches, and he does, and he looks calm. But my sense is that he's dramatically more comfortable in small groups. Many of these guys are, actually. Not all of them. But an awful lot of them."

Indeed, according to a famous study by the influential management theorist Jim Collins, many of the best-performing companies of the late twentieth century were run by what he calls "Level 5 Leaders." These exceptional CEOs were known not for their flash or charisma but for extreme humility coupled with intense professional will. In his influential book *Good to Great*, Collins tells the story of Darwin Smith, who in his twenty years as head of Kimberly-Clark turned it into the leading paper company in the world and generated stock returns more than four times higher than the market average.

Smith was a shy and mild-mannered man who wore J.C. Penney suits and nerdy black-rimmed glasses, and spent his vacations puttering around his Wisconsin farm by himself. Asked by a *Wall Street Journal* reporter to describe his management style, Smith stared back for an uncomfortably long time and answered with a single word: "Eccentric." But his soft demeanor concealed a fierce resolve. Soon after being appointed CEO, Smith made a dramatic decision to sell the mills that produced the company's core business of coated paper and invest instead in the consumer-paper-products industry, which he believed had better economics and a brighter future. Everyone said this was a huge mistake, and Wall Street downgraded Kimberly-Clark's stock. But Smith, unmoved by the crowd, did what he thought was right. As a result, the company grew stronger and soon outpaced its rivals. Asked later about his strategy, Smith replied that he never stopped trying to become qualified for the job.

Collins hadn't set out to make a point about quiet leadership. When he started his research, all he wanted to know was what characteristics made a company outperform its competition. He selected eleven standout companies to research in depth. Initially he ignored the question of leadership altogether, because he wanted to avoid simplistic answers. But when he analyzed what the highest-performing companies had in common, the nature of their CEOs jumped out at him. *Every single one of them was led by an unassuming man like Darwin Smith.* Those who worked with these leaders tended to describe them with the following words: quiet, humble, modest, reserved, shy, gracious, mild-mannered, self-effacing, understated.

The lesson, says Collins, is clear. We don't need giant personalities to transform companies. We need leaders who build not their own egos but the institutions they run.

~

So what do introverted leaders do differently from—and sometimes better than—extroverts?

One answer comes from the work of Wharton management professor Adam Grant, who has spent considerable time consulting with Fortune 500 executives and military leaders—from Google to the U.S. Army and Navy. When we first spoke, Grant was teaching at the Ross School of Business at the University of Michigan, where he'd become convinced that the existing research, which showed a correlation between extroversion and leadership, didn't tell the whole story.

Grant told me about a wing commander in the U.S. Air Force—one rank below general, in command of thousands of people, charged with protecting a high-security missile base—who was one of the most classically introverted people, as well as one of the finest leaders, Grant had ever met. This man lost focus when he interacted too much with people, so he carved out time for thinking and recharging. He spoke quietly, without much variation in his vocal inflections or facial expressions. He was more interested in listening and gathering information than in asserting his opinion or dominating a conversation.

He was also widely admired; when he spoke, everyone listened. This was not necessarily remarkable—if you're at the top of the military hierarchy, people are supposed to listen to you. But in the case of this commander, says Grant, people respected not just his formal authority, but also the way he led: by supporting his employees' efforts to take the initiative. He gave subordinates input into key decisions, implementing the ideas that made sense, while making it clear that he had the final authority. He wasn't concerned with getting credit or even with being in charge; he simply assigned work to those who could perform it best. This meant delegating some of his most interesting, meaningful, and important tasks—work that other leaders would have kept for themselves.

Why did the research not reflect the talents of people like the wing commander? Grant thought he knew what the problem was. First, when he looked closely at the existing studies on personality and leadership, he found that the correlation between extroversion and leadership was modest. Second, these studies were often based on people's perceptions of who made a good leader, as opposed to actual results. And personal opinions are often a simple reflection of cultural bias.

But most intriguing to Grant was that the existing research didn't differentiate among the various kinds of situations a leader might face. It might be that certain organizations or contexts were better suited to introverted leadership styles, he thought, and others to extroverted approaches, but the studies didn't make such distinctions.

Grant had a theory about which kinds of circumstances would call for introverted leadership. His hypothesis was that extroverted leaders enhance group performance when employees are passive, but that introverted leaders are more effective with proactive employees. To test his idea, he and two colleagues, professors Francesca Gino of Harvard Business School and David Hofman of the Kenan-Flagler Business School at the University of North Carolina, carried out a pair of studies of their own.

In the first study, Grant and his colleagues analyzed data from one of the five biggest pizza chains in the United States. They discovered that the weekly profits of the stores managed by extroverts were 16 percent higher than the profits of those led by introverts—but only when the employees were passive types who tended to do their job *without exercising initiative*. Introverted leaders had the exact opposite results. When they worked with employees who actively tried to improve work procedures, their stores outperformed those led by extroverts by more than 14 percent.

In the second study, Grant's team divided 163 college students into competing teams charged with folding as many T-shirts as possible in ten minutes. Unbeknownst to the participants, each team included two actors. In some teams, the two actors acted passively, following the leader's instructions. In other teams, one of the actors said, "I wonder if there's a more efficient way to do this." The other actor replied that he had a friend from Japan who had a faster way to fold shirts. "It might take a minute or two to teach you," the actor told the leader, "but do we want to try it?"

The results were striking. The introverted leaders were 20 percent more likely to follow the suggestion—and their teams had 24 percent better results than the teams of the extroverted leaders. When the followers were not proactive, though—when they simply did as the leader instructed without suggesting their own shirt-folding methods—the teams led by extroverts outperformed those led by the introverts by 22 percent.

Why did these leaders' effectiveness turn on whether their employees were passive or proactive? Grant says it makes sense that introverts are uniquely good at leading initiative-takers. Because of their inclination to listen to others and lack of interest in dominating social situations, introverts are more likely to hear and implement suggestions. Having benefited from the talents of their followers, they are then likely to motivate them to be even more proactive. Introverted leaders create a virtuous circle of proactivity, in other words. In the T-shirt-folding study, the team members reported perceiving the introverted leaders as more open and receptive to their ideas, which motivated them to work harder and to fold more shirts.

Extroverts, on the other hand, can be so intent on putting their own stamp on events that they risk losing others' good ideas along the way and allowing workers to lapse into passivity. "Often the leaders end up doing a lot of the talking," says Francesca Gino, "and not listening to any of the ideas that the followers are trying to provide." But with their natural ability to inspire, extroverted leaders are better at getting results from more passive workers.

This line of research is still in its infancy. But under the auspices of Grant—an especially proactive fellow himself—it may grow quickly. (One of his colleagues has described Grant as the kind of person who "can make things happen twenty-eight minutes before they're scheduled to begin.") Grant is especially excited about the implications of these findings because proactive employees who take advantage of opportunities in a fast-moving, 24/7 business environment, without waiting for a leader to tell them what to do, are increasingly vital to organizational success. To understand how to maximize these employees' contributions is an important tool for all leaders. It's also important for companies to groom listeners as well as talkers for leadership roles.

The popular press, says Grant, is full of suggestions that introverted leaders practice their public speaking skills and smile more. But Grant's research suggests that in at least one important regard—encouraging employees to take initiative—introverted leaders would do well to go on doing what they do naturally. Extroverted leaders, on the other hand, "may wish to adopt a more reserved, quiet style," Grant writes. They may want to learn to sit down so that others might stand up.

Which is just what a woman named Rosa Parks did naturally.

~

For years before the day in December 1955 when Rosa Parks refused to give up her seat on a Montgomery bus, she worked behind the scenes for the NAACP, even receiving training in nonviolent resistance. Many things had inspired her political commitment. The time the Ku Klux Klan marched in front of her childhood house. The time her brother, a private in the U.S. Army who'd saved the lives of white soldiers, came home from World War II only to be spat upon. The time a black eighteen-year-old delivery boy was framed for rape and sent to the electric chair. Parks organized NAACP records, kept track of membership payments, read to little kids in her neighborhood. She was diligent and honorable, but no one thought of her as a leader. Parks, it seemed, was more of a foot soldier.

Not many people know that twelve years before her showdown with the Montgomery bus driver, she'd had another encounter with the same man, possibly on the very same bus. It was a November afternoon in

1943, and Parks had entered through the front door of the bus because the back was too crowded. The driver, a well-known bigot named James Blake, told her to use the rear and started to push her off the bus. Parks asked him not to touch her. She would leave on her own, she said quietly. "Get off my bus," Blake sputtered in response.

Parks complied, but not before deliberately dropping her purse on her way out and sitting on a "white" seat as she picked it up. "Intuitively, she had engaged in an act of passive resistance, a precept named by Leo Tolstoy and embraced by Mahatma Gandhi," writes the historian Douglas Brinkley in a wonderful biography of Parks. It was more than a decade before King popularized the idea of nonviolence and long before Parks's own training in civil disobedience, but, Brinkley writes, "such principles were a perfect match for her own personality."

Parks was so disgusted by Blake that she refused to ride his bus for the next twelve years. On the day she finally did, the day that turned her into the "Mother of the Civil Rights Movement," she got back on that bus, according to Brinkley, only out of sheer absentmindedness.

Parks's actions that day were brave and singular, but it was in the legal fallout that her quiet strength truly shone. Local civil rights leaders sought her out as a test case to challenge the city's bus laws, pressing her to file a lawsuit. This was no small decision. Parks had a sickly mother who depended on her; to sue would mean losing her job and her husband's. It would mean running the very real risk of being lynched from "the tallest telephone pole in town," as her husband and mother put it. "Rosa, the white folks will kill you," pleaded her husband. "It was one thing to be arrested for an isolated bus incident," writes Brinkley; "it was quite another, as historian Taylor Branch would put it, to 'reenter that forbidden zone by choice.'"

But because of her nature, Parks was the perfect plaintiff. Not only because she was a devout Christian, not only because she was an upstanding citizen, but also because she was gentle. "They've messed with the wrong one now!" the boycotters would declare as they traipsed miles to work and school. The phrase became a rallying cry. Its power lay in how paradoxical it was. Usually such a phrase implies that you've messed with a local heavy, with some bullying giant. But it was Parks's quiet strength that made her unassailable. "The slogan served as a reminder that the woman who had inspired the boycott was the sort of soft-spoken martyr God would not abandon," writes Brinkley.

Parks took her time coming to a decision, but ultimately agreed to sue. She also lent her presence at a rally held on the evening of her trial, the night when a young Martin Luther King Jr., the head of the brand-new Montgomery Improvement Association, roused all of Montgomery's black community to boycott the buses. "Since it had to happen," King told the crowd, "I'm happy it happened to a person like Rosa Parks, for nobody can doubt the boundless outreach of her integrity. Nobody can doubt the height of her character. Mrs. Parks is unassuming, and yet there is integrity and character there."

Later that year Parks agreed to go on a fund-raising speaking tour with King and other civil rights leaders. She suffered insomnia, ulcers, and homesickness along the way. She met her idol, Eleanor Roosevelt, who wrote of their encounter in her newspaper column: "She is a very quiet, gentle person and it is difficult to imagine how she ever could take such a positive and independent stand." When the boycott finally ended, over a year later, the buses integrated by decree of the Supreme Court, Parks was overlooked by the press. The *New York Times* ran two front-page stories that celebrated King but didn't mention her. Other papers photographed the boycott leaders sitting in front of buses, but Parks was not invited to sit for these pictures. She didn't mind. On the day the buses were integrated, she preferred to stay home and take care of her mother.

~

Parks's story is a vivid reminder that we have been graced with limelight-avoiding leaders throughout history. Moses, for example, was not, according to some interpretations of his story, the brash, talkative type who would organize road trips and hold forth in a classroom at Harvard Business School. On the contrary, by today's standards he was dreadfully timid. He spoke with a stutter and considered himself inarticulate. The book of Numbers describes him as "very meek, above all the men which were upon the face of the earth."

When God first appeared to him in the form of a burning bush, Moses was employed as a shepherd by his father-in-law; he wasn't even ambitious enough to own his own sheep. And when God revealed to Moses his role as liberator of the Jews, did Moses leap at the opportunity? Send someone else to do it, he said. "Who am I, that I should go to Pharaoh?" he pleaded. "I have never been eloquent. I am slow of speech and tongue."

It was only when God paired him up with his extroverted brother Aaron that Moses agreed to take on the assignment. Moses would be the speechwriter, the behind-the-scenes guy, the Cyrano de Bergerac; Aaron would be the public face of the operation. "It will be as if he were your mouth," said God, "and as if you were God to him."

Complemented by Aaron, Moses led the Jews from Egypt, provided for them in the desert for the next forty years, and brought the Ten Commandments down from Mount Sinai. And he did all this using strengths that are classically associated with introversion: climbing a mountain in search of wisdom and writing down carefully, on two stone tablets, everything he learned there.

We tend to write Moses' true personality out of the Exodus story. (Cecil B. DeMille's classic, *The Ten Commandments*, portrays him as a swashbuckling figure who does all the talking, with no help from Aaron.) We don't ask why God chose as his prophet a stutterer with a public speaking phobia. But we should. The book of Exodus is short on explication, but its stories suggest that introversion plays yin to the yang of extroversion; that the medium is not always the message; and that people followed Moses because his words were thoughtful, not because he spoke them well.

~

If Parks spoke through her actions, and if Moses spoke through his brother Aaron, today another type of introverted leader speaks using the Internet.

In his book *The Tipping Point*, Malcolm Gladwell explores the influence of "Connectors"—people who have a "special gift for bringing the world together" and "an instinctive and natural gift for making social connections." He describes a "classic Connector" named Roger Horchow, a charming and successful businessman and backer of Broadway hits such as *Les Misérables*, who "collects people the same way others collect stamps." "If you sat next to Roger Horchow on a plane ride across the Atlantic," writes Gladwell, "he would start talking as the plane taxied to the runway, you would be laughing by the time the seatbelt sign was turned off, and when you landed at the other end you'd wonder where the time went."

We generally think of Connectors in just the way that Gladwell describes Horchow: chatty, outgoing, spellbinding even. But consider for a moment a modest, cerebral man named Craig Newmark. Short, balding, and bespectacled, Newmark was a systems engineer for seventeen years at IBM. Before that, he had consuming interests in dinosaurs, chess, and physics. If you sat next to him on a plane, he'd probably keep his nose buried in a book.

Yet Newmark also happens to be the founder and majority owner of Craigslist, the eponymous website that—well—connects people with each other. As of May 28, 2011, Craigslist was the seventh-largest English language website in the world. Its users in over 700 cities in seventy countries find jobs, dates, and even kidney donors on Newmark's site. They join singing groups. They read one another's haikus. They confess their affairs. Newmark describes the site not as a business but as a public commons.

"Connecting people to fix the world over time is the deepest spiritual value you can have," Newmark has said. After Hurricane Katrina, Craigslist helped stranded families find new homes. During the New York City transit strike of 2005, Craigslist was the go-to place for ride-share listings. "Yet another crisis, and Craigslist commands the community," wrote one blogger about Craigslist's role in the strike. "How come Craig organically can touch lives on so many personal levels—and Craig's users can touch each other's lives on so many levels?"

Here's one answer: social media has made new forms of leadership possible for scores of people who don't fit the Harvard Business School mold.

On August 10, 2008, Guy Kawasaki, the best-selling author, speaker, serial entrepreneur, and Silicon Valley legend, tweeted, "You may find this hard to believe, but I am an introvert. I have a 'role' to play, but I fundamentally am a loner." Kawasaki's tweet set the world of social media buzzing. "At the time," wrote one blogger, "Guy's avatar featured him wearing a pink boa from a large party he threw at his house. Guy Kawasaki an introvert? Does not compute."

On August 15, 2008, Pete Cashmore, the founder of Mashable, the online guide to social media, weighed in. "Wouldn't it be a great irony," he asked, "if the leading proponents of the 'it's about people' mantra weren't so enamored with meeting large groups of people in real life? Perhaps social media affords us the control we lack in real life socializing: the screen as a barrier between us and the world." Then Cashmore outed himself. "Throw me firmly in the 'introverts' camp with Guy," he posted.

Studies have shown that, indeed, introverts are more likely than extroverts to express intimate facts about themselves online that their family and friends would be surprised to read, to say that they can express the "real me" online, and to spend more time in certain kinds of online discussions. They welcome the chance to communicate digitally. The same person who would never raise his hand in a lecture hall of two hundred people might blog to two thousand, or two million, without thinking twice. The same person who finds it difficult to introduce himself to strangers might establish a presence online and *then* extend these relationships into the real world.

~

What would have happened if the Subarctic Survival Situation had been conducted online, with the benefit of all the voices in the room—the Rosa Parkses and the Craig Newmarks and the Darwin Smiths? What if it had been a group of proactive castaways led by an introvert with a gift for calmly encouraging them to contribute? What if there had been an introvert and an extrovert sharing the helm, like Rosa Parks and Martin Luther King Jr.? Might they have reached the right result?

It's impossible to say. No one has ever run these studies, as far as I know—which is a shame. It's understandable that the HBS model of leadership places such a high premium on confidence and quick decision-making. If assertive people tend to get their way, then it's a useful skill for leaders whose work depends on influencing others. Decisiveness inspires confidence, while wavering (or even appearing to waver) can threaten morale.

But one can take these truths too far; in some circumstances quiet, modest styles of leadership may be equally or more effective. As I left the HBS campus, I stopped by a display of notable *Wall Street Journal* cartoons in the Baker Library lobby. One showed a haggard executive looking at a chart of steeply falling profits.

"It's all because of Fradkin," the executive tells his colleague. "He has terrible business sense but great leadership skills, and everyone is following him down the road to ruin."

Does God Love Introverts? An Evangelical's Dilemma

If Harvard Business School is an East Coast enclave for the global elite, my next stop was an institution that's much the opposite. It sits on a sprawling, 120-acre campus in the former desert and current exurb of Lake Forest, California. Unlike Harvard Business School, it admits anyone who wants to join. Families stroll the palm-tree-lined plazas and walkways in good-natured clumps. Children frolic in man-made streams and waterfalls. Staff wave amiably as they cruise by in golf carts. Wear whatever you want: sneakers and flip-flops are perfectly fine. This campus is presided over not by nattily attired professors wielding words like *protagonist* and *case method*, but by a benign Santa Claus–like figure in a Hawaiian shirt and sandy-haired goatee.

With an average weekly attendance of 22,000 and counting, Saddleback Church is one of the largest and most influential evangelical churches in the nation. Its leader is Rick Warren, author of *The Purpose Driven Life*, one of the best-selling books of all time, and the man who delivered the invocation at President Obama's inauguration. Saddleback doesn't cater to world-famous leaders the way HBS does, but it plays no less mighty a role in society. Evangelical leaders have the ear of presidents; dominate thousands of hours of TV time; and run multimillion-dollar businesses, with the most prominent boasting their own production companies, recording studios, and distribution deals with media giants like Time Warner.

Saddleback also has one more thing in common with Harvard Business School: its debt to—and propagation of—the Culture of Personality.

It's a Sunday morning in August 2006, and I'm standing at the center of a dense hub of sidewalks on Saddleback's campus. I consult a signpost, the kind you see at Walt Disney World, with cheerful arrows pointing every which way: Worship Center, Plaza Room, Terrace Café, Beach Café. A nearby poster features a beaming young man in bright red polo shirt and sneakers: "Looking for a new direction? Give traffic ministry a try!"

I'm searching for the open-air bookstore, where I'll be meeting Adam McHugh, a local evangelical pastor with whom I've been corresponding. McHugh is an avowed introvert, and we've been having a cross-country conversation about what it feels like to be a quiet and cerebral type in the evangelical movement—especially as a leader. Like HBS, evangelical churches often make extroversion a prerequisite for leadership, sometimes explicitly. "The priest must be . . . an extrovert who enthusiastically engages members and newcomers, a team player," reads an ad for a position as associate rector of a 1,400-member parish. A senior priest at another church confesses online that he has advised parishes recruiting a new rector to ask what his or her Myers-Briggs score is. "If the first letter isn't an 'E' [for extrovert]," he tells them, "think twice . . . I'm sure our Lord was [an extrovert]."

McHugh doesn't fit this description. He discovered his introversion as a junior at Claremont McKenna College, when he realized he was getting up early in the morning just to savor time alone with a steaming cup of coffee. He enjoyed parties, but found himself leaving early. "Other people would get louder and louder, and I would get quieter and quieter," he told me. He took a Myers-Briggs personality test and found out that there was a word, *introvert*, that described the type of person who likes to spend time as he did.

At first McHugh felt good about carving out more time for himself. But then he got active in evangelicalism and began to feel guilty about all that solitude. He even believed that God disapproved of his choices and, by extension, of him.

"The evangelical culture ties together faithfulness with extroversion," McHugh explained. "The emphasis is on community, on participating in more and more programs and events, on meeting more and more people. It's a constant tension for many introverts that they're not living that out. And in a religious world, there's more at stake when you feel that tension. It doesn't feel like 'I'm not doing as well as I'd like.' It feels like 'God isn't pleased with me.'"

From outside the evangelical community, this seems an astonishing confession. Since when is solitude one of the Seven Deadly Sins? But to a fellow evangelical, McHugh's sense of spiritual failure would make perfect sense. Contemporary evangelicalism says that every person you fail to meet and proselytize is another soul you might have saved. It also emphasizes building community among confirmed believers, with many churches encouraging (or even requiring) their members to join extra-curricular groups organized around every conceivable subject—cooking, real-estate investing, skateboarding. So every social event McHugh left early, every morning he spent alone, every group he failed to join, meant wasted chances to connect with others.

But, ironically, if there was one thing McHugh knew, it was that he *wasn't* alone. He looked around and saw a vast number of people in the evangelical community who felt just as conflicted as he did. He became ordained as a Presbyterian minister and worked with a team of student leaders at Claremont College, many of whom were introverts. The team became a kind of laboratory for experimenting with introverted forms of leadership and ministry. They focused on one-on-one and small group interactions rather than on large groups, and McHugh helped the students find rhythms in their lives that allowed them to claim the solitude they needed and enjoyed, and to have social energy left over for leading others. He urged them to find the courage to speak up and take risks in meeting new people.

A few years later, when social media exploded and evangelical bloggers started posting about their experiences, written evidence of the schism between introverts and extroverts within the evangelical church finally emerged. One blogger wrote about his "cry from the heart wondering *how* to fit in as an introvert in a church that prides itself on extroverted evangelism. There are probably quite a few [of you] out there who are put on guilt trips each time [you] get a personal evangelism push at church. There's a place in God's kingdom for sensitive, reflective types. It's not easy to claim, but it's there." Another wrote about his simple desire "to serve the Lord but not serve on a parish committee. In a universal church, there should be room for the un-gregarious."

McHugh added his own voice to this chorus, first with a blog calling for greater emphasis on religious practices of solitude and contemplation, and later with a book called *Introverts in the Church: Finding Our Place in an Extroverted Culture*. He argues that evangelism means listening as well as talking, that evangelical churches should incorporate silence and mystery into religious worship, and that they should make room for introverted leaders who might be able to demonstrate a quieter path to God. After all, hasn't prayer always been about contemplation as well as community? Religious leaders from Jesus to Buddha, as well as the lesser-known saints, monks, shamans, and prophets, have always gone off alone to experience the revelations they later shared with the rest of us.

~

When finally I find my way to the bookstore, McHugh is waiting with a serene expression on his face. He's in his early thirties, tall and broad-shouldered, dressed in jeans, a black polo shirt, and black flip-flops. With his short brown hair, reddish goatee, and sideburns, McHugh looks like a typical Gen Xer, but he speaks in the soothing, considered tones of a college professor. McHugh doesn't preach or worship at Saddleback, but we've chosen to meet here because it's such an important symbol of evangelical culture.

Since services are just about to start, there's little time to chat. Saddleback offers six different "worship venues," each housed in its own building or tent and set to its own beat: Worship Center, Traditional, OverDrive Rock, Gospel, Family, and something called Ohana Island Style Worship. We head to the main Worship Center, where Pastor Warren is about to preach. With its sky-high ceiling crisscrossed with klieg lights, the auditorium looks like a rock concert venue, save for the unobtrusive wooden cross hanging on the side of the room.

A man named Skip is warming up the congregation with a song. The lyrics are broadcast on five Jumbotron screens, interspersed with photos of shimmering lakes and Caribbean sunsets. Miked-up tech guys sit on a thronelike dais at the center of the room, training their video cameras on the audience. The cameras linger on a teenage girl—long, silky blond hair, electric smile, and shining blue eyes—who's singing her heart out. I can't help but think of Tony Robbins's "Unleash the Power Within" seminar. Did Tony base his program on megachurches like Saddleback, I wonder, or is it the other way around?

"Good morning, everybody!" beams Skip, then urges us to greet those seated near us. Most people oblige with wide smiles and glad hands, including McHugh, but there's a hint of strain beneath his smile.

Pastor Warren takes the stage. He's wearing a short-sleeved polo shirt and his famous goatee. Today's sermon will be based on the book of Jeremiah, he tells us. "It would be foolish to start a business without a business plan," Warren says, "but most people have no life plan. If you're a business leader, you need to read the book of Jeremiah over and over, because he was a genius CEO." There are no Bibles at our seats, only pencils and note cards, with the key points from the sermon preprinted, and blanks to fill in as Warren goes along.

Like Tony Robbins, Pastor Warren seems truly well-meaning; he's created this vast Saddleback ecosystem out of nothing, and he's done good works around the world. But at the same time I can see how hard it must be, inside this world of Luau worship and Jumbotron prayer, for Saddleback's introverts to feel good about themselves. As the service wears on, I feel the same sense of alienation that McHugh has described. Events like this don't give me the sense of oneness others seem to enjoy; it's always been private occasions that make me feel connected to the joys and sorrows of the world, often in the form of communion with writers and musicians I'll never meet in person. Proust called these moments of unity between writer and reader "that fruitful miracle of a communication in the midst of solitude." His use of religious language was surely no accident.

McHugh, as if reading my mind, turns to me when the service is over. "Everything in the service involved communication," he says with gentle exasperation. "Greeting people, the lengthy sermon, the singing. There was no emphasis on quiet, liturgy, ritual, things that give you space for contemplation."

McHugh's discomfort is all the more poignant because he genuinely admires Saddleback and all that it stands for. "Saddleback is doing amazing things around the world and in its own community," he says. "It's a friendly, hospitable place that genuinely seeks to connect with newcomers. That's an impressive mission given how colossal the church is, and how easy it would be for people to remain completely disconnected from others. Greeters, the informal atmosphere, meeting people around you—these are all motivated by good desires."

Yet McHugh finds practices like the mandatory smile-and-good-morning at the start of the service to be painful—and though he personally is willing to endure it, even sees the value in it, he worries about how many other introverts will not.

"It sets up an extroverted atmosphere that can be difficult for introverts like me," he explains. "Sometimes I feel like I'm going through the motions. The outward enthusiasm and passion that seems to be part and parcel of Saddleback's culture doesn't feel natural. Not that introverts can't be eager and enthusiastic, but we're not as overtly expressive as extroverts. At a place like Saddleback, you can start questioning your own experience of God. Is it really as strong as that of other people who look the part of the devout believer?"

Evangelicalism has taken the Extrovert Ideal to its logical extreme, McHugh is telling us. If you don't love Jesus out loud, then it must not be real love. It's not enough to forge your own spiritual connection to the divine; *it must be displayed publicly*. Is it any wonder that introverts like Pastor McHugh start to question their own hearts?

It's brave of McHugh, whose spiritual and professional calling depends on his connection to God, to confess his self-doubt. He does so because he wants to spare others the inner conflict he has struggled with, and because he loves evangelicalism and wants it to grow by learning from the introverts in its midst.

But he knows that meaningful change will come slowly to a religious culture that sees extroversion not only as a personality trait but also as an indicator of virtue. Righteous behavior is not so much the good we do behind closed doors when no one is there to praise us; it is what we "put out into the world." Just as Tony Robbins's aggressive upselling is OK with his fans because spreading helpful ideas is part of being a good person, and just as HBS expects its students to be talkers because this is seen as a prerequisite of leadership, so have many evangelicals come to associate godliness with sociability.

WHEN COLLABORATION KILLS CREATIVITY

The Rise of the New Groupthink and the Power of Working Alone

I am a horse for a single harness, not cut out for tandem or team-work . . . for well I know that in order to attain any definite goal, it is imperative that one person do the thinking and the commanding.

—ALBERT EINSTEIN

March 5, 1975. A cold and drizzly evening in Menlo Park, California. Thirty unprepossessing-looking engineers gather in the garage of an unemployed colleague named Gordon French. They call themselves the Homebrew Computer Club, and this is their first meeting. Their mission: to make computers accessible to regular people—no small task at a time when most computers are temperamental SUV-sized machines that only universities and corporations can afford.

The garage is drafty, but the engineers leave the doors open to the damp night air so people can wander inside. In walks an uncertain young man of twenty-four, a calculator designer for Hewlett-Packard. Serious and bespectacled, he has shoulder-length hair and a brown beard. He takes a chair and listens quietly as the others marvel over a new build-it-yourself computer called the Altair 8800, which recently made the cover of *Popular Electronics*. The Altair isn't a true personal computer; it's hard to use, and appeals only to the type of person who shows up at a garage on a rainy Wednesday night to talk about microchips. But it's an important first step.

The young man, whose name is Stephen Wozniak, is thrilled to hear of the Altair. He's been obsessed with electronics since the age of three. When he was eleven he came across a magazine article about the first computer, the ENIAC, or Electronic Numerical Integrator and Computer, and ever since, his dream has been to build a machine so small and easy to use that you could keep it at home. And now, inside this garage, here is news that The Dream—he thinks of it with capital letters—might one day materialize.

As he'll later recall in his memoir, *iWoz*, where most of this story appears, Wozniak is also excited to be surrounded by kindred spirits. To the Homebrew crowd, computers are a tool for social justice, and he feels the same way. Not that he talks to anyone at this first meeting—he's way too shy for that. But that night he goes home and sketches his first design for a personal computer, with a keyboard and a screen just like the kind we use today. Three months later he builds a prototype of that machine. And ten months after that, he and Steve Jobs cofound Apple Computer.

Today Steve Wozniak is a revered figure in Silicon Valley—there's a street in San Jose, California, named Woz's Way—and is sometimes called the nerd soul of Apple. He has learned over time to open up and speak publicly, even appearing as a contestant on *Dancing with the Stars*, where he displayed an endearing mixture of stiffness and good cheer. I once saw Wozniak speak at a bookstore in New York City. A standing-room-only crowd showed up bearing their 1970s Apple operating manuals, in honor of all that he had done for them.

~

But the credit is not Wozniak's alone; it also belongs to Homebrew. Wozniak identifies that first meeting as the beginning of the computer revolution and one of the most important nights of his life. So if you wanted to replicate the conditions that made Woz so productive, you might point to Homebrew, with its collection of like-minded souls. You might decide that Wozniak's achievement was a shining example of the collaborative approach to creativity. You might conclude that people who hope to be innovative should work in highly social workplaces.

And you might be wrong.

Consider what Wozniak did right after the meeting in Menlo Park. Did he huddle with fellow club members to work on computer design? No. (Although he did keep attending the meetings, every other Wednesday.) Did he seek out a big, open office space full of cheerful pandemonium in which ideas would cross-pollinate? No. When you read his account of his work process on that first PC, the most striking thing is that *he was always by himself*.

Wozniak did most of the work inside his cubicle at Hewlett-Packard. He'd arrive around 6:30 a.m. and, alone in the early morning, read engineering magazines, study chip manuals, and prepare designs in his head. After work, he'd go home, make a quick spaghetti or TV dinner, then drive back to the office and work late into the night. He describes this period of quiet midnights and solitary sunrises as "the biggest high ever." His efforts paid off on the night of June 29, 1975, at around 10:00 p.m., when Woz finished building a prototype of his machine. He hit a few keys on the keyboard—and letters appeared on the screen in front of him. It was the sort of breakthrough moment that most of us can only dream of. And he was alone when it happened.

Intentionally so. In his memoir, he offers this advice to kids who aspire to great creativity:

> Most inventors and engineers I've met are like me—they're shy and they live in their heads. They're almost like artists. In fact, the very best of them *are* artists. *And artists work best alone* where they can control an invention's design without a lot of other people designing it for marketing or some other committee. I don't believe anything really revolutionary has been invented by committee. If you're that rare engineer who's an inventor and also an artist, I'm going to give you some advice that might be hard to take. That advice is: *Work alone. You're going to be best able to design revolu-*

tionary products and features if you're working on your own. Not on a committee. Not on a team.

~

From 1956 to 1962, an era best remembered for its ethos of stultifying conformity, the Institute of Personality Assessment and Research at the University of California, Berkeley, conducted a series of studies on the nature of creativity. The researchers sought to identify the most spectacularly creative people and then figure out what made them different from everybody else. They assembled a list of architects, mathematicians, scientists, engineers, and writers who had made major contributions to their fields, and invited them to Berkeley for a weekend of personality tests, problem-solving experiments, and probing questions.

Then the researchers did something similar with members of the same professions whose contributions were decidedly less groundbreaking.

One of the most interesting findings, echoed by later studies, was that the more creative people tended to be socially poised introverts. They were interpersonally skilled but "not of an especially sociable or participative temperament." They described themselves as independent and individualistic. As teens, many had been shy and solitary.

These findings don't mean that introverts are always more creative than extroverts, but they do suggest that in a group of people who have been extremely creative throughout their lifetimes, you're likely to find a lot of introverts. Why should this be true? Do quiet personalities come with some ineffable quality that fuels creativity? Perhaps, as we'll see in chapter 6.

But there's a less obvious yet surprisingly powerful explanation for introverts' creative advantage—an explanation that everyone can learn from: *introverts prefer to work independently, and solitude can be a catalyst to innovation.* As the influential psychologist Hans Eysenck once observed, introversion "concentrates the mind on the tasks in hand, and prevents the dissipation of energy on social and sexual matters unrelated to work." In other words, if you're in the backyard sitting under a tree while everyone else is clinking glasses on the patio, you're more likely to have an apple fall on your head. (Newton was one of the world's great introverts. William Wordsworth described him as "A mind forever / Voyaging through strange seas of Thought alone.")

~

If this is true—if solitude is an important key to creativity—then we might all want to develop a taste for it. We'd want to teach our kids to work independently. We'd want to give employees plenty of privacy and autonomy. Yet increasingly we do just the opposite.

We like to believe that we live in a grand age of creative individualism. We look back at the midcentury era in which the Berkeley researchers conducted their creativity studies, and feel superior. Unlike the starched-shirted conformists of the 1950s, *we* hang posters of Einstein on our walls, his tongue stuck out iconoclastically. *We* consume indie music and films, and generate our own online content. *We* "think different" (even if we got the idea from Apple Computer's famous ad campaign).

But the way we organize many of our most important institutions—our schools and our workplaces—tells a very different story. It's the story of a contemporary phenomenon that I call the New Groupthink—a phenomenon that has the potential to stifle productivity at work and to deprive schoolchildren of the skills they'll need to achieve excellence in an increasingly competitive world.

The New Groupthink elevates teamwork above all else. It insists that creativity and intellectual achievement come from a gregarious place. It has many powerful advocates. "Innovation—the heart of the knowledge economy—is fundamentally social," writes the prominent journalist Malcolm Gladwell. "None of us is as smart as all of us," declares the organizational consultant Warren Bennis, in his book *Organizing Genius*, whose opening chapter heralds the rise of the "Great Group" and "The End of the Great Man." "Many jobs that we regard as the province of a single mind actually require a crowd," muses Clay Shirky in his influential book *Here Comes Everybody*. Even "Michelangelo had assistants paint part of the Sistine Chapel ceiling." (Never mind that the assistants were likely interchangeable, while Michelangelo was not.)

The New Groupthink is embraced by many corporations, which increasingly organize workforces into teams, a practice that gained popularity in the early 1990s. By 2000 an estimated half of all U.S. organizations used teams, and today virtually all of them do, according to the management professor Frederick Morgeson. A recent survey found that 91 percent of high-level managers believe that teams are the key to success. The consultant Stephen Harvill told me that of the thirty major organizations he worked with in 2010, including J.C. Penney, Wells Fargo, Dell Computers, and Prudential, he couldn't think of a single one that didn't use teams.

Some of these teams are virtual, working together from remote locations, but others demand a tremendous amount of face-to-face interaction, in the form of team-building exercises and retreats, shared online calendars that announce employees' availability for meetings, and physical workplaces that afford little privacy. Today's employees inhabit open office plans, in which no one has a room of his or her own, the only walls are the ones holding up the building, and senior executives operate from the center of the boundary-less floor along with everyone else. In fact, over 70 percent of today's employees work in an open plan; companies using them include Procter & Gamble, Ernst & Young, GlaxoSmith-Kline, Alcoa, and H.J. Heinz.

The amount of space per employee shrank from 500 square feet in the 1970s to 200 square feet in 2010, according to Peter Miscovich, a managing director at the real estate brokerage firm Jones Lang LaSalle. "There has been a shift from 'I' to 'we' work," Steelcase CEO James Hackett told *Fast Company* magazine in 2005. "Employees used to work alone in 'I' settings. Today, working in teams and groups is highly valued. We are designing products to facilitate that." Rival office manufacturer Herman Miller, Inc., has not only introduced new furniture designed to accommodate "the move toward collaboration and teaming in the workplace" but also moved its own top executives from private offices to an open space. In 2006, the Ross School of Business at the University of

Michigan demolished a classroom building in part because it wasn't set up for maximum group interaction.

The New Groupthink is also practiced in our schools, via an increasingly popular method of instruction called "cooperative" or "small group" learning. In many elementary schools, the traditional rows of seats facing the teacher have been replaced with "pods" of four or more desks pushed together to facilitate countless group learning activities. Even subjects like math and creative writing, which would seem to depend on solo flights of thought, are often taught as group projects. In one fourth-grade classroom I visited, a big sign announced the "Rules for Group Work," including, YOU CAN'T ASK A TEACHER FOR HELP UNLESS EVERYONE IN YOUR GROUP HAS THE SAME QUESTION.

According to a 2002 nationwide survey of more than 1,200 fourth- and eighth-grade teachers, 55 percent of fourth-grade teachers prefer cooperative learning, compared to only 26 percent who favor teacher-directed formats. Only 35 percent of fourth-grade and 29 percent of eighth-grade teachers spend more than half their classroom time on traditional instruction, while 42 percent of fourth-grade and 41 percent of eighth-grade teachers spend at least a quarter of class time on group work. Among younger teachers, small-group learning is even more popular, suggesting that the trend will continue for some time to come.

The cooperative approach has politically progressive roots—the theory is that students take ownership of their education when they learn from one another—but according to elementary school teachers I interviewed at public and private schools in New York, Michigan, and Georgia, it also trains kids to express themselves in the team culture of corporate America. "This style of teaching reflects the business community," one fifth-grade teacher in a Manhattan public school told me, "where people's respect for others is based on their verbal abilities, not their originality or insight. You have to be someone who speaks well and calls attention to yourself. It's an elitism based on something other than merit." "Today the world of business works in groups, so now the kids do it in school," a third-grade teacher in Decatur, Georgia, explained. "Cooperative learning enables skills in working as teams—skills that are in dire demand in the workplace," writes the educational consultant Bruce Williams.

Williams also identifies leadership training as a primary benefit of cooperative learning. Indeed, the teachers I met seemed to pay close attention to their students' managerial skills. In one public school I visited in downtown Atlanta, a third-grade teacher pointed out a quiet student who likes to "do his own thing." "But we put him in charge of safety patrol one morning, so he got the chance to be a leader, too," she assured me.

This teacher was kind and well-intentioned, but I wonder whether students like the young safety officer would be better off if we appreciated that not everyone *aspires* to be a leader in the conventional sense of the word—that some people wish to fit harmoniously into the group, and others to be independent of it. Often the most highly creative people are in the latter category. As Janet Farrall and Leonie Kronborg write in *Leadership Development for the Gifted and Talented*:

> While extroverts tend to attain leadership in public domains, introverts tend to attain leadership in theoretical and aesthetic fields. Outstanding introverted leaders, such as Charles Darwin, Marie Curie, Patrick White and Arthur Boyd, who have created either new fields of thought or rearranged existing knowledge, have spent long periods of their lives in solitude. Hence leadership does not only apply in social situations, but also occurs in more solitary situations such as developing new techniques in the arts, creating new philosophies, writing profound books and making scientific breakthroughs.

The New Groupthink did not arise at one precise moment. Cooperative learning, corporate teamwork, and open office plans emerged at different times and for different reasons. But the mighty force that pulled these trends together was the rise of the World Wide Web, which lent both cool and gravitas to the idea of collaboration. On the Internet, wondrous creations were produced via shared brainpower: Linux, the open-source operating system; Wikipedia, the online encyclopedia; MoveOn.org, the grassroots political movement. These collective productions, exponentially greater than the sum of their parts, were so awe-inspiring that we came to revere the hive mind, the wisdom of crowds, the miracle of crowdsourcing. *Collaboration* became a sacred concept—the key multiplier for success.

But then we took things a step further than the facts called for. We came to value transparency and to knock down walls—not only online but also in person. We failed to realize that what makes sense for the asynchronous, relatively anonymous interactions of the Internet might not work as well inside the face-to-face, politically charged, acoustically noisy confines of an open-plan office. Instead of distinguishing between online and in-person interaction, we used the lessons of one to inform our thinking about the other.

That's why, when people talk about aspects of the New Groupthink such as open office plans, they tend to invoke the Internet. "Employees are putting their whole lives up on Facebook and Twitter and everywhere else anyway. There's no reason they should hide behind a cubicle wall," Dan Lafontaine, CFO of the social marketing firm Mr. Youth, told NPR. Another management consultant told me something similar: "An office wall is exactly what it sounds like—a barrier. The fresher your methodologies of thinking, the less you want boundaries. The companies who use open office plans are new companies, just like the World Wide Web, which is still a teenager."

The Internet's role in promoting face-to-face group work is especially ironic because the early Web was a medium that enabled bands of often introverted individualists—people much like the solitude-craving thought leaders Farrall and Kronborg describe—to come together to subvert and transcend the usual ways of problem-solving. A significant majority of the earliest computer enthusiasts were introverts, according to a study of 1,229 computer professionals working in the U.S., the U.K., and Australia between 1982 and 1984. "It's a truism in tech that open source attracts introverts," says Dave W. Smith, a consultant and software developer in Silicon Valley, referring to the practice of producing software by opening the source code to the online public and allowing anyone to copy, improve upon, and distribute it. Many of these people were motivated by a desire to contribute to the broader good, and to see their achievements recognized by a community they valued.

But the earliest open-source creators didn't share office space—often they didn't even live in the same country. Their collaborations took place largely in the ether. This is not an insignificant detail. If you had gathered the same people who created Linux, installed them in a giant conference room for a year, and asked them to devise a new operating system, it's doubtful that anything so revolutionary would have occurred—for reasons we'll explore in the rest of this chapter.

~

When the research psychologist Anders Ericsson was fifteen, he took up chess. He was pretty good at it, he thought, trouncing all his classmates during lunchtime matches. Until one day a boy who'd been one of the worst players in the class started to win every match.

Ericsson wondered what had happened. "I really thought about this a lot," he recalls in an interview with Daniel Coyle, author of *The Talent Code*. "Why could that boy, whom I had beaten so easily, now beat me just as easily? I knew he was studying, going to a chess club, but what had happened, really, underneath?"

This is the question that drives Ericsson's career: How do extraordinary achievers get to be so great at what they do? Ericsson has searched for answers in fields as diverse as chess, tennis, and classical piano.

In a now-famous experiment, he and his colleagues compared three groups of expert violinists at the elite Music Academy in West Berlin. The researchers asked the professors to divide the students into three groups: the "best violinists," who had the potential for careers as international soloists; the "good violinists"; and a third group training to be violin teachers rather than performers. Then they interviewed the musicians and asked them to keep detailed diaries of their time.

They found a striking difference among the groups. All three groups spent the same amount of time—over fifty hours a week—participating in music-related activities. All three had similar classroom requirements making demands on their time. But the two best groups spent most of their music-related time *practicing in solitude*: 24.3 hours a week, or 3.5 hours a day, for the best group, compared with only 9.3 hours a week, or 1.3 hours a day, for the worst group. The best violinists rated "practice alone" as the most important of all their music-related activities. Elite musicians—even those who perform in groups—describe practice sessions with their chamber group as "leisure" compared with solo practice, where the real work gets done.

Ericsson and his cohorts found similar effects of solitude when they studied other kinds of expert performers. "Serious study alone" is the strongest predictor of skill for tournament-rated chess players, for example; grandmasters typically spend a whopping five thousand hours—almost five times as many hours as intermediate-level players—studying the game by themselves during their first ten years of learning to play. College students who tend to study alone learn more over time than those who work in groups. Even elite athletes in team sports often spend unusual amounts of time in solitary practice.

What's so magical about solitude? In many fields, Ericsson told me, it's only when you're alone that you can engage in Deliberate Practice, which he has identified as the key to exceptional achievement. When you practice deliberately, you identify the tasks or knowledge that are just out of your reach, strive to upgrade your performance, monitor your progress, and revise accordingly. Practice sessions that fall short of this standard are not only less useful—they're counterproductive. They reinforce existing cognitive mechanisms instead of improving them.

Deliberate Practice is best conducted alone for several reasons. It takes intense concentration, and other people can be distracting. It requires deep motivation, often self-generated. But most important, it involves working on the task that's most challenging to *you* personally. Only when you're alone, Ericsson told me, can you "go directly to the part that's challenging to you. If you want to improve what you're doing, *you* have to be the one who generates the move. Imagine a group class—you're the one generating the move only a small percentage of the time."

To see Deliberate Practice in action, we need look no further than the story of Stephen Wozniak. The Homebrew meeting was the catalyst that inspired him to build that first PC, but the knowledge base and work habits that made it possible came from another place entirely: Woz had deliberately practiced engineering ever since he was a little kid. (Ericsson says that it takes approximately ten thousand hours of Deliberate Practice to gain true expertise, so it helps to start young.)

In *iWoz*, Wozniak describes his childhood passion for electronics, and unintentionally recounts all the elements of Deliberate Practice that Ericsson emphasizes. First, he was motivated: his father, a Lockheed engineer, had taught Woz that engineers could change people's lives and were "among the key people in the world." Second, he built his expertise step by painstaking step. Because he entered countless science fairs, he says,

> I acquired a central ability that was to help me through my entire career: patience. I'm serious. Patience is usually so underrated. I mean, for all those projects, from third grade all the way to eighth grade, I just learned things gradually, figuring out how to put electronic devices together without so much as cracking a book. . . . I learned to not worry so much about the outcome, but to concentrate on the step I was on and to try to do it as perfectly as I could when I was doing it.

Third, Woz often worked alone. This was not necessarily by choice. Like many technically inclined kids, he took a painful tumble down the social ladder when he got to junior high school. As a boy he'd been admired for his science prowess, but now nobody seemed to care. He hated small talk, and his interests were out of step with those of his peers. A black-and-white photo from this period shows Woz, hair closely cropped, grimacing intensely, pointing proudly at his "science-fair-winning Adder/ Subtractor," a boxlike contraption of wires, knobs, and gizmos. But the awkwardness of those years didn't deter him from pursuing his dream; it probably nurtured it. He would never have learned so much about computers, Woz says now, if he hadn't been too shy to leave the house.

No one would choose this sort of painful adolescence, but the fact is that the solitude of Woz's teens, and the single-minded focus on what would turn out to be a lifelong passion, is typical for highly creative people. According to the psychologist Mihaly Csikszentmihalyi, who between 1990 and 1995 studied the lives of ninety-one exceptionally creative people in the arts, sciences, business, and government, many of his subjects were on the social margins during adolescence, partly because "intense curiosity or focused interest seems odd to their peers." Teens who are too gregarious to spend time alone often fail to cultivate their talents "because practicing music or studying math requires a solitude they dread." Madeleine L'Engle, the author of the classic young adult novel *A Wrinkle in Time* and more than sixty other books, says that she would never have developed into such a bold thinker had she not spent so much of her childhood alone with books and ideas. As a young boy, Charles Darwin made friends easily but preferred to spend his time taking long, solitary nature walks. (As an adult he was no different. "My dear Mr. Babbage," he wrote to the famous mathematician who had invited him to a dinner party, "I am very much obliged to you for sending me cards for your parties, but I am afraid of accepting them, for I should meet some people there, to whom I have sworn by all the saints in Heaven, I never go out.")

But exceptional performance depends not only on the groundwork we lay through Deliberate Practice; it also requires the right working conditions. And in contemporary workplaces, these are surprisingly hard to come by.

~

One of the side benefits of being a consultant is getting intimate access to many different work environments. Tom DeMarco, a principal of the Atlantic Systems Guild team of consultants, had walked around a good number of offices in his time, and he noticed that some workspaces were a lot more densely packed than others. He wondered what effect all that social interaction had on performance.

To find out, DeMarco and his colleague Timothy Lister devised a study called the Coding War Games. The purpose of the games was to identify the characteristics of the best and worst computer programmers; more than six hundred developers from ninety-two different companies participated. Each designed, coded, and tested a program, working in his normal office space during business hours. Each participant was also assigned a partner from the same company. The partners worked separately, however, without any communication, a feature of the games that turned out to be critical.

When the results came in, they revealed an enormous performance gap. The best outperformed the worst by a 10:1 ratio. The top programmers were also about 2.5 times better than the median. When DeMarco and Lister tried to figure out what accounted for this astonishing range, the factors that you'd think would matter—such as years of experience, salary, even the time spent completing the work—had little correlation to outcome. Programmers with ten years' experience did no better than those with two years. The half who performed above the median earned *less* than 10 percent more than the half below—even though they were almost twice as good. The programmers who turned in "zero-defect" work took slightly less, not more, time to complete the exercise than those who made mistakes.

It was a mystery with one intriguing clue: programmers from the same companies performed at more or less the same level, *even though they hadn't worked together*. That's because top performers overwhelmingly worked for companies that gave their workers the most privacy, personal space, control over their physical environments, and freedom from interruption. Sixty-two percent of the best performers said that their workspace was acceptably private, compared to only 19 percent of the worst performers; 76 percent of the worst performers but only 38 percent of the top performers said that people often interrupted them needlessly.

The Coding War Games are well known in tech circles, but DeMarco and Lister's findings reach beyond the world of computer programmers. A mountain of recent data on open-plan offices from many different industries corroborates the results of the games. Open-plan offices have been found to reduce productivity and impair memory. They're associated with high staff turnover. They make people sick, hostile, unmotivated, and insecure. Open-plan workers are more likely to suffer from high blood pressure and elevated stress levels and to get the flu; they argue more with their colleagues; they worry about coworkers eavesdropping on their phone calls and spying on their computer screens. They have fewer personal and confidential conversations with colleagues. They're often subject to loud and uncontrollable noise, which raises heart rates; releases cortisol, the body's fight-or-flight "stress" hormone; and makes people socially distant, quick to anger, aggressive, and slow to help others.

Indeed, excessive stimulation seems to impede learning: a recent study found that people learn better after a quiet stroll through the woods than after a noisy walk down a city street. Another study, of 38,000 knowledge workers across different sectors, found that the simple act of being interrupted is one of the biggest barriers to productivity. Even multitasking, that prized feat of modern-day office warriors, turns out to be a myth. Scientists now know that the brain is incapable of paying attention to two things at the same time. What looks like multitasking is really switching back and forth between multiple tasks, which reduces productivity and increases mistakes by up to 50 percent.

Many introverts seem to know these things instinctively, and resist being herded together. Backbone Entertainment, a video game design company in Oakland, California, initially used an open office plan but found that their game developers, many of whom were introverts, were unhappy. "It was one big warehouse space, with just tables, no walls, and everyone could see each other," recalls Mike Mika, the former creative director. "We switched over to cubicles and were worried about it—you'd think in a creative environment that people would hate that. But it turns out they prefer having nooks and crannies they can hide away in and just be away from everybody."

Something similar happened at Reebok International when, in 2000, the company consolidated 1,250 employees in their new headquarters in Canton, Massachusetts. The managers assumed that their shoe designers would want office space with plenty of access to each other so they could brainstorm (an idea they probably picked up when they were getting their MBAs). Luckily, they consulted first with the shoe designers themselves, who told them that actually what they needed was peace and quiet so they could concentrate.

This would not have come as news to Jason Fried, cofounder of the web application company 37signals. For ten years, beginning in 2000, Fried asked hundreds of people (mostly designers, programmers, and writers) where they liked to work when they needed to get something done. He found that they went anywhere *but* their offices, which were too noisy and full of interruptions. That's why, of Fried's sixteen employees, only eight live in Chicago, where 37signals is based, and even they are not required to show up for work, even for meetings. Especially not for meetings, which Fried views as "toxic." Fried is not anti-collaboration—37signals' home page touts its products' ability to make collaboration productive and pleasant. But he prefers passive forms of collaboration like e-mail, instant messaging, and online chat tools. His advice for other employers? "Cancel your next meeting," he advises. "Don't reschedule it. Erase it from memory." He also suggests "No-Talk Thursdays," one day a week in which employees aren't allowed to speak to each other.

The people Fried interviewed were saying out loud what creative people have always known. Kafka, for example, couldn't bear to be near even his adoring fiancée while he worked:

> You once said that you would like to sit beside me while I write. Listen, in that case I could not write at all. For writing means revealing oneself to excess; that utmost of self-revelation and surrender, in which a human being, when involved with others, would feel he was losing himself, and from which, therefore, he will always shrink as long as he is in his right mind. . . . That is why one can never be alone enough when one writes, why there can never be enough silence around one when one writes, why even night is not night enough.

Even the considerably more cheerful Theodor Geisel (otherwise known as Dr. Seuss) spent his workdays ensconced in his private studio, the walls lined with sketches and drawings, in a bell-tower outside his La Jolla, California, house. Geisel was a much more quiet man than his jocular rhymes suggest. He rarely ventured out in public to meet his young readership, fretting that kids would expect a merry, outspoken, Cat in the Hat–like figure, and would be disappointed with his reserved personality. "In mass, [children] terrify me," he admitted.

~

If personal space is vital to creativity, so is freedom from "peer pressure." Consider the story of the legendary advertising man Alex Osborn. Today

Osborn's name rings few bells, but during the first half of the twentieth century he was the kind of larger-than-life renaissance man who mesmerized his contemporaries. Osborn was a founding partner of the advertising agency Batten, Barton, Durstine, and Osborn (BBDO), but it was as an author that he really made his mark, beginning with the day in 1938 that a magazine editor invited him to lunch and asked what his hobby was.

"Imagination," replied Osborn.

"Mr. Osborn," said the editor, "you must do a book on that. It's a job that has been waiting to be done all these years. There is no subject of greater importance. You must give it the time and energy and thoroughness it deserves."

And so Mr. Osborn did. He wrote several books during the 1940s and 1950s, in fact, each tackling a problem that had vexed him in his capacity as head of BBDO: his employees were not creative enough. They had good ideas, Osborn believed, but were loath to share them for fear of their colleagues' judgment.

For Osborn, the solution was not to have his employees work alone, but rather to remove the threat of criticism from group work. He invented the concept of brainstorming, a process in which group members generate ideas in a nonjudgmental atmosphere. Brainstorming had four rules:

1. Don't judge or criticize ideas.
2. Be freewheeling. The wilder the idea, the better.
3. Go for quantity. The more ideas you have, the better.
4. Build on the ideas of fellow group members.

Osborn believed passionately that groups—once freed from the shackles of social judgment—produced more and better ideas than did individuals working in solitude, and he made grand claims for his favored method. "The quantitative results of group brainstorming are beyond question," he wrote. "One group produced 45 suggestions for a home-appliance promotion, 56 ideas for a money-raising campaign, 124 ideas on how to sell more blankets. In another case, 15 groups brainstormed one and the same problem and produced over 800 ideas."

Osborn's theory had great impact, and company leaders took up brainstorming with enthusiasm. To this day, it's common for anyone who spends time in corporate America to find himself occasionally cooped up with colleagues in a room full of whiteboards, markers, and a preternaturally peppy facilitator encouraging everyone to free-associate.

There's only one problem with Osborn's breakthrough idea: group brainstorming doesn't actually work. One of the first studies to demonstrate this was conducted in 1963. Marvin Dunnette, a psychology professor at the University of Minnesota, gathered forty-eight research scientists and forty-eight advertising executives, all of them male employees of Minnesota Mining and Manufacturing (otherwise known as 3M, inventors of the Post-it), and asked them to participate in both solitary and group brainstorming sessions. Dunnette was confident that the executives would benefit from the group process. He was less sure that the research scientists, whom he considered more introverted, would profit from group work.

Dunnette divided each set of forty-eight men into twelve groups of four. Each foursome was given a problem to brainstorm, such as the benefits or difficulties that would arise from being born with an extra thumb. Each man was also given a similar problem to brainstorm on his own. Then Dunnette and his team counted all the ideas, comparing those produced by the groups with those generated by people working individually. In order to compare apples with apples, Dunnette pooled the ideas of each individual together with those of three other individuals, as if they had been working in "nominal" groups of four. The researchers also measured the quality of the ideas, rating them on a "Probability Scale" of 0 through 4.

The results were unambiguous. The men in twenty-three of the twenty-four groups produced more ideas when they worked on their own than when they worked as a group. They also produced ideas of equal or higher quality when working individually. And the advertising executives were no better at group work than the presumably introverted research scientists.

Since then, some forty years of research has reached the same startling conclusion. Studies have shown that performance gets worse as group size increases: groups of nine generate fewer and poorer ideas compared to groups of six, which do worse than groups of four. The "evidence from science suggests that business people must be insane to use brainstorming groups," writes the organizational psychologist Adrian Furnham. "If you have talented and motivated people, they should be encouraged to work alone when creativity or efficiency is the highest priority."

The one exception to this is online brainstorming. Groups brainstorming electronically, when properly managed, not only do better than individuals, research shows; the larger the group, the better it performs. The same is true of academic research—professors who work together electronically, from different physical locations, tend to produce research that is more influential than those either working alone or collaborating face-to-face.

This shouldn't surprise us; as we've said, it was the curious power of electronic collaboration that contributed to the New Groupthink in the first place. What created Linux, or Wikipedia, if not a gigantic electronic brainstorming session? But we're so impressed by the power of online collaboration that we've come to overvalue *all* group work at the expense of solo thought. We fail to realize that participating in an online working group is a form of solitude all its own. Instead we assume that the success of online collaborations will be replicated in the face-to-face world.

Indeed, after all these years of evidence that conventional brainstorming groups don't work, they remain as popular as ever. Participants in brainstorming sessions usually believe that their group performed much better than it actually did, which points to a valuable reason for their continued popularity—group brainstorming makes people feel attached. A worthy goal, so long as we understand that social glue, as opposed to creativity, is the principal benefit.

~

Psychologists usually offer three explanations for the failure of group brainstorming. The first is *social loafing*: in a group, some individuals tend to sit back and let others do the work. The second is *production blocking*: only one person can talk or produce an idea at once, while the other group members are forced to sit passively. And the third is *evaluation apprehension*, meaning the fear of looking stupid in front of one's peers.

Osborn's "rules" of brainstorming were meant to neutralize this anxiety, but studies show that the fear of public humiliation is a potent force. During the 1988–89 basketball season, for example, two NCAA basketball teams played eleven games without any spectators, owing to a measles outbreak that led their schools to quarantine all students. Both teams played much better (higher free-throw percentages, for example) without any fans, even adoring home-team fans, to unnerve them.

The behavioral economist Dan Ariely noticed a similar phenomenon when he conducted a study asking thirty-nine participants to solve anagram puzzles, either alone at their desks or with others watching. Ariely predicted that the participants would do better in public because they'd be more motivated. But they performed worse. An audience may be rousing, but it's also stressful.

The problem with evaluation apprehension is that there's not much we can do about it. You'd think you could overcome it with will or training or a set of group process rules like Alex Osborn's. But recent research in neuroscience suggests that the fear of judgment runs much deeper and has more far-reaching implications than we ever imagined.

Between 1951 and 1956, just as Osborn was promoting the power of group brainstorming, a psychologist named Solomon Asch conducted a series of now-famous experiments on the dangers of group influence. Asch gathered student volunteers into groups and had them take a vision test. He showed them a picture of three lines of varying lengths and asked questions about how the lines compared with one another: which was longer, which one matched the length of a fourth line, and so on. His questions were so simple that 95 percent of students answered every question correctly.

But when Asch planted actors in the groups, and the actors confidently volunteered the same incorrect answer, the number of students who gave all correct answers plunged to 25 percent. That is, a staggering 75 percent of the participants went along with the group's wrong answer to at least one question.

The Asch experiments demonstrated the power of conformity at exactly the time that Osborn was trying to release us from its chains. What they didn't tell us was *why* we were so prone to conform. What was going on in the minds of the kowtowers? Had their *perception* of the lines' lengths been altered by peer pressure, or did they knowingly give wrong answers for fear of being the odd one out? For decades, psychologists puzzled over this question.

Today, with the help of brain-scanning technology, we may be getting closer to the answer. In 2005 an Emory University neuroscientist named Gregory Berns decided to conduct an updated version of Asch's experiments. Berns and his team recruited thirty-two volunteers, men and women between the ages of nineteen and forty-one. The volunteers played a game in which each group member was shown two different three-dimensional objects on a computer screen and asked to decide whether the first object could be rotated to match the second. The experimenters used an fMRI scanner to take snapshots of the volunteers' brains as they conformed to or broke with group opinion.

The results were both disturbing and illuminating. First, they corroborated Asch's findings. When the volunteers played the game on their own, they gave the wrong answer only 13.8 percent of the time. But when they played with a group whose members gave unanimously wrong answers, they agreed with the group 41 percent of the time.

But Berns's study also shed light on exactly *why* we're such conformists. When the volunteers played alone, the brain scans showed activity in a network of brain regions including the occipital cortex and parietal cortex, which are associated with visual and spatial perception, and in the frontal cortex, which is associated with conscious decision-making. But when they went along with their group's wrong answer, their brain activity revealed something very different.

Remember, what Asch wanted to know was whether people conformed despite knowing that the group was wrong, or whether their perceptions had been *altered* by the group. If the former was true, Berns and his team reasoned, then they should see more brain activity in the decision-making prefrontal cortex. That is, the brain scans would pick up the volunteers deciding consciously to abandon their own beliefs to fit in with the group. But if the brain scans showed heightened activity in regions associated with visual and spatial perception, this would suggest that the group had somehow managed to change the individual's perceptions.

That was exactly what happened—the conformists showed less brain activity in the frontal, decision-making regions and more in the areas of the brain associated with perception. Peer pressure, in other words, is not only unpleasant, but can actually change your view of a problem.

These early findings suggest that groups are like mind-altering substances. If the group thinks the answer is A, you're much more likely to believe that A is correct, too. It's not that you're saying consciously, "Hmm, I'm not sure, but they all think the answer's A, so I'll go with that." Nor are you saying, "I want them to like me, so I'll just pretend that the answer's A." No, you are doing something much more unexpected—and dangerous. Most of Berns's volunteers reported having gone along with the group because "they thought that they had arrived serendipitously at the same correct answer." They were utterly blind, in other words, to how much their peers had influenced them.

What does this have to do with social fear? Well, remember that the volunteers in the Asch and Berns studies didn't always conform. Sometimes they picked the right answer despite their peers' influence. And Berns and his team found something very interesting about these moments. They were linked to heightened activation in the amygdala, a small organ in the brain associated with upsetting emotions such as the fear of rejection.

Berns refers to this as "the pain of independence," and it has serious implications. Many of our most important civic institutions, from elections to jury trials to the very idea of majority rule, depend on dissenting voices. But when the group is literally capable of changing our perceptions, and when to stand alone is to activate primitive, powerful, and unconscious feelings of rejection, then the health of these institutions seems far more vulnerable than we think.

~

But of course I've been simplifying the case against face-to-face collaboration. Steve Wozniak collaborated with Steve Jobs, after all; without their pairing, there would be no Apple today. Every pair bond between mother and father, between parent and child, is an act of creative collaboration. Indeed, studies show that face-to-face interactions create trust in a way that online interactions can't. Research also suggests that population density is correlated with innovation; despite the advantages of quiet walks in the woods, people in crowded cities benefit from the web of interactions that urban life offers.

I have experienced this phenomenon personally. When I was getting ready to write this book, I carefully set up my home office, complete with uncluttered desk, file cabinets, free counter space, and plenty of natural light—and then felt too cut off from the world to type a single keystroke there. Instead, I wrote most of this book on a laptop at my favorite densely packed neighborhood café. I did this for exactly the reasons that champions of the New Groupthink might suggest: the mere presence of other people helped my mind to make associative leaps. The coffee shop was full of people bent over their own computers, and if the expressions of rapt concentration on their faces were any indication, I wasn't the only one getting a lot of work done.

But the café worked as my office because it had specific attributes that are absent from many modern schools and workplaces. It was social, yet its casual, come-and-go-as-you-please nature left me free from unwelcome entanglements and able to "deliberately practice" my writing. I could toggle back and forth between observer and social actor as much as I wanted. I could also control my environment. Each day I chose the location of my table—in the center of the room or along the perimeter—depending on whether I wanted to be seen as well as to see. And I had the option to leave whenever I wanted peace and quiet to edit what I'd written that day. Usually I was ready to exercise this right after only a few hours—not the eight, ten, or fourteen hours that many office dwellers put in.

The way forward, I'm suggesting, is not to stop collaborating face-to-face, but to refine the way we do it. For one thing, we should actively seek out symbiotic introvert-extrovert relationships, in which leadership and other tasks are divided according to people's natural strengths and temperaments. The most effective teams are composed of a healthy mix of introverts and extroverts, studies show, and so are many leadership structures.

We also need to create settings in which people are free to circulate in a shifting kaleidoscope of interactions, and to disappear into their private workspaces when they want to focus or simply be alone. Our schools should teach children the skills to work with others—cooperative learning can be effective when practiced well and in moderation—but also the time and training they need to deliberately practice on their own. It's also vital to recognize that many people—especially introverts like Steve Wozniak—need extra quiet and privacy in order to do their best work.

Some companies are starting to understand the value of silence and solitude, and are creating "flexible" open plans that offer a mix of solo workspaces, quiet zones, casual meeting areas, cafés, reading rooms, computer hubs, and even "streets" where people can chat casually with each other without interrupting others' workflow. At Pixar Animation Studios, the sixteen-acre campus is built around a football-field-sized atrium housing mailboxes, a cafeteria, and even bathrooms. The idea is to encourage as many casual, chance encounters as possible. At the same time, employees are encouraged to make their individual offices, cubicles, desks, and work areas their own and to decorate them as they wish. Similarly, at Microsoft, many employees enjoy their own private offices, yet they come with sliding doors, movable walls, and other features that allow occupants to decide when they want to collaborate and when they need private time to think. These kinds of diverse workspaces benefit introverts as well as extroverts, the systems design researcher Matt Davis told me, because they offer more spaces to retreat to than traditional open-plan offices.

I suspect that Wozniak himself would approve of these developments. Before he created the Apple PC, Woz designed calculators at Hewlett-Packard, a job he loved in part because HP made it so easy to chat with others. Every day at 10:00 a.m. and 2:00 p.m. management wheeled in donuts and coffee, and people would socialize and swap ideas. What set these interactions apart was how low-key and relaxed they were. In *iWoz*, he recalls HP as a meritocracy where it didn't matter what you looked like, where there was no premium on playing social games, and where no one pushed him from his beloved engineering work into management. That was what collaboration meant for Woz: the ability to share a donut and a brainwave with his laid-back, nonjudgmental, poorly dressed colleagues—who minded not a whit when he disappeared into his cubicle to get the real work done.

Part

Two

YOUR BIOLOGY, YOUR SELF?

4

IS TEMPERAMENT DESTINY?

Nature, Nurture, and the Orchid Hypothesis

Some people are more certain of everything than I am of anything.
—ROBERT RUBIN, *In an Uncertain World*

ALMOST TEN YEARS AGO

It's 2:00 a.m., I can't sleep, and I want to die.

I'm not normally the suicidal type, but this is the night before a big speech, and my mind races with horrifying what-if propositions. What if my mouth dries up and I can't get any words out? What if I bore the audience? What if I throw up onstage?

My boyfriend (now my husband), Ken, watches me toss and turn. He's bewildered by my distress. A former UN peacekeeper, he once was ambushed in Somalia, yet I don't think he felt as scared then as I do now.

"Try to think of happy things," he says, caressing my forehead.

I stare at the ceiling, tears welling. What happy things? Who could be happy in a world of podiums and microphones?

"There are a billion people in China who don't give a rat's ass about your speech," Ken offers sympathetically.

This helps, for approximately five seconds. I turn over and watch the alarm clock. Finally it's six thirty. At least the worst part, the night-before part, is over; this time tomorrow, I'll be free. But first I have to get through today. I dress grimly and put on a coat. Ken hands me a sports water bottle filled with Baileys Irish Cream. I'm not a big drinker, but I like Baileys because it tastes like a chocolate milkshake. "Drink this fifteen minutes before you go on," he says, kissing me good-bye.

I take the elevator downstairs and settle into the car that waits to ferry me to my destination, a big corporate headquarters in suburban New Jersey. The drive gives me plenty of time to wonder how I allowed myself to get into this situation. I recently left my job as a Wall Street lawyer to start my own consulting firm. Mostly I've worked one-on-one or in small groups, which feels comfortable. But when an acquaintance who is general counsel at a big media company asked me to run a seminar for his entire executive team, I agreed—enthusiastically, even!—for reasons I can't fathom now. I find myself praying for calamity—a flood or a small earthquake, maybe—anything so I don't have to go through with this. Then I feel guilty for involving the rest of the city in my drama.

The car pulls up at the client's office and I step out, trying to project the peppy self-assurance of a successful consultant. The event organizer escorts me to the auditorium. I ask for directions to the bathroom, and, in the privacy of the stall, gulp from the water bottle. For a few moments I stand still, waiting for the alcohol to work its magic. But nothing happens—I'm still terrified. Maybe I should take another swig. No, it's only nine in the morning—what if they smell the liquor on my breath? I reapply my lipstick and make my way back to the event room, where I arrange my notecards at the podium as the room fills with important-looking businesspeople. *Whatever you do, try not to vomit*, I tell myself.

Some of the executives glance up at me, but most of them stare fixedly at their BlackBerrys. Clearly, I'm taking them away from very pressing work. How am I going to hold their attention long enough for them to stop pounding out urgent communiqués into their tiny typewriters? I vow, right then and there, that I will never make another speech.

~

Well, since then I've given plenty of them. I haven't completely over-come my anxiety, but over the years I've discovered strategies that can help anyone with stage fright who needs to speak in public. More about that in chapter 5.

In the meantime, I've told you my tale of abject terror because it lies at the heart of some of my most urgent questions about introversion. On some deep level, my fear of public speaking seems connected to other aspects of my personality that I appreciate, especially my love of all things gentle and cerebral. This strikes me as a not-uncommon constellation of traits. But are they truly connected, and if so, how? Are they the result of "nurture"—the way I was raised? Both of my parents are soft-spoken, reflective types; my mother hates public speaking too. Or are they my "nature"—something deep in my genetic makeup?

I've been puzzling over these questions for my entire adult life. Fortunately, so have researchers at Harvard, where scientists are probing the human brain in an attempt to discover the biological origins of human temperament.

One such scientist is an eighty-two-year-old man named Jerome Kagan, one of the great developmental psychologists of the twentieth century. Kagan devoted his career to studying the emotional and cognitive development of children. In a series of groundbreaking longitudinal studies, he followed children from infancy through adolescence, documenting their physiologies and personalities along the way. Longitudinal studies like these are time-consuming, expensive, and therefore rare—but when they pay off, as Kagan's did, they pay off big.

For one of those studies, launched in 1989 and still ongoing, Professor Kagan and his team gathered five hundred four-month-old infants in his Laboratory for Child Development at Harvard, predicting they'd be able to tell, on the strength of a forty-five-minute evaluation, which babies were more likely to turn into introverts or extroverts. If you've seen a four-month-old baby lately, this may seem an audacious claim. But Kagan had been studying temperament for a long time, and he had a theory.

Kagan and his team exposed the four-month-olds to a carefully chosen set of new experiences. The infants heard tape-recorded voices and balloons popping, saw colorful mobiles dance before their eyes, and inhaled the scent of alcohol on cotton swabs. They had wildly varying reactions to the new stimuli. About 20 percent cried lustily and pumped their arms and legs. Kagan called this group "high-reactive." About 40 percent stayed quiet and placid, moving their arms or legs occasionally, but without all the dramatic limb-pumping. This group Kagan called "low-reactive." The remaining 40 percent fell between these two extremes. In a startlingly counterintuitive hypothesis, Kagan predicted that it was the infants in the high-reactive group—the lusty arm-pumpers— who were most likely to grow into quiet teenagers.

When they were two, four, seven, and eleven years old, many of the children returned to Kagan's lab for follow-up testing of their reactions to new people and events. At the age of two, the children met a lady wearing a gas mask and a lab coat, a man dressed in a clown costume, and a radio-controlled robot. At seven, they were asked to play with kids they'd never met before. At eleven, an unfamiliar adult interviewed them about their personal lives. Kagan's team observed how the children reacted to these strange situations, noting their body language and recording how often and spontaneously they laughed, talked, and smiled. They also interviewed the kids and their parents about what the children were like outside the laboratory. Did they prefer one or two close friends to a merry band? Did they like visiting new places? Were they risk-takers or were they more cautious? Did they consider themselves shy or bold?

Many of the children turned out exactly as Kagan had expected. The high-reactive infants, the 20 percent who'd hollered at the mobiles bobbing above their heads, were more likely to have developed serious, careful personalities. The low-reactive infants—the quiet ones—were more likely to have become relaxed and confident types. High and low reactivity tended to correspond, in other words, to introversion and extroversion. As Kagan mused in his 1998 book, *Galen's Prophecy*, "Carl Jung's descriptions of the introvert and extrovert, written over seventy-five years ago, apply with uncanny accuracy to a proportion of our high- and low-reactive adolescents."

Kagan describes two of those adolescents—reserved Tom and extroverted Ralph—and the differences between the two are striking. Tom, who was unusually shy as a child, is good at school, watchful and quiet, devoted to his girlfriend and parents, prone to worry, and loves learning on his own and thinking about intellectual problems. He plans to be a scientist. "Like . . . other famous introverts who were shy children," writes

Kagan, comparing Tom to T. S. Eliot and the mathematician-philosopher Alfred North Whitehead, Tom "has chosen a life of the mind."

Ralph, in contrast, is relaxed and self-assured. He engages the interviewer from Kagan's team as a peer, not as an authority figure twenty-five years his senior. Though Ralph is very bright, he recently failed his English and science classes because he'd been goofing around. But nothing much bothers Ralph. He admits his flaws cheerfully.

Psychologists often discuss the difference between "temperament" and "personality." Temperament refers to inborn, biologically based behavioral and emotional patterns that are observable in infancy and early childhood; personality is the complex brew that emerges after cultural influence and personal experience are thrown into the mix. Some say that temperament is the foundation, and personality is the building. Kagan's work helped link certain infant temperaments with adolescent personality styles like those of Tom and Ralph.

~

But how did Kagan know that the arm-thrashing infants would likely turn into cautious, reflective teens like Tom, or that the quiet babies were more likely to become forthright, too-cool-for-school Ralphs? The answer lies in their physiologies.

In addition to observing the children's behaviors in strange situations, Kagan's team measured their heart rates, blood pressure, finger temperature, and other properties of the nervous system. Kagan chose these measures because they're believed to be controlled by a potent organ inside the brain called the amygdala. The amygdala is located deep in the limbic system, an ancient brain network found even in primitive animals like mice and rats. This network—sometimes called the "emotional brain"—underlies many of the basic instincts we share with these animals, such as appetite, sex drive, and fear.

The amygdala serves as the brain's emotional switchboard, receiving information from the senses and then signaling the rest of the brain and nervous system how to respond. One of its functions is to instantly detect new or threatening things in the environment—from an airborne Frisbee to a hissing serpent—and send rapid-fire signals through the body that trigger the fight-or-flight response. When the Frisbee looks like it's headed straight for your nose, it's your amygdala that tells you to duck. When the rattlesnake prepares to bite, it's the amygdala that makes sure you run.

Kagan hypothesized that infants born with an especially excitable amygdala would wiggle and howl when shown unfamiliar objects—and grow up to be children who were more likely to feel vigilant when meeting new people. And this is just what he found. In other words, the four-month-olds who thrashed their arms like punk rockers did so not because they were extroverts in the making, but because their little bodies reacted strongly—they were "high-reactive"—to new sights, sounds, and smells. The quiet infants were silent not because they were future introverts—just the opposite—but because they had nervous systems that were unmoved by novelty.

The more reactive a child's amygdala, the higher his heart rate is likely to be, the more widely dilated his eyes, the tighter his vocal cords, the more cortisol (a stress hormone) in his saliva—the more jangled he's likely to *feel* when he confronts something new and stimulating. As high-reactive infants grow up, they continue to confront the unknown in many different contexts, from visiting an amusement park for the first time to meeting new classmates on the first day of kindergarten. We tend to notice most a child's reaction to unfamiliar people—how does he behave on the first day of school? Does she seem uncertain at birthday parties full of kids she doesn't know? But what we're really observing is a child's sensitivity to novelty in general, not just to people.

High- and low-reactivity are probably not the only biological routes to introversion and extroversion. There are plenty of introverts who do not have the sensitivity of a classic high-reactive, and a small percentage of high-reactives grow up to be extroverts. Still, Kagan's decades-long series of discoveries mark a dramatic breakthrough in our understanding of these personality styles—including the value judgments we make. Extroverts are sometimes credited with being "pro-social"—meaning caring about others—and introverts disparaged as people who don't like people. But the reactions of the infants in Kagan's tests had nothing to do with people. These babies were shouting (or not shouting) over Q-tips. They were pumping their limbs (or staying calm) in response to popping balloons. The high-reactive babies were not misanthropes in the making; they were simply sensitive to their environments.

Indeed, the sensitivity of these children's nervous systems seems to be linked not only to noticing scary things, but to noticing in general. High-reactive children pay what one psychologist calls "alert attention" to people and things. They literally use more eye movements than others to compare choices before making a decision. It's as if they process more deeply—sometimes consciously, sometimes not—the information they take in about the world. In one early series of studies, Kagan asked a group of first-graders to play a visual matching game. Each child was shown a picture of a teddy bear sitting on a chair, alongside six other similar pictures, only one of which was an exact match. The high-reactive children spent more time than others considering all the alternatives, and were more likely to make the right choice. When Kagan asked these same kids to play word games, he found that they also read more accurately than impulsive children did.

High-reactive kids also tend to think and feel deeply about what they've noticed, and to bring an extra degree of nuance to everyday experiences. This can be expressed in many different ways. If the child is socially oriented, she may spend a lot of time pondering her observations of others—why Jason didn't want to share his toys today, why Mary got so mad at Nicholas when he bumped into her accidentally. If he has a particular interest—in solving puzzles, making art, building sand castles—he'll often concentrate with unusual intensity. If a high-reactive toddler breaks another child's toy by mistake, studies show, she often experiences a more intense mix of guilt and sorrow than a lower-reactive child would. All kids notice their environments and feel emotions, of course, but high-reactive kids seem to see and feel things more. If you ask a high-reactive seven-year-old how a group of kids should share a coveted toy, writes the science journalist Winifred Gallagher, he'll tend to come up with sophisticated strategies like "Alphabetize their last names, and let the person closest to A go first."

"Putting theory into practice is hard for them," writes Gallagher, "because their sensitive natures and elaborate schemes are unsuited to the heterogeneous rigors of the schoolyard." Yet as we'll see in the chapters to come, these traits—alertness, sensitivity to nuance, complex emotionality—turn out to be highly underrated powers.

~

Kagan has given us painstakingly documented evidence that high reactivity is one biological basis of introversion (we'll explore another likely route in chapter 7), but his findings are powerful in part because they confirm what we've sensed all along. Some of Kagan's studies even venture into the realm of cultural myth. For example, he believes, based on his data, that high reactivity is associated with physical traits such as blue eyes, allergies, and hay fever, and that high-reactive men are more likely than others to have a thin body and narrow face. Such conclusions are speculative and call to mind the nineteenth-century practice of divining a man's soul from the shape of his skull. But whether or not they turn out to be accurate, it's interesting that these are just the physical characteristics we give fictional characters when we want to suggest that they're quiet, introverted, cerebral. It's as if these physiological tendencies are buried deep in our cultural unconscious.

Take Disney movies, for example: Kagan and his colleagues speculate that Disney animators unconsciously understood high reactivity when they drew sensitive figures like Cinderella, Pinocchio, and Dopey with blue eyes, and brasher characters like Cinderella's stepsisters, Grumpy, and Peter Pan with darker eyes. In many books, Hollywood films, and TV shows, too, the stock character of a reedy, nose-blowing young man is shorthand for the hapless but thoughtful kid who gets good grades, is a bit overwhelmed by the social whirl, and is talented at introspective activities like poetry or astrophysics. (Think Ethan Hawke in *Dead Poets Society*.) Kagan even speculates that some men prefer women with fair skin and blue eyes because they unconsciously code them as sensitive.

Other studies of personality also support the premise that extroversion and introversion are physiologically, even genetically, based. One of the most common ways of untangling nature from nurture is to compare the personality traits of identical and fraternal twins. Identical twins develop from a single fertilized egg and therefore have exactly the same genes, while fraternal twins come from separate eggs and share only 50 percent of their genes on average. So if you measure introversion or extroversion levels in pairs of twins and find more correlation in identical twins than in fraternal pairs—which scientists do, in study after study, even of twins raised in separate households—you can reasonably conclude that the trait has some genetic basis.

None of these studies is perfect, but the results have consistently suggested that introversion and extroversion, like other major personality traits such as agreeableness and conscientiousness, are about 40 to 50 percent heritable.

But are biological explanations for introversion wholly satisfying? When I first read Kagan's book *Galen's Prophecy*, I was so excited that I couldn't sleep. Here, inside these pages, were my friends, my family, myself—all of humanity, in fact!—neatly sorted through the prism of a quiescent nervous system versus a reactive one. It was as if centuries of philosophical inquiry into the mystery of human personality had led to this shining moment of scientific clarity. There was an easy answer to the nature-nurture question after all—we are born with prepackaged temperaments that powerfully shape our adult personalities.

But it couldn't be that simple—could it? Can we really reduce an introverted or extroverted personality to the nervous system its owner was born with? I would guess that I inherited a high-reactive nervous system, but my mother insists I was an easy baby, not the kind to kick and wail over a popped balloon. I'm prone to wild flights of self-doubt, but I also have a deep well of courage in my own convictions. I feel horribly uncomfortable on my first day in a foreign city, but I love to travel. I was shy as a child, but have outgrown the worst of it. Furthermore, I don't think these contradictions are so unusual; many people have dissonant aspects to their personalities. And people change profoundly over time, don't they? What about free will—do we have no control over who we are, and whom we become?

I decided to track down Professor Kagan to ask him these questions in person. I felt drawn to him not only because his research findings were so compelling, but also because of what he represents in the great nature-nurture debate. He'd launched his career in 1954 staunchly on the side of nurture, a view in step with the scientific establishment of the day. Back then, the idea of inborn temperament was political dynamite, evoking the specter of Nazi eugenics and white supremacism. By contrast, the notion of children as blank slates for whom anything was possible appealed to a nation built on democracy.

But Kagan had changed his mind along the way. "I have been dragged, kicking and screaming, by my data," he says now, "to acknowledge that temperament is more powerful than I thought and wish to believe." The publication of his early findings on high-reactive children in *Science* magazine in 1988 helped to legitimize the idea of inborn temperament, partly because his "nurturist" reputation was so strong.

If anyone could help me untangle the nature-nurture question, I hoped, it was Jerry Kagan.

~

Kagan ushers me inside his office in Harvard's William James Hall, surveying me unblinkingly as I sit down: not unkind, but definitely discerning. I had imagined him as a gentle, white-lab-coated scientist in a cartoon, pouring chemicals from one test tube to another until—*poof! Now, Susan, you know exactly who you are.* But this isn't the mild-mannered old professor I'd imagined. Ironically for a scientist whose books are infused with humanism and who describes himself as having been an anxious, easily frightened boy, I find him downright intimidating. I kick off our interview by asking a background question whose premise he disagrees with. "No, no, no!" he thunders, as if I weren't sitting just across from him.

The high-reactive side of my personality kicks into full gear. I'm always soft-spoken, but now I have to force my voice to come out louder than a whisper (on the tape recording of our conversation, Kagan's voice sounds booming and declamatory, mine much quieter). I'm aware that I'm holding my torso tensely, one of the telltale signs of the high-reactive. It feels strange to know that Kagan must be observing this too—he says as much, nodding at me as he notes that many high-reactives become writers or pick other intellectual vocations where "you're in charge: you close the door, pull down the shades and do your work. You're protected from encountering unexpected things." (Those from less educated backgrounds tend to become file clerks and truck drivers, he says, for the same reasons.)

I mention a little girl I know who is "slow to warm up." She studies new people rather than greeting them; her family goes to the beach every weekend, but it takes her ages to dip a toe into the surf. A classic high-reactive, I remark.

"No!" Kagan exclaims. "Every behavior has more than one cause. Don't ever forget that! For every child who's slow to warm up, yes, there will be statistically more high-reactives, but you can be slow to warm up because of how you spent the first three and a half years of your life! When writers and journalists talk, they want to see a one-to-one relationship—one behavior, one cause. But it's really important that you see, for behaviors like slow-to-warm-up, shyness, impulsivity, there are many routes to that."

He reels off examples of environmental factors that could produce an introverted personality independently of, or in concert with, a reactive nervous system: A child might enjoy having new ideas about the world, say, so she spends a lot of time inside her head. Or health problems might direct a child inward, to what's going on inside his body.

My fear of public speaking might be equally complex. Do I dread it because I'm a high-reactive introvert? Maybe not. Some high-reactives love public speaking and performing, and plenty of extroverts have stage fright; public speaking is the number-one fear in America, far more common than the fear of death. Public speaking phobia has many causes, including early childhood setbacks, that have to do with our unique personal histories, not inborn temperament.

In fact, public speaking anxiety may be primal and quintessentially human, not limited to those of us born with a high-reactive nervous system. One theory, based on the writings of the sociobiologist E. O. Wilson, holds that when our ancestors lived on the savannah, being watched intently meant only one thing: a wild animal was stalking us. And when we think we're about to be eaten, do we stand tall and hold forth confidently? No. We run. In other words, hundreds of thousands of years of evolution urge us to get the hell off the stage, where we can mistake the gaze of the spectators for the glint in a predator's eye. Yet the audience expects not only that we'll stay put, but that we'll act relaxed and assured. This conflict between biology and protocol is one reason that speechmaking can be so fraught. It's also why exhortations to imagine the audience in the nude don't help nervous speakers; naked lions are just as dangerous as elegantly dressed ones.

But even though all human beings may be prone to mistaking audience members for predators, each of us has a different threshold for triggering the fight-or-flight response. How threateningly must the eyes of the audience members narrow before you feel they're about to pounce? Does it happen before you've even stepped onstage, or does it take a few really good hecklers to trigger that adrenaline rush? You can see how a highly sensitive amygdala would make you more susceptible to frowns and bored sighs and people who check their BlackBerrys while you're in mid-sentence. And indeed, studies do show that introverts are significantly more likely than extroverts to fear public speaking.

Kagan tells me about the time he watched a fellow scientist give a wonderful talk at a conference. Afterward, the speaker asked if they could have lunch. Kagan agreed, and the scientist proceeded to tell him that he gives lectures every month and, despite his capable stage persona, is terrified each time. Reading Kagan's work had had a big impact on him, however.

"You changed my life," he told Kagan. "All this time I've been blaming my mother, but now I think I'm a high-reactive."

~

So am I introverted because I inherited my parents' high reactivity, copied their behaviors, or both? Remember that the heritability statistics derived from twin studies show that introversion-extroversion is only 40 to 50 percent heritable. This means that, in a group of people, on average half of the variability in introversion-extroversion is caused by genetic factors. To make things even more complex, there are probably many genes at work, and Kagan's framework of high reactivity is likely one of many physiological routes to introversion. Also, averages are tricky. A heritability rate of 50 percent doesn't necessarily mean that my introversion is 50 percent inherited from my parents, or that half of the difference in extroversion between my best friend and me is genetic. One hundred percent of my introversion might come from genes, or none at all—or more likely some unfathomable combination of genes and experience. To ask whether it's nature or nurture, says Kagan, is like asking whether a blizzard is caused by temperature or humidity. It's the intricate interaction between the two that makes us who we are.

So perhaps I've been asking the wrong question. Maybe the mystery of what percent of personality is nature and what percent nurture is less important than the question of *how* your inborn temperament interacts with the environment and with your own free will. To what degree is temperament destiny?

On the one hand, according to the theory of gene-environment interaction, people who inherit certain traits tend to seek out life experiences that reinforce those characteristics. The most low-reactive kids, for example, court danger from the time they're toddlers, so that by the time they grow up they don't bat an eye at grown-up-sized risks. They "climb a few fences, become desensitized, and climb up on the roof," the late psychologist David Lykken once explained in an *Atlantic* article. "They'll have all sorts of experiences that other kids won't. Chuck Yeager (the first pilot to break the sound barrier) could step down from the belly of the bomber into the rocketship and push the button not because he was born with that difference between him and me, but because for the previous thirty years his temperament impelled him to work his way up from climbing trees through increasing degrees of danger and excitement."

Conversely, high-reactive children may be more likely to develop into artists and writers and scientists and thinkers because their aversion to novelty causes them to spend time inside the familiar—and intellectually fertile—environment of their own heads. "The university is filled with introverts," observes the psychologist Jerry Miller, director of the Center for the Child and the Family at the University of Michigan. "The stereotype of the university professor is accurate for so many people on campus. They like to read; for them there's nothing more exciting than ideas. And some of this has to do with how they spent their time when they were growing up. If you spend a lot of time charging around, then you have less time for reading and learning. There's only so much time in your life."

On the other hand, there is also a wide range of possible outcomes for each temperament. Low-reactive, extroverted children, if raised by attentive families in safe environments, can grow up to be energetic achievers with big personalities—the Richard Bransons and Oprahs of this world. But give those same children negligent caregivers or a bad neighborhood, say some psychologists, and they can turn into bullies, juvenile delinquents, or criminals. Lykken has controversially called psychopaths and heroes "twigs on the same genetic branch."

Consider the mechanism by which kids acquire their sense of right and wrong. Many psychologists believe that children develop a conscience when they do something inappropriate and are rebuked by their caregivers. Disapproval makes them feel anxious, and since anxiety is unpleasant, they learn to steer clear of antisocial behavior. This is known as internalizing their parents' standards of conduct, and its core is anxiety.

But what if some kids are less prone to anxiety than others, as is true of extremely low-reactive kids? Often the best way to teach these children values is to give them positive role models and to channel their fearlessness into productive activities. A low-reactive child on an ice-hockey team enjoys his peers' esteem when he charges at his opponents with a lowered shoulder, which is a "legal" move. But if he goes too far, raises his elbow, and gives another guy a concussion, he lands in the penalty box. Over time he learns to use his appetite for risk and assertiveness wisely.

Now imagine this same child growing up in a dangerous neighborhood with few organized sports or other constructive channels for his boldness. You can see how he might fall into delinquency. It may be that some disadvantaged kids who get into trouble suffer not solely from poverty or neglect, say those who hold this view, but also from the tragedy of a bold and exuberant temperament deprived of healthy outlets.

~

The destinies of the most high-reactive kids are also influenced by the world around them—perhaps even more so than for the average child, according to a groundbreaking new theory dubbed "the orchid hypothesis" by David Dobbs in a wonderful article in *The Atlantic*. This theory holds that many children are like dandelions, able to thrive in just about any environment. But others, including the high-reactive types that Kagan studied, are more like orchids: they wilt easily, but under the right conditions can grow strong and magnificent.

According to Jay Belsky, a leading proponent of this view and a psychology professor and child care expert at the University of London, the reactivity of these kids' nervous systems makes them quickly overwhelmed by childhood adversity, but also able to benefit from a nurturing environment more than other children do. In other words, orchid children are more strongly affected by all experience, both positive and negative.

Scientists have known for a while that high-reactive temperaments come with risk factors. These kids are especially vulnerable to challenges like marital tension, a parent's death, or abuse. They're more likely than their peers to react to these events with depression, anxiety, and shyness. Indeed, about a quarter of Kagan's high-reactive kids suffer from some degree of the condition known as "social anxiety disorder," a chronic and disabling form of shyness.

What scientists *haven't* realized until recently is that these risk factors have an upside. In other words, the sensitivities and the strengths are a package deal. High-reactive kids who enjoy good parenting, child care, and a stable home environment tend to have *fewer* emotional problems and more social skills than their lower-reactive peers, studies show. Often they're exceedingly empathic, caring, and cooperative. They work well with others. They are kind, conscientious, and easily disturbed by cruelty, injustice, and irresponsibility. They're successful at the things that matter to them. They don't necessarily turn into class presidents or stars of the school play, Belsky told me, though this can happen, too: "For some it's becoming the leader of their class. For others it takes the form of doing well academically or being well-liked."

The upsides of the high-reactive temperament have been documented in exciting research that scientists are only now beginning to pull together. One of the most interesting findings, also reported in Dobbs's *Atlantic* article, comes from the world of rhesus monkeys, a species that shares about 95 percent of its DNA with humans and has elaborate social structures that resemble our own.

In these monkeys as well as in humans, a gene known as the serotonin-transporter (SERT) gene, or 5-HTTLPR, helps to regulate the processing of serotonin, a neurotransmitter that affects mood. A particular variation, or allele, of this gene, sometimes referred to as the "short" allele, is thought to be associated with high reactivity and introversion, as well as a heightened risk of depression in humans who have had difficult lives. When baby monkeys with a similar allele were subjected to stress—in one experiment they were taken from their mothers and raised as orphans—they processed serotonin less efficiently (a risk factor for depression and anxiety) than monkeys with the long allele who endured similar privations. But young monkeys with the same risky genetic profile who were raised by nurturing mothers did as well as or *better* than their long-allele brethren—even those raised in similarly secure environments—at key social tasks, like finding playmates, building alliances, and handling conflicts. They often became leaders of their troops. They also processed serotonin more efficiently.

Stephen Suomi, the scientist who conducted these studies, has speculated that these high-reactive monkeys owed their success to the enormous amounts of time they spent watching rather than participating in the group, absorbing on a deep level the laws of social dynamics. (This is a hypothesis that might ring true to parents whose high-reactive children hover observantly on the edges of their peer group, sometimes for weeks or months, before edging successfully inside.)

Studies in humans have found that adolescent girls with the short allele of the SERT gene are 20 percent more likely to be depressed than long-allele girls when exposed to stressful family environments, but 25 percent *less* likely to be depressed when raised in stable homes. Similarly, short allele adults have been shown to have more anxiety in the evening than others when they've had stressful days, but *less* anxiety on calm days. High-reactive four-year-olds give more pro-social responses than other children when presented with moral dilemmas—but this difference remains at age five only if their mothers used gentle, not harsh, discipline. High-reactive children raised in supportive environments are even more resistant than other kids to the common cold and other respiratory illnesses, but get sick more easily if they're raised in stressful conditions. The short allele of the SERT gene is also associated with higher performance on a wide range of cognitive tasks.

These findings are so dramatic that it's remarkable no one arrived at them until recently. Remarkable, but perhaps not surprising. Psychologists are trained to heal, so their research naturally focuses on problems and pathology. "It is almost as if, metaphorically speaking, sailors are so busy—and wisely—looking under the water line for extensions of icebergs that could sink their ship," writes Belsky, "that they fail to appreciate that by climbing on top of the iceberg it might prove possible to chart a clear passage through the ice-laden sea."

The parents of high-reactive children are exceedingly lucky, Belsky told me. "The time and effort they invest will actually make a difference. Instead of seeing these kids as vulnerable to adversity, parents should see them as malleable—for worse, but also for better." He describes eloquently a high-reactive child's ideal parent: someone who "can read your cues and respect your individuality; is warm and firm in placing demands on you without being harsh or hostile; promotes curiosity, academic achievement, delayed gratification, and self-control; and is not harsh, neglectful, or inconsistent." This advice is terrific for all parents, of course, but it's crucial for raising a high-reactive child. (If you think your child might be high-reactive, you're probably already asking yourself what else you can do to cultivate your son or daughter. Chapter 11 has some answers.)

But even orchid children can withstand some adversity, Belsky says. Take divorce. In general, it will disrupt orchid kids more than others: "If the parents squabble a lot, and put their kid in the middle, then watch out—this is the kid who will succumb." But if the divorcing parents get along, if they provide their child with the other psychological nutrients he needs, then even an orchid child can do just fine.

Most people would appreciate the flexibility of this message, I think; few of us had problem-free childhoods.

But there's another kind of flexibility that we all hope applies to the question of who we are and what we become. We want the freedom to map our own destinies. We want to preserve the advantageous aspects of our temperaments and improve, or even discard, the ones we dislike—such as a horror of public speaking. In addition to our inborn temperaments, beyond the luck of the draw of our childhood experience, we want to believe that we—as adults—can shape our selves and make what we will of our lives.

Can we?

BEYOND TEMPERAMENT

The Role of Free Will (and the Secret of Public Speaking for Introverts)

Enjoyment appears at the boundary between boredom and anxiety, when the challenges are just balanced with the person's capacity to act.

—MIHALY CSIKSZENTMIHALYI

Deep inside the bowels of the Athinoula A. Martinos Center for Bio-medical Imaging at Massachusetts General Hospital, the hallways are nondescript, dingy even. I'm standing outside the locked door of a win-dowless room with Dr. Carl Schwartz, the director of the Developmental Neuroimaging and Psychopathology Research Lab. Schwartz has bright, inquisitive eyes, graying brown hair, and a quietly enthusiastic manner. Despite our unprepossessing surroundings, he prepares with some fanfare to unlock the door.

The room houses a multimillion-dollar fMRI (functional magnetic resonance imaging) machine, which has made possible some of the greatest breakthroughs in modern neuroscience. An fMRI machine can measure which parts of the brain are active when you're thinking a par-ticular thought or performing a specific task, allowing scientists to per-form the once unimaginable task of mapping the functions of the human brain. A principal inventor of the fMRI technique, says Dr. Schwartz, was a brilliant but unassuming scientist named Kenneth Kwong, who works inside this very building. This whole place is full of quiet and modest people doing extraordinary things, Schwartz adds, waving his hand appreciatively at the empty hallway.

Before Schwartz opens the door, he asks me to take off my gold hoop earrings and set aside the metal tape recorder I've been using to record our conversation. The magnetic field of the fMRI machine is 100,000 times stronger than the earth's gravitational pull—so strong, Schwartz says, that it could rip the earrings right out of my ears if they were magnetic and send them flying across the room. I worry about the metal fasteners of my bra, but I'm too embarrassed to ask. I point instead to my shoe buckle, which I figure has the same amount of metal as the bra strap. Schwartz says it's all right, and we enter the room.

We gaze reverently at the fMRI scanner, which looks like a gleaming rocketship lying on its side. Schwartz explains that he asks his subjects—who are in their late teens—to lie down with their heads in the scanner while they look at photographs of faces and the machine tracks how their brains respond. He's especially interested in activity in the amygdala—the same powerful organ inside the brain that Kagan found played such an important role in shaping some introverts' and extroverts' personalities.

Schwartz is Kagan's colleague and protégé, and his work picks up just where Kagan's longitudinal studies of personality left off. The infants Kagan once categorized as high- and low-reactive have now grown up, and Schwartz is using the fMRI machine to peer inside their brains. Kagan followed his subjects from infancy into adolescence, but Schwartz wanted to see what happened to them after that. Would the footprint of temperament be detectable, all those years later, in the adult brains of Kagan's high- and low-reactive infants? Or would it have been erased by some combination of environment and conscious effort?

Interestingly, Kagan cautioned Schwartz against doing the study. In the competitive field of science research, you don't want to waste time conducting studies that may not yield significant findings. And Kagan worried that there were no results to be found—that the link between temperament and destiny would be severed by the time an infant reached adulthood.

"He was trying to take care of me," Schwartz tells me. "It was an interesting paradox. Because here Jerry was doing all these early observations of infants, and seeing that it wasn't just their social behavior that was different in the extremes—everything about these kids was different. Their eyes dilated more widely when they were solving problems, their vocal cords became more tense while uttering words, their heart rate patterns were unique: there were all these channels that suggested there was something different physiologically about these kids. And I think, in spite of this, because of his intellectual heritage, he had the feeling that environmental factors are so complex that it would be really hard to pick up that footprint of temperament later in life."

But Schwartz, who believes that he's a high-reactive himself and was drawing partly on his own experience, had a hunch that he'd find that footprint even farther along the longitudinal timeline than Kagan had.

He demonstrates his research by allowing me to act as if I were one of his subjects, albeit not inside the fMRI scanner. As I sit at a desk, a computer monitor flashes photos at me, one after another, each showing an unfamiliar face: disembodied black-and-white heads floating against a dark background. I think I can feel my pulse quicken as the photos start coming at me faster and faster. I also notice that Schwartz has slipped in some repeats and that I feel more relaxed as the faces start to look familiar. I describe my reactions to Schwartz, who nods. The slide show is designed, he says, to mimic an environment that corresponds to the sense that high-reactive people get when they walk into a crowded room of strangers and feel "Geez! Who are these people?"

I wonder if I'm imagining my reactions, or exaggerating them, but Schwartz tells me that he's gotten back the first set of data on a group of high-reactive children Kagan studied from four months of age—and sure enough, the amygdalae of those children, now grown up, had turned out to be more sensitive to the pictures of unfamiliar faces than did the amygdalae of those who'd been bold toddlers. Both groups reacted to the pictures, but the formerly shy kids reacted more. In other words, *the footprint of a high- or low-reactive temperament never disappeared in adulthood.* Some high-reactives grew into socially fluid teenagers who were not outwardly rattled by novelty, but they never shed their genetic inheritance.

Schwartz's research suggests something important: we can stretch our personalities, but only up to a point. Our inborn temperaments influence us, regardless of the lives we lead. A sizable part of who we are is ordained by our genes, by our brains, by our nervous systems. And yet the elasticity that Schwartz found in some of the high-reactive teens also suggests the converse: we have free will and can use it to shape our personalities.

These seem like contradictory principles, but they are not. Free will can take us far, suggests Dr. Schwartz's research, but it cannot carry us infinitely beyond our genetic limits. Bill Gates is never going to be Bill Clinton, no matter how he polishes his social skills, and Bill Clinton can never be Bill Gates, no matter how much time he spends alone with a computer.

We might call this the "rubber band theory" of personality. We are like rubber bands at rest. We are elastic and can stretch ourselves, but only so much.

~

To understand why this might be so for high-reactives, it helps to look at what happens in the brain when we greet a stranger at a cocktail party. Remember that the amygdala, and the limbic system of which it's a key part, is an ancient part of the brain—so old that primitive mammals have their own versions of this system. But as mammals became more complex, an area of the brain called the neocortex developed around the limbic system. The neocortex, and particularly the frontal cortex in humans, performs an astonishing array of functions, from deciding which brand of toothpaste to buy, to planning a meeting, to pondering the nature of reality. One of these functions is to soothe unwarranted fears.

If you were a high-reactive baby, then your amygdala may, for the rest of your life, go a bit wild every time you introduce yourself to a stranger at a cocktail party. But if you feel relatively skilled in company, that's partly because your frontal cortex is there to tell you to calm down, extend a handshake, and smile. In fact, a recent fMRI study shows that when people use self-talk to reassess upsetting situations, activity in their prefrontal cortex increases in an amount correlated with a decrease of activity in their amygdala.

But the frontal cortex isn't all-powerful; it doesn't switch the amygdala off altogether. In one study, scientists conditioned a rat to associate a certain sound with an electrical shock. Then they played that sound over and over again *without* administering the shock, until the rats lost their fear.

But it turned out that this "unlearning" was not as complete as the scientists first thought. When they severed the neural connections between the rats' cortex and amygdala, the rats became afraid of the sound again. This was because the fear conditioning had been suppressed by the activity of the cortex, but was still present in the amygdala. In humans with unwarranted fears, like batophobia, or fear of heights, the same thing happens. Repeated trips to the top of the Empire State Building seem to extinguish the fear, but it may come roaring back during times of stress—when the cortex has other things to do than soothe an excitable amygdala.

This helps explain why many high-reactive kids retain some of the fearful aspects of their temperament all the way into adulthood, no matter how much social experience they acquire or free will they exercise. My colleague Sally is a good example of this phenomenon. Sally is a thoughtful and talented book editor, a self-described shy introvert, and one of the most charming and articulate people I know. If you invite her to a party, and later ask your other guests whom they most enjoyed meeting, chances are they'll mention Sally. She's so sparkly, they'll tell you. So witty! So adorable!

Sally is conscious of how well she comes across—you can't be as appealing as she is without being aware of it. But that doesn't mean her amygdala knows it. When she arrives at a party, Sally often wishes she could hide behind the nearest couch—until her prefrontal cortex takes over and she remembers what a good conversationalist she is. Even so, her amygdala, with its lifetime of stored associations between strangers and anxiety, sometimes prevails. Sally admits that sometimes she drives an hour to a party and then leaves five minutes after arriving.

When I think of my own experiences in light of Schwartz's findings, I realize it's not true that I'm no longer shy; I've just learned to talk myself down from the ledge (thank you, prefrontal cortex!). By now I do it so automatically that I'm hardly aware it's happening. When I talk with a stranger or a group of people, my smile is bright and my manner direct, but there's a split second that feels like I'm stepping onto a high wire. By now I've had so many thousands of social experiences that I've learned that the high wire is a figment of my imagination, or that I won't die if I fall. I reassure myself so instantaneously that I'm barely aware I'm doing it. But the reassurance process is still happening—and occasionally it doesn't work. The word that Kagan first used to describe high-reactive people was *inhibited*, and that's exactly how I still feel at some dinner parties.

~

This ability to stretch ourselves—within limits—applies to extroverts, too. One of my clients, Alison, is a business consultant, mother, and wife with the kind of extroverted personality—friendly, forthright, perpetually on the go—that makes people describe her as a "force of nature." She has a happy marriage, two daughters she adores, and her own consulting firm that she built from scratch. She's rightly proud of what she's accomplished in life.

But she hasn't always felt so satisfied. The year she graduated from high school, she took a good look at herself and didn't like what she saw. Alison is extremely bright, but you couldn't see that from her high school transcript. She'd had her heart set on attending an Ivy League school, and had thrown that chance away.

And she knew why. She'd spent high school socializing—Alison was involved in practically every extracurricular activity her school had to offer—and that didn't leave much time for academics. Partly she blamed her parents, who were so proud of their daughter's social gifts that they hadn't insisted she study more. But mostly she blamed herself.

As an adult, Alison is determined not to make similar mistakes. She knows how easy it would be to lose herself in a whirl of PTA meetings and business networking. So Alison's solution is to look to her family for adaptive strategies. She happens to be the only child of two introverted parents, to be married to an introvert, and to have a younger daughter who is a strong introvert herself.

Alison has found ways to tap into the wavelength of the quiet types around her. When she visits her parents, she finds herself meditating and writing in her journal, just the way her mother does. At home she relishes peaceful evenings with her homebody husband. And her younger daughter, who enjoys intimate backyard talks with her mother, has Alison spending her afternoons engaged in thoughtful conversation.

Alison has even created a network of quiet, reflective friends. Although her best friend in the world, Amy, is a highly charged extrovert just like her, most of her other friends are introverts. "I so appreciate people who listen well," says Alison. "They are the friends I go have coffee with. They give me the most spot-on observations. Sometimes I haven't even realized I was doing something counterproductive, and my introverted friends will say, 'Here's what you're doing, and here are fifteen examples of when you did that same thing,' whereas my friend Amy wouldn't even notice. But my introverted friends are sitting back and observing, and we can really connect over that."

Alison remains her boisterous self, but she has also discovered how to be, and to benefit from, quiet.

~

Even though we can reach for the outer limits of our temperaments, it can often be better to situate ourselves squarely inside our comfort zones.

Consider the story of my client Esther, a tax lawyer at a large corporate law firm. A tiny brunette with a springy step and blue eyes as bright as headlamps, Esther was not shy and never had been. But she was decidedly introverted. Her favorite part of the day was the quiet ten minutes when she walked to the bus along the tree-lined streets of her neighborhood. Her second favorite part was when she got to close the door to her office and dig into her work.

Esther had chosen her career well. A mathematician's daughter, she loved to think about intimidatingly complex tax problems, and could discuss them with ease. (In chapter 7, I examine why introverts are so good at complex, focused problem-solving.) She was the youngest member of a close-knit working group operating inside a much larger law firm. This group comprised five other tax lawyers, all of whom supported one another's careers. Esther's work consisted of thinking deeply about questions that fascinated her and working closely with trusted colleagues.

But it happened that Esther's small group of tax lawyers periodically had to give presentations to the rest of the law firm. These talks were a source of misery for Esther, not because she was afraid of public speaking, but because she wasn't comfortable speaking extemporaneously. Esther's colleagues, in contrast—all of whom happened to be extroverts—were spontaneous talkers who decided what they'd say on their way to the presentation and were somehow able to convey their thoughts intelligibly and engagingly by the time they arrived.

Esther was fine if given a chance to prepare, but sometimes her colleagues failed to mention that they'd be delivering a talk until she arrived at work that morning. She assumed that their ability to speak improvisationally was a function of their superior understanding of tax law and that, as she gained more experience, she too would be able to "wing it." But as Esther became more senior and more knowledgeable, she still couldn't do it.

To solve Esther's problem, let's focus on another difference between introverts and extroverts: their preference for stimulation.

For several decades, beginning in the late 1960s, an influential research psychologist named Hans Eysenck hypothesized that human beings seek "just right" levels of stimulation—not too much and not too little. Stimulation is the amount of input we have coming in from the outside world. It can take any number of forms, from noise to social life to flashing lights. Eysenck believed that extroverts prefer more stimulation than introverts do, and that this explained many of their differences: introverts enjoy shutting the doors to their offices and plunging into their work, because for them this sort of quiet intellectual activity is optimally stimulating, while extroverts function best when engaged in higher-wattage activities like organizing team-building workshops or chairing meetings.

Eysenck also thought that the basis of these differences might be found in a brain structure called the ascending reticular activating system (ARAS). The ARAS is a part of the brain stem that has connections leading up to the cerebral cortex and other parts of the brain. The brain has excitatory mechanisms that cause us to feel awake, alert, and energetic—"aroused," in the parlance of psychologists. It also has calming mechanisms that do the opposite. Eysenck speculated that the ARAS regulates the balance between over- and under-arousal by controlling the amount of sensory stimulation that flows into the brain; sometimes the channels are wide open, so a lot of stimulation can get in, and sometimes they're constricted, so the brain is less stimulated. Eysenck thought that the ARAS functioned differently in introverts and extroverts: introverts have wide-open information channels, causing them to be flooded with stimulation and over-aroused, while extroverts have tighter channels, making them prone to under-arousal. Over-arousal doesn't produce anxiety so much as the sense that you can't think straight—that you've had enough and would like to go home now. Under-arousal is something like cabin fever. Not enough is happening: you feel itchy, restless, and sluggish, like you need to get out of the house already.

Today we know that the reality is far more complex. For one thing, the ARAS doesn't turn stimulation on and off like a fire truck's hose, flooding the entire brain at once; different parts of the brain are aroused more than others at different times. Also, high arousal levels in the brain don't always correlate with how aroused we *feel*. And there are many different kinds of arousal: arousal by loud music is not the same as arousal by mortar fire, which is not the same as arousal by presiding at a meeting; you might be more sensitive to one form of stimulation than to another. It's also too simple to say that we always seek moderate levels of arousal: excited fans at a soccer game crave hyperstimulation, while people who visit spas for relaxation treatments seek low levels.

Still, more than a thousand studies conducted by scientists worldwide have tested Eysenck's theory that cortical arousal levels are an important clue to the nature of introversion and extroversion, and it appears to be what the personality psychologist David Funder calls "half-right"—in very important ways. Whatever the underlying cause, there's a host of evidence that introverts *are* more sensitive than extroverts to various kinds of stimulation, from coffee to a loud bang to the dull roar of a networking event—and that introverts and extroverts often need very different levels of stimulation to function at their best.

In one well-known experiment, dating all the way back to 1967 and still a favorite in-class demonstration in psychology courses, Eysenck placed lemon juice on the tongues of adult introverts and extroverts to find out who salivated more. Sure enough, the introverts, being more aroused by sensory stimuli, were the ones with the watery mouths.

In another famous study, introverts and extroverts were asked to play a challenging word game in which they had to learn, through trial and error, the governing principle of the game. While playing, they wore headphones that emitted random bursts of noise. They were asked to adjust the volume of their headsets up or down to the level that was "just right." On average, the extroverts chose a noise level of 72 decibels, while the introverts selected only 55 decibels. When working at the volume that they had selected—loud for the extroverts, quiet for the introverts—the two types were about equally aroused (as measured by their heart rates and other indicators). They also played equally well.

When the introverts were asked to work at the noise level preferred by the extroverts, and vice versa, everything changed. Not only were the introverts *over*-aroused by the loud noise, but they also *under*performed—taking an average of 9.1 trials rather than 5.8 to learn the game. The opposite was true for the extroverts—they were *under*-aroused (and possibly bored) by the quieter conditions, and took an average of 7.3 trials, compared with the 5.4 they'd averaged under noisier conditions.

~

When combined with Kagan's findings on high reactivity, this line of studies offers a very empowering lens through which to view your personality. Once you understand introversion and extroversion as preferences for certain levels of stimulation, you can begin consciously trying to situate yourself in environments favorable to your own personality—neither overstimulating nor understimulating, neither boring nor anxiety-making.

You can organize your life in terms of what personality psychologists call "optimal levels of arousal" and what I call "sweet spots," and by doing so feel more energetic and alive than before.

Your sweet spot is the place where you're optimally stimulated. You probably seek it out already without being aware that you're doing so. Imagine that you're lying contentedly in a hammock reading a great novel. This is a sweet spot. But after half an hour you realize that you've read the same sentence five times; now you're understimulated. So you call a friend and go out for brunch—in other words, you ratchet up your stimulation level—and as you laugh and gossip over blueberry pancakes, you're back, thank goodness, inside your sweet spot. But this agreeable state lasts only until your friend—an extrovert who needs much more stimulation than you do—persuades you to accompany her to a block party, where you're now confronted by loud music and a sea of strangers.

Your friend's neighbors seem affable enough, but you feel pressured to make small talk above the din of music. Now—bang, just like that— you've fallen out of your sweet spot, except this time you're *over*stimulated. And you'll probably feel that way until you pair off with someone on the periphery of the party for an in-depth conversation, or bow out altogether and return to your novel.

Imagine how much better you'll be at this sweet-spot game once you're aware of playing it. You can set up your work, your hobbies, and your social life so that you spend as much time inside your sweet spot as possible. People who are aware of their sweet spots have the power to leave jobs that exhaust them and start new and satisfying businesses. They can hunt for homes based on the temperaments of their family members—with cozy window seats and other nooks and crannies for the introverts, and large, open living-dining spaces for the extroverts.

Understanding your sweet spot can increase your satisfaction in every arena of your life, but it goes even further than that. Evidence suggests that sweet spots can have life-or-death consequences. According to a recent study of military personnel conducted through the Walter Reed Army Institute of Research, introverts function better than extroverts when sleep deprived, which is a cortically de-arousing condition (because losing sleep makes us less alert, active, and energetic). Drowsy extroverts behind the wheel should be especially careful—at least until they increase their arousal levels by chugging coffee or cranking up the radio. Conversely, introverts driving in loud, overly arousing traffic noise should work to stay focused, since the noise may impair their thinking.

Now that we know about optimal levels of stimulation, Esther's problem—winging it at the podium—also makes sense. Overarousal interferes with attention and short-term memory—key components of the ability to speak on the fly. And since public speaking is an inherently stimulating activity—even for those, like Esther, who suffer no stage fright—introverts can find their attention impaired just when they need it most. Esther could live to be a one-hundred-year-old lawyer, in other words, the most knowledgeable practitioner in her field, and she might never be comfortable speaking extemporaneously. She might find herself perpetually unable, at speech time, to draw on the massive body of data sitting inside her long-term memory.

But once Esther understands herself, she can insist to her colleagues that they give her advance notice of any speaking events. She can practice her speeches and find herself well inside her sweet spot when finally she reaches the podium. She can prepare the same way for client meetings, networking events, even casual meetings with her colleagues—any situation of heightened intensity in which her short-term memory and the ability to think on her feet might be a little more compromised than usual.

~

Esther managed to solve her problem from the comfort of her sweet spot. Yet sometimes stretching beyond it is our only choice. Some years ago I decided that I wanted to conquer my fear of public speaking. After much hemming and hawing, I signed up for a workshop at the Public Speaking–Social Anxiety Center of New York. I had my doubts; I felt like a garden-variety shy person, and I didn't like the pathological sound of the term "social anxiety." But the class was based on desensitization training, an approach that made sense to me. Often used as a way to conquer phobias, desensitization involves exposing yourself (and your amygdala) to the thing you're afraid of over and over again, in manageable doses. This is very different from the well-meaning but unhelpful advice that you should just jump in at the deep end and try to swim—an approach that *might* work, but more likely will produce panic, further encoding in your brain a cycle of dread, fear, and shame.

I found myself in good company. There were about fifteen people in the class, which was led by Charles di Cagno, a wiry, compact man with warm brown eyes and a sophisticated sense of humor. Charles is himself a veteran of exposure therapy. Public speaking anxiety doesn't keep him up at night anymore, he says, but fear is a wily enemy and he's always working to get the better of it.

The workshop had been in session for a few weeks before I joined, but Charles assured me that newcomers were welcome. The group was more diverse than I expected. There was a fashion designer with long, curly hair, bright lipstick, and pointy snakeskin boots; a secretary with thick glasses and a clipped, matter-of-fact manner, who talked a lot about her Mensa membership; a couple of investment bankers, tall and athletic; an actor with black hair and vivid blue eyes who bounded cheerfully across the room in his Puma sneakers but claimed to be terrified the entire time; a Chinese software designer with a sweet smile and a nervous laugh. A regular cross-section of New Yorkers, really. It might have been a class in digital photography or Italian cooking.

Except that it wasn't. Charles explained that each of us would speak in front of the group, but at an anxiety level we could handle.

A martial arts instructor named Lateesha was first up that evening. Lateesha's assignment was to read aloud to the class from a Robert Frost poem. With her dreadlocks and wide smile, Lateesha looked as if she wasn't afraid of anything. But as she got ready to speak, her book propped open at the podium, Charles asked how anxious she was, on a scale of 1 to 10.

"At least seven," said Lateesha.

"Take it slow," he said. "There are only a few people out there who can completely overcome their fears, and they all live in Tibet."

Lateesha read the poem clearly and quietly, with only the slightest tremor in her voice. When she was finished, Charles beamed proudly.

"Stand up please, Lisa," he said, addressing an attractive young marketing director with shiny black hair and a gleaming engagement ring. "It's your turn to offer feedback. Did Lateesha look nervous?"

"No," said Lisa.

"I was really scared, though," Lateesha said.

"Don't worry, no one could tell," Lisa assured her.

The others nodded their heads vigorously. *Couldn't tell at all*, they echoed. Lateesha sat down, looking pleased.

Next it was my turn. I stood at a makeshift podium—really a music stand—and faced the group. The only sound in the room was the ticking of the ceiling fan and the blare of traffic outside. Charles asked me to introduce myself. I took a deep breath.

"HELLOOO!!!!" I shouted, hoping to sound dynamic.

Charles looked alarmed. "Just be yourself," he said.

My first exercise was simple. All I had to do was answer a few questions that people called out: Where do you live? What do you do for a living? What did you do this weekend?

I answered the questions in my normal, soft-spoken way. The group listened carefully.

"Does anyone have any more questions for Susan?" asked Charles. The group shook their heads.

"Now, Dan," said Charles, nodding at a strapping red-haired fellow who looked like one of those CNBC journalists reporting directly from the New York Stock Exchange, "you're a banker and you have tough standards. Tell me, did Susan look nervous?"

"Not at all," said Dan.

The rest of the group nodded. *Not nervous at all*, they murmured—just as they had for Lateesha.

You seem so outgoing, they added.

You came across as really confident!

You're lucky because you never run out of things to say.

I sat down feeling pretty good about myself. But soon I saw that Lateesha and I weren't the only ones to get that kind of feedback. A few others did as well. "You looked so calm!" these speakers were told, to their visible relief. "No one would ever know if they didn't know! What are you doing in this class?"

At first I wondered why I prized these reassurances so highly. Then I realized that I was attending the workshop because I wanted to stretch myself to the outer limits of my temperament. I wanted to be the best and bravest speaker I could be. The reassurances were evidence that I was on my way toward achieving this goal. I suspected that the feedback I was getting was overly charitable, but I didn't care. What mattered was that I'd addressed an audience that had received me well, and I felt good about the experience. I had begun to desensitize myself to the horrors of public speaking.

Since then, I've done plenty of speaking, to groups of ten and crowds of hundreds. I've come to embrace the power of the podium. For me this involves taking specific steps, including treating every speech as a creative project, so that when I get ready for the big day, I experience that delving-deep sensation I enjoy so much. I also speak on topics that matter to me deeply, and have found that I feel much more centered when I truly care about my subject.

This isn't always possible, of course. Sometimes speakers need to talk about subjects that don't interest them much, especially at work. I believe this is harder for introverts, who have trouble projecting artificial enthusiasm. But there's a hidden advantage to this inflexibility: it can motivate us to make tough but worthwhile career changes if we find ourselves compelled to speak too often about topics that leave us cold. There is no one more courageous than the person who speaks with the courage of his convictions.

"FRANKLIN WAS A POLITICIAN, BUT ELEANOR SPOKE OUT OF CONSCIENCE"

Why Cool Is Overrated

*A shy man no doubt dreads the notice of strangers, but can hardly be said
to be afraid of them. He may be as bold as a hero in battle, and yet have
no self-confidence about trifles in the presence of strangers.*

—CHARLES DARWIN

Easter Sunday, 1939. The Lincoln Memorial. Marian Anderson, one of
the most extraordinary singers of her generation, takes the stage, the
statue of the sixteenth president rising up behind her. A regal woman
with toffee-colored skin, she gazes at her audience of 75,000: men in
brimmed hats, ladies in their Sunday best, a great sea of black and white
faces. "My country 'tis of thee," she begins, her voice soaring, each word
pure and distinct. "Sweet land of liberty." The crowd is rapt and tearful.
They never thought this day would come to pass.

And it wouldn't have, without Eleanor Roosevelt. Earlier that year,
Anderson had planned to sing at Constitution Hall in Washington,
D.C., but the Daughters of the American Revolution, who owned the
hall, rejected her because of her race. Eleanor Roosevelt, whose family
had fought in the Revolution, resigned from the DAR, helped arrange
for Anderson to sing at the Lincoln Memorial—and ignited a national

firestorm. Roosevelt was not the only one to protest, but she brought political clout to the issue, risking her own reputation in the process.

For Roosevelt, who seemed constitutionally unable to look away from other people's troubles, such acts of social conscience were nothing unusual. But others appreciated how remarkable they were. "This was something unique," recalled the African-American civil rights leader James Farmer of Roosevelt's brave stand. "Franklin was a politician. He weighed the political consequences of every step that he took. He was a good politician, too. But Eleanor spoke out of conscience, and acted as a conscientious person. That was different."

It was a role she played throughout their life together: Franklin's adviser, Franklin's conscience. He may have chosen her for just this reason; in other ways they were such an unlikely pair.

They met when he was twenty. Franklin was her distant cousin, a sheltered Harvard senior from an upper-crust family. Eleanor was only nineteen, also from a moneyed clan, but she had chosen to immerse herself in the sufferings of the poor, despite her family's disapproval. As a volunteer at a settlement house on Manhattan's impoverished Lower East Side, she had met children who were forced to sew artificial flowers in windowless factories to the point of exhaustion. She took Franklin with her one day. He couldn't believe that human beings lived in such miserable conditions—or that a young woman of his own class had been the one to open his eyes to this side of America. He promptly fell in love with her.

But Eleanor wasn't the light, witty type he'd been expected to marry. Just the opposite: she was slow to laugh, bored by small talk, serious-minded, shy. Her mother, a fine-boned, vivacious aristocrat, had nicknamed her "Granny" because of her demeanor. Her father, the charming and popular younger brother of Theodore Roosevelt, doted on her when he saw her, but he was drunk most of the time, and died when Eleanor was nine. By the time Eleanor met Franklin, she couldn't believe that someone like *him* would be interested in *her*. Franklin was everything that she was not: bold and buoyant, with a wide, irrepressible grin, as easy with people as she was cautious. "He was young and gay and good looking," Eleanor recalled, "and I was shy and awkward and thrilled when he asked me to dance."

At the same time, many told Eleanor that Franklin wasn't good enough for her. Some saw him as a lightweight, a mediocre scholar, a frivolous man-about-town. And however poor Eleanor's own self-image, she did not lack for admirers who appreciated her gravitas. Some of her suitors wrote grudging letters of congratulations to Franklin when he won her hand. "I have more respect and admiration for Eleanor than any girl I have ever met," one letter-writer said. "You are mighty lucky. Your future wife is such as it is the privilege of few men to have," said another.

But public opinion was beside the point for Franklin and Eleanor. Each had strengths that the other craved—her empathy, his bravado. "E is an Angel," Franklin wrote in his journal. When she accepted his marriage proposal in 1903, he proclaimed himself the happiest man alive. She responded with a flood of love letters. They were married in 1905 and went on to have six children.

Despite the excitement of their courtship, their differences caused trouble from the start. Eleanor craved intimacy and weighty conversations; he loved parties, flirting, and gossip. The man who would declare that he had nothing to fear but fear itself could not understand his wife's struggles with shyness. When Franklin was appointed assistant secretary of the navy in 1913, the pace of his social life grew ever more frenzied and the settings more gilded—elite private clubs, his Harvard friends' mansions. He caroused later and later into the night. Eleanor went home earlier and earlier.

In the meantime, Eleanor found herself with a full calendar of social duties. She was expected to pay visits to the wives of other Washington luminaries, leaving calling cards at their doors and holding open houses in her own home. She didn't relish this role, so she hired a social secretary named Lucy Mercer to help her. Which seemed a good idea—until the summer of 1917, when Eleanor took the children to Maine for the summer, leaving Franklin behind in Washington with Mercer. The two began a lifelong affair. Lucy was just the kind of lively beauty Franklin had been expected to marry in the first place.

Eleanor found out about Franklin's betrayal when she stumbled on a packet of love letters in his suitcase. She was devastated, but stayed in the marriage. And although they never rekindled the romantic side of their relationship, she and Franklin replaced it with something formidable: a union of his confidence with her conscience.

~

Fast-forward to our own time, where we'll meet another woman of similar temperament, acting out of her own sense of conscience. Dr. Elaine Aron is a research psychologist who, since her first scientific publication in 1997, has singlehandedly reframed what Jerome Kagan and others call high reactivity (and sometimes "negativity" or "inhibition"). She calls it "sensitivity," and along with her new name for the trait, she's transformed and deepened our understanding of it.

When I hear that Aron will be the keynote speaker at an annual weekend gathering of "highly sensitive people" at Walker Creek Ranch in Marin County, California, I quickly buy plane tickets. Jacquelyn Strickland, a psychotherapist and the founder and host of the event, explains that she created these weekends so that sensitive people could benefit from being in one another's presence. She sends me an agenda explaining that we'll be sleeping in rooms designated for "napping, journaling, puttering, meditating, organizing, writing, and reflecting."

"Please do socialize very quietly in your room (with consent of your roommate), or preferably in the group areas on walks and at mealtimes," says the agenda. The conference is geared to people who enjoy meaningful discussions and sometimes "move a conversation to a deeper level, only to find out we are the only ones there." There will be plenty of time for serious talk this weekend, we're assured. But we'll also be free to come and go as we please. Strickland knows that most of us will have weathered a lifetime of mandatory group activities, and she wants to show us a different model, if only for a few days.

Walker Creek Ranch sits on 1,741 acres of unspoiled Northern California wilderness. It offers hiking trails and wildlife and vast crystalline skies, but at its center is a cozy, barnlike conference center where about thirty of us gather on a Thursday afternoon in the middle of June. The

Buckeye Lodge is outfitted with grey industrial carpets, large white-boards, and picture windows overlooking sunny redwood forests. Along-side the usual piles of registration forms and name badges, there's a flip chart where we're asked to write our name and Myers-Briggs personality type. I scan the list. Everyone's an introvert except for Strickland, who is warm, welcoming, and expressive. (According to Aron's research, the majority, though not all, of sensitive people are introverts.)

The tables and chairs in the room are organized in a big square so that we can all sit and face one another. Strickland invites us—participation optional—to share what brought us here. A software engineer named Tom kicks off, describing with great passion his relief at learning that there was "a physiological basis for the trait of sensitivity. Here's the re-search! This is how I am! I don't have to try to meet anyone's expecta-tions anymore. I don't need to feel apologetic or defensive in any way." With his long, narrow face, brown hair, and matching beard, Tom re-minds me of Abraham Lincoln. He introduces his wife, who talks about how compatible she and Tom are, and how together they stumbled across Aron's work.

When it's my turn, I talk about how I've never been in a group envi-ronment in which I didn't feel obliged to present an unnaturally rah-rah version of myself. I say that I'm interested in the connection between introversion and sensitivity. Many people nod.

On Saturday morning, Dr. Aron appears in the Buckeye Lodge. She waits playfully behind an easel containing a flip chart while Strickland introduces her to the audience. Then she emerges smiling—ta-da!—from behind the easel, sensibly clad in a blazer, turtleneck, and corduroy skirt. She has short, feathery brown hair and warm, crinkly blue eyes that look as if they don't miss a thing. You can see immediately the dignified scholar Aron is today, as well as the awkward schoolgirl she must once have been. You can see, too, her respect for her audience.

Getting right down to business, she informs us that she has five dif-ferent subtopics she can discuss, and asks us to raise our hands to vote for our first, second, and third choice of subjects. Then she performs, rapid-fire, an elaborate mathematical calculation from which she deter-mines the three subtopics for which we've collectively voted. The crowd settles down amiably. It doesn't really matter which subtopics we've chosen; we know that Aron is here to talk about sensitivity, and that she's taking our preferences into consideration.

Some psychologists make their mark by doing unusual research experiments. Aron's contribution is to think differently, radically differently, about studies that others have done. When she was a girl, Aron was often told that she was "too sensitive for her own good." She had two hardy elder siblings and was the only child in her family who liked to daydream, and play inside, and whose feelings were easily hurt. As she grew older and ventured outside her family's orbit, she continued to notice things about herself that seemed different from the norm. She could drive alone for hours and never turn on the radio. She had strong, sometimes disturbing dreams at night. She was "strangely intense," and often beset by powerful emotions, both positive and negative. She had trouble finding the sacred in the everyday; it seemed to be there only when she withdrew from the world.

Aron grew up, became a psychologist, and married a robust man who loved these qualities. To her husband, Art, Aron was creative, intuitive, and a deep thinker. She appreciated these things in herself, too, but saw them as "acceptable surface manifestations of a terrible, hidden flaw I had been aware of all my life." She thought it was a miracle that Art loved her in spite of this flaw.

But when one of her fellow psychologists casually described Aron as "highly sensitive," a lightbulb went on in her head. It was as if these two words described her mysterious failing, except that the psychologist hadn't been referring to a flaw at all. It had been a neutral description.

Aron pondered this new insight, and then set out to research this trait called "sensitivity." She came up mostly dry, so she pored over the vast literature on introversion, which seemed to be intimately related: Kagan's work on high-reactive children, and the long line of experiments on the tendency of introverts to be more sensitive to social and sensory stimulation. These studies gave her glimpses of what she was looking for, but Aron thought that there was a missing piece in the emerging portrait of introverted people.

"The problem for scientists is that we try to observe behavior, and these are things that you cannot observe," she explains. Scientists can easily report on the behavior of extroverts, who can often be found laughing, talking, or gesticulating. But "if a person is standing in the corner of a room, you can attribute about fifteen motivations to that person. But you don't really know what's going on inside."

Yet inner behavior was still behavior, thought Aron, even if it was difficult to catalog. So what *is* the inner behavior of people whose most visible feature is that when you take them to a party they aren't very pleased about it? She decided to find out.

First Aron interviewed thirty-nine people who described themselves as being either introverted or easily overwhelmed by stimulation. She asked them about the movies they liked, their first memories, relationships with parents, friendships, love lives, creative activities, philosophical and religious views. Based on these interviews, she created a voluminous questionnaire that she gave to several large groups of people. Then she boiled their responses down to a constellation of twenty-seven attributes. She named the people who embodied these attributes "highly sensitive."

Some of these twenty-seven attributes were familiar from Kagan and others' work. For example, highly sensitive people tend to be keen observers who look before they leap. They arrange their lives in ways that limit surprises. They're often sensitive to sights, sounds, smells, pain, coffee. They have difficulty when being observed (at work, say, or performing at a music recital) or judged for general worthiness (dating, job interviews).

But there were also new insights. The highly sensitive tend to be philosophical or spiritual in their orientation, rather than materialistic or hedonistic. They dislike small talk. They often describe themselves as creative or intuitive (just as Aron's husband had described her). They dream vividly, and can often recall their dreams the next day. They love music, nature, art, physical beauty. They feel exceptionally strong emotions—sometimes acute bouts of joy, but also sorrow, melancholy, and fear.

Highly sensitive people also process information about their environments—both physical and emotional—unusually deeply. They tend to notice subtleties that others miss—another person's shift in mood, say, or a lightbulb burning a touch too brightly.

Recently a group of scientists at Stony Brook University tested this finding by showing two pairs of photos (of a fence and some bales of hay) to eighteen people lying inside fMRI machines. In one pair the photos were noticeably different from each other, and in the other pair the difference was much more subtle. For each pair, the scientists asked whether the second photo was the same as the first. They found that sensitive people spent more time than others looking at the photos with the subtle differences. Their brains also showed more activity in regions that help to make associations between those images and other stored information. In other words, the sensitive people were processing the photos at a more elaborate level than their peers, reflecting more on those fenceposts and haystacks.

This study is very new, and its conclusions still need to be replicated and explored in other contexts. But it echoes Jerome Kagan's findings that high-reactive first graders spend more time than other children comparing choices when they play matching games or reading unfamiliar words. And it suggests, says Jadzia Jagiellowicz, the lead scientist at Stony Brook, that sensitive types think in an unusually complex fashion. It may also help explain why they're so bored by small talk. "If you're thinking in more complicated ways," she told me, "then talking about the weather or where you went for the holidays is not quite as interesting as talking about values or morality."

The other thing Aron found about sensitive people is that sometimes they're highly empathic. It's as if they have thinner boundaries separating them from other people's emotions and from the tragedies and cruelties of the world. They tend to have unusually strong consciences. They avoid violent movies and TV shows; they're acutely aware of the consequences of a lapse in their own behavior. In social settings they often focus on subjects like personal problems, which others consider "too heavy."

Aron realized that she was on to something big. Many of the characteristics of sensitive people that she'd identified—such as empathy and responsiveness to beauty—were believed by psychologists to be characteristic of other personality traits like "agreeableness" and "openness to experience." But Aron saw that they were also a fundamental part of sensitivity. Her findings implicitly challenged accepted tenets of personality psychology.

She started publishing her results in academic journals and books, and speaking publicly about her work. At first this was difficult. Audience members told her that her ideas were fascinating, but that her uncertain delivery was distracting. But Aron had a great desire to get her message out. She persevered, and learned to speak like the authority she was. By the time I saw her at Walker Creek Ranch, she was practiced, crisp, and sure. The only difference between her and your typical speaker was how conscientious she seemed about answering every last audience question. She lingered afterward with the group, even though, as an extreme introvert, she must have been itching to get home.

Aron's description of highly sensitive people sounds as if she's talking about Eleanor Roosevelt herself. Indeed, in the years since Aron first published her findings, scientists have found that when you put people whose genetic profiles have been tentatively associated with sensitivity and introversion (people with the gene variant of 5-HTTLPR that characterized the rhesus monkeys of chapter 3) inside an fMRI machine and show them pictures of scared faces, accident victims, mutilated bodies, and polluted scenery, the amygdala—the part of the brain that plays such an important role in processing emotions—becomes strongly activated. Aron and a team of scientists have also found that when sensitive people see faces of people experiencing strong feelings, they have more activation than others do in areas of the brain associated with empathy and with trying to control strong emotions.

It's as if, like Eleanor Roosevelt, they can't help but feel what others feel.

~

In 1921, FDR contracted polio. It was a terrible blow, and he considered retiring to the country to live out his life as an invalid gentleman. But Eleanor kept his contacts with the Democratic Party alive while he recovered, even agreeing to address a party fund-raiser. She was terrified of public speaking, and not much good at it—she had a high-pitched voice and laughed nervously at all the wrong times. But she trained for the event and made her way through the speech.

After that, Eleanor was still unsure of herself, but she began working to fix the social problems she saw all around her. She became a champion of women's issues and forged alliances with other serious-minded people. By 1928, when FDR was elected governor of New York, she was the director of the Bureau of Women's Activities for the Democratic Party and one of the most influential women in American politics. She and Franklin were now a fully functioning partnership of his savoir faire and her social conscience. "I knew about social conditions, perhaps more than he did," Eleanor recalled with characteristic modesty. "But he knew about government and how you could use government to improve things. And I think we began to get an understanding of teamwork."

FDR was elected president in 1933. It was the height of the Depression, and Eleanor traveled the country—in a single three-month period she covered 40,000 miles—listening to ordinary people tell their hard-luck stories. People opened up to her in ways they didn't for other powerful figures. She became for Franklin the voice of the dispossessed. When she returned home from her trips, she often told him what she'd seen and pressed him to act. She helped orchestrate government programs for half-starved miners in Appalachia. She urged FDR to include women and African-Americans in his programs to put people back to work. And she helped arrange for Marian Anderson to sing at the Lincoln Memorial. "She kept at him on issues which he might, in the rush of things, have wanted to overlook," the historian Geoff Ward has said. "She kept him to a high standard. Anyone who ever saw her lock eyes with him and say, 'Now Franklin, you should . . .' never forgot it."

The shy young woman who'd been terrified of public speaking grew to love public life. Eleanor Roosevelt became the first First Lady to hold a press conference, address a national convention, write a newspaper column, and appear on talk radio. Later in her career she served as a U.S. delegate to the United Nations, where she used her unusual brand of political skills and hard-won toughness to help win passage of the Universal Declaration of Human Rights.

She never did outgrow her vulnerability; all her life she suffered dark "Griselda moods," as she called them (named for a princess in a medieval legend who withdrew into silence), and struggled to "develop skin as tough as rhinoceros hide." "I think people who are shy remain shy always, but they learn how to overcome it," she said. But it was perhaps this sensitivity that made it easy for her to relate to the disenfranchised, and conscientious enough to act on their behalf. FDR, elected at the start of the Depression, is remembered for his compassion. But it was Eleanor who made sure he knew how suffering Americans *felt*.

~

The connection between sensitivity and conscience has long been observed. Imagine the following experiment, performed by the developmental psychologist Grazyna Kochanska. A kind woman hands a toy to a toddler, explaining that the child should be very careful because it's one of the woman's favorites. The child solemnly nods assent and begins to play with the toy. Soon afterward, it breaks dramatically in two, having been rigged to do so.

The woman looks upset and cries, "Oh my!" Then she waits to see what the child does next.

Some children, it turns out, feel a lot more guilty about their (supposed) transgression than others. They look away, hug themselves, stammer out confessions, hide their faces. And it's the kids we might call the most sensitive, the most high-reactive, the ones who are likely to be introverts who feel the guiltiest. Being unusually sensitive to all experience, both positive and negative, they seem to feel both the sorrow of the woman whose toy is broken and the anxiety of having done something bad. (In case you're wondering, the woman in the experiments quickly returned to the room with the toy "fixed" and reassurances that the child had done nothing wrong.)

In our culture, guilt is a tainted word, but it's probably one of the building blocks of conscience. The anxiety these highly sensitive toddlers feel upon apparently breaking the toy gives them the motivation to avoid harming someone's plaything the next time. By age four, according to Kochanska, these same kids are less likely than their peers to cheat or break rules, *even when they think they can't be caught*. And by six or seven, they're more likely to be described by their parents as having high levels of moral traits such as empathy. They also have fewer behavioral problems in general.

"Functional, moderate guilt," writes Kochanska, "may promote future altruism, personal responsibility, adaptive behavior in school, and harmonious, competent, and prosocial relationships with parents, teachers, and friends." This is an especially important set of attributes at a time when a 2010 University of Michigan study shows that college students today are 40 percent less empathetic than they were thirty years ago, with much of the drop having occurred since 2000. (The study's authors speculate that the decline in empathy is related to the prevalence of social media, reality TV, and "hyper-competitiveness.")

Of course, having these traits doesn't mean that sensitive children are angels. They have selfish streaks like everyone else. Sometimes they act aloof and unfriendly. And when they're overwhelmed by negative emotions like shame or anxiety, says Aron, they can be positively oblivious of other people's needs.

But the same receptivity to experience that can make life difficult for the highly sensitive also builds their consciences. Aron tells of one sensitive teen who persuaded his mother to feed a homeless person he'd met in the park, and of another eight-year-old who cried not only when *she* felt embarrassed, but also when her peers were teased.

We know this type of person well from literature, probably because so many writers are sensitive introverts themselves. He "had gone through life with one skin fewer than most men," the novelist Eric Malpass writes of his quiet and cerebral protagonist, also an author, in the novel *The Long Long Dances*. "The troubles of others moved him more, as did also the teeming beauty of life: moved him, compelled him, to seize a pen and write about them. [He was moved by] walking in the hills, listening to a Schubert impromptu, watching nightly from his armchair the smashing of bone and flesh that made up so much of the nine o'clock news."

The description of such characters as thin-skinned is meant metaphorically, but it turns out that it's actually quite literal. Among the tests researchers use to measure personality traits are skin conductance tests, which record how much people sweat in response to noises, strong emotions, and other stimuli. High-reactive introverts sweat more; low-reactive extroverts sweat less. Their skin is literally "thicker," more impervious to stimuli, cooler to the touch. In fact, according to some of the scientists I spoke to, this is where our notion of being socially "cool" comes from; the lower-reactive you are, the cooler your skin, the cooler you *are*. (Incidentally, sociopaths lie at the extreme end of this coolness barometer, with extremely low levels of arousal, skin conductance, and anxiety. There is some evidence that sociopaths have damaged amygdalae.)

Lie detectors (polygraphs) are partially skin conductance tests. They operate on the theory that lying causes anxiety, which triggers the skin to perspire imperceptibly. When I was in college, I applied for a summer job as a secretary at a large jewelry company. I had to take a lie detector test as part of the application process. The test was administered in a small, dingily lit room with linoleum floors, by a thin, cigarette-puffing man with pocked yellow skin. The man asked me a series of warm-up questions: my name, address, and so on, to establish my baseline level of skin conductance. Then the questions grew more probing and the examiner's manner harsher. Had I been arrested? Had I ever shoplifted? Had I used cocaine? With this last question my interrogator peered at me intently. As it happens, I never *had* tried cocaine. But he seemed to think I had. The accusing look on his face was the equivalent of the old policeman's trick where they tell the suspect that they have the damning evidence and there's no point denying it.

I knew the man was mistaken, but I still felt myself blush. And sure enough, the test came back showing I'd lied on the cocaine question. My skin is so thin, apparently, that it sweats in response to imaginary crimes!

We tend to think of coolness as a pose that you strike with a pair of sunglasses, a nonchalant attitude, and drink in hand. But maybe we didn't choose these social accessories at random. Maybe we've adopted dark glasses, relaxed body language, and alcohol as signifiers precisely because they camouflage signs of a nervous system on overdrive. Sunglasses prevent others from seeing our eyes dilate with surprise or fear; we know from Kagan's work that a relaxed torso is a hallmark of low reactivity; and alcohol removes our inhibitions and lowers our arousal levels. When you go to a football game and someone offers you a beer, says the personality psychologist Brian Little, "they're really saying hi, have a glass of extroversion."

Teenagers understand instinctively the physiology of cool. In Curtis Sittenfeld's novel *Prep*, which explores the adolescent social rituals of boarding-school life with uncanny precision, the protagonist, Lee, is invited unexpectedly to the dorm room of Aspeth, the coolest girl in school. The first thing she notices is how physically stimulating Aspeth's world is. "From outside the door, I could hear pounding music," she observes. "White Christmas lights, currently turned on, were taped high up along all the walls, and on the north wall they'd hung an enormous orange and green tapestry. . . . I felt overstimulated and vaguely irritated. The room I shared with [my roommate] seemed so quiet and plain, our lives seemed so quiet and plain. Had Aspeth been born cool, I wondered, or had someone taught her, like an older sister or a cousin?"

Jock cultures sense the low-reactive physiology of cool, too. For the early U.S. astronauts, having a low heart rate, which is associated with low reactivity, was a status symbol. Lieutenant Colonel John Glenn, who became the first American to orbit the Earth and would later run for president, was admired by his comrades for his supercool pulse rate during liftoff (only 110 beats per minute).

~

But physical lack of cool may be more socially valuable than we think. That deep blush when a hard-bitten tester puts his face an inch from yours and asks if you've ever used cocaine turns out to be a kind of social glue. In a recent experiment, a team of psychologists led by Corine Dijk asked sixty-odd participants to read accounts of people who'd done something morally wrong, like driving away from a car crash, or something embarrassing, like spilling coffee on someone. The participants were shown photographs of the wrongdoers, who had one of four different facial expressions: shame or embarrassment (head and eyes down); shame/embarrassment plus a blush; neutral; or neutral with a blush. Then they were asked to rate how sympathetic and trustworthy the transgressors were.

It turned out that the offenders who blushed were judged a lot more positively than those who didn't. This was because the blush signified concern for others. As Dacher Keltner, a psychologist at the University of California, Berkeley, who specializes in positive emotions, put it to the *New York Times*, "A blush comes online in two or three seconds and says, 'I care; I know I violated the social contract.'"

In fact, the very thing that many high-reactives hate most about blushing—its uncontrollability—is what makes it so socially useful. "Because it is impossible to control the blush intentionally," Dijk speculates, blushing is an authentic sign of embarrassment. And embarrassment, according to Keltner, is a moral emotion. It shows humility, modesty, and a desire to avoid aggression and make peace. It's not about isolating the person who feels ashamed (which is how it sometimes feels to easy blushers), but about bringing people together.

Keltner has tracked the roots of human embarrassment and found that after many primates fight, they try to make up. They do this partly by making gestures of embarrassment of the kind we see in humans—looking away, which acknowledges wrongdoing and the intention to stop; lowering the head, which shrinks one's size; and pressing the lips together, a sign of inhibition. These gestures in humans have been called "acts of devotion," writes Keltner. Indeed, Keltner, who is trained in reading people's faces, has studied photos of moral heroes like Gandhi and the Dalai Lama and found that they feature just such controlled smiles and averted eyes.

In his book, *Born to Be Good*, Keltner even says that if he had to choose his mate by asking a single question at a speed-dating event, the question he would choose is: "What was your last embarrassing experience?" Then he would watch very carefully for lip-presses, blushing, and averted eyes. "The elements of the embarrassment are fleeting statements the individual makes about his or her respect for the judgment of others," he writes. "Embarrassment reveals how much the individual cares about the rules that bind us to one another."

In other words, you want to make sure that your spouse cares what other people think. It's better to mind too much than to mind too little.

~

No matter how great the benefits of blushing, the phenomenon of high sensitivity raises an obvious question. How did the highly sensitive manage to survive the harsh sorting-out process of evolution? If the bold and aggressive generally prevail (as it sometimes seems), why were the sensitive not selected out of the human population thousands of years ago, like tree frogs colored orange? For you may, like the protagonist of *The Long Long Dances*, be moved more deeply than the next person by the opening chords of a Schubert impromptu, and you may flinch more than others at the smashing of bone and flesh, and you may have been the sort of child who squirmed horribly when you thought you'd broken someone's toy, but evolution doesn't reward such things.

Or does it?

Elaine Aron has an idea about this. She believes that high sensitivity was not itself selected for, but rather the careful, reflective style that tends to accompany it. "The type that is 'sensitive' or 'reactive' would reflect a strategy of observing carefully before acting," she writes, "thus avoiding dangers, failures, and wasted energy, which would require a nervous system specially designed to observe and detect subtle differences. It is a strategy of 'betting on a sure thing' or 'looking before you leap.' In contrast, the active strategy of the [other type] is to be first, without complete information and with the attendant risks—the strategy of 'taking a long shot' because the 'early bird catches the worm' and 'opportunity only knocks once.'"

In truth, many people Aron considers sensitive have some of the twenty-seven attributes associated with the trait, but not all of them. Maybe they're sensitive to light and noise, but not to coffee or pain; maybe they're not sensitive to anything sensory, but they're deep thinkers with a rich inner life. Maybe they're not even introverts—only 70 percent of sensitive people are, according to Aron, while the other 30 percent are extroverts (although this group tends to report craving more downtime and solitude than your typical extrovert). This, speculates Aron, is because sensitivity arose as a by-product of survival strategy, and you need only some, not all, of the traits to pull off the strategy effectively.

There's a great deal of evidence for Aron's point of view. Evolutionary biologists once believed that every animal species evolved to fit an ecological niche, that there was one ideal set of behaviors for that niche, and that species members whose behavior deviated from that ideal would die off. But it turns out that it's not only humans that divide into those who "watch and wait" and others who "just do it." *More than a hundred species in the animal kingdom are organized in roughly this way.*

From fruit flies to house cats to mountain goats, from sunfish to bushbaby primates to Eurasian tit birds, scientists have discovered that approximately 20 percent of the members of many species are "slow to warm up," while the other 80 percent are "fast" types who venture forth boldly without noticing much of what's going on around them. (Intriguingly, the percentage of infants in Kagan's lab who were born high-reactive was also, you'll recall, about twenty.)

If "fast" and "slow" animals had parties, writes the evolutionary biologist David Sloan Wilson, "some of the fasts would bore everyone with their loud conversation, while others would mutter into their beer that they don't get any respect. Slow animals are best described as shy, sensitive types. They don't assert themselves, but they are observant and notice things that are invisible to the bullies. They are the writers and artists at the party who have interesting conversations out of earshot of the bullies. They are the inventors who figure out new ways to behave, while the bullies steal their patents by copying their behavior."

Once in a while, a newspaper or TV program runs a story about animal personalities, casting shy behavior as unseemly and bold behavior as attractive and admirable. (*That's our kind of fruit fly!*) But Wilson, like Aron, believes that both types of animals exist because they have radically different survival strategies, each of which pays off differently and at different times. This is what's known as the trade-off theory of evolution, in which a particular trait is neither all good nor all bad, but a mix of pros and cons whose survival value varies according to circumstance.

"Shy" animals forage less often and widely for food, conserving en-

ergy, sticking to the sidelines, and surviving when predators come calling. Bolder animals sally forth, swallowed regularly by those farther up
the food chain but surviving when food is scarce and they need to assume
more risk. When Wilson dropped metal traps into a pond full of pumpkinseed fish, an event he says must have seemed to the fish as unsettling
as a flying saucer landing on Earth, the bold fish couldn't help but inves-
tigate—and rushed headlong into Wilson's traps. The shy fish hovered
judiciously at the edge of the pond, making it impossible for Wilson to
catch them.

On the other hand, after Wilson succeeded in trapping both types of
fish with an elaborate netting system and carrying them back to his lab,
the bold fish acclimated quickly to their new environment and started
eating a full five days earlier than did their shy brethren. "There is no
single best . . . [animal] personality," writes Wilson, "but rather a diversity of personalities maintained by natural selection."

Another example of the trade-off theory of evolution is a species
known as Trinidadian guppies. These guppies develop personalities—
with astonishing speed, in evolutionary terms—to suit the microcli-
mates in which they live. Their natural predators are pike. But some
guppy neighborhoods, upstream of a waterfall for example, are pike-free.
If you're a guppy who grew up in such a charmed locale, then chances
are you have a bold and carefree personality well suited to *la dolce vita*.
In contrast, if your guppy family came from a "bad neighborhood" down-
stream from the waterfall, where pike cruise the waterways menacingly,
then you probably have a much more circumspect style, just right for
avoiding the bad guys.

The interesting thing is that these differences are heritable, not
learned, so that the offspring of bold guppies who move into bad neighborhoods inherit their parents' boldness—even though this puts them
at a severe disadvantage compared to their vigilant peers. It doesn't take
long for their genes to mutate, though, and descendants who manage
to survive tend to be careful types. The same thing happens to vigilant
guppies when the pike suddenly disappear; it takes about twenty years for
their descendants to evolve into fish who act as if they haven't a care in
the world.

~

The trade-off theory seems to apply equally to humans. Scientists have found that nomads who inherited the form of a particular gene linked to extroversion (specifically, to novelty-seeking) are better nourished than those without this version of the gene. But in *settled* populations, people with this same gene form have *poorer* nutrition. The same traits that make a nomad fierce enough to hunt and to defend livestock against raiders may hinder more sedentary activities like farming, selling goods at the market, or focusing at school.

Or consider this trade-off: human extroverts have more sex partners than introverts do—a boon to any species wanting to reproduce itself—but they commit more adultery and divorce more frequently, which is not a good thing for the children of all those couplings. Extroverts exercise more, but introverts suffer fewer accidents and traumatic injuries. Extroverts enjoy wider networks of social support, but commit more crimes. As Jung speculated almost a century ago about the two types, "the one [extroversion] consists in a high rate of fertility, with low powers of defense and short duration of life for the single individual; the other [introversion] consists in equipping the individual with numerous means of self-preservation plus a low fertility rate."

The trade-off theory may even apply to entire species. Among evolutionary biologists, who tend to subscribe to the vision of lone individuals hell-bent on reproducing their own DNA, the idea that species include individuals whose traits promote group survival is hotly debated and, not long ago, could practically get you kicked out of the academy. But this view is slowly gaining acceptance. Some scientists even speculate that the evolutionary basis for traits like sensitivity is heightened compassion for the suffering of other members of one's species, especially one's family.

But you don't have to go that far. As Aron explains, it makes sense that animal groups depend on their sensitive members for survival. "Suppose a herd of antelope . . . has a few members who are constantly stopping their grazing to use their keen senses to watch for predators," she writes. "Herds with such sensitive, watchful individuals would survive better, and so continue to breed, and so continue to have some sensitive individuals born in the group."

And why should it be any different for humans? We need our Eleanor Roosevelts as surely as grazing herds depend on their sensitive antelopes.

In addition to "shy" and "bold" animals, and to "fast" and "slow" ones, biologists sometimes speak of the "hawk" and "dove" members of a given species. Great tit birds, for example, some of whom are much more aggressive than others, often act like case studies in an international relations class. These birds feed on beech tree nuts, and in years when nuts are scarce, the hawkish female birds do better, just as you'd expect, because they're quick to challenge nut-eating competitors to a duel. But in seasons when there are plenty of beech nuts to go around, the female "doves"—who, incidentally, tend to make more attentive mothers—do better than the "hawks," because the hawks waste time and bodily health getting into fights for no good reason.

Male great tits, on the other hand, have the opposite pattern. This is because their main role in life is not to find food but to defend territory. In years when food is scarce, so many of their fellow tit birds die of hunger that there's enough space for all. The hawkish males then fall into the same trap as their female comrades during nutty seasons—they brawl, squandering precious resources with each bloody battle. But in good years, when competition for nesting territory heats up, aggression pays for the hawkish male tit bird.

~

During times of war or fear—the human equivalent of a bad nut season for female tit birds—it might seem that what we need most are aggressive heroic types. But if our entire population consisted of warriors, there would be no one to notice, let alone battle, potentially deadly but far quieter threats like viral disease or climate change.

Consider Vice President Al Gore's decades-long crusade to raise awareness of global warming. Gore is, by many accounts, an introvert. "If you send an introvert into a reception or an event with a hundred other people he will emerge with less energy than he had going in," says a former aide. "Gore needs a rest after an event." Gore acknowledges that his skills are not conducive to stumping and speechmaking. "Most people in politics draw energy from backslapping and shaking hands and all that," he has said. "I draw energy from discussing ideas."

But combine that passion for thought with attention to subtlety—both common characteristics of introverts—and you get a very powerful mix. In 1968, when Gore was a college student at Harvard, he took a class with an influential oceanographer who presented early evidence linking the burning of fossil fuels with the greenhouse effect. Gore's ears perked up.

He tried to tell others what he knew. But he found that people wouldn't listen. It was as if they couldn't hear the alarm bells that rang so loudly in his ears.

"When I went to Congress in the middle of the 1970s, I helped organize the first hearings on global warming," he recalls in the Oscar-winning movie *An Inconvenient Truth*—a film whose most stirring action scenes involve the solitary figure of Gore wheeling his suitcase through a midnight airport. Gore seems genuinely puzzled that no one paid attention: "I actually thought and believed that the story would be compelling enough to cause a real sea change in the way Congress reacted to that issue. I thought they would be startled, too. And they weren't."

But if Gore had known then what we know now about Kagan's research, and Aron's, he might have been less surprised by his colleagues' reactions. He might even have used his insight into personality psychology to get them to listen. Congress, he could have safely assumed, is made up of some of the least sensitive people in the country—people who, if they'd been kids in one of Kagan's experiments, would have marched up to oddly attired clowns and strange ladies wearing gas masks without so much as a backward glance at their mothers. Remember Kagan's introverted Tom and extroverted Ralph? Well, Congress is full of Ralphs—it was *designed* for people like Ralph. Most of the Toms of the world do not want to spend their days planning campaigns and schmoozing with lobbyists.

These Ralph-like Congressmen can be wonderful people—exuberant, fearless, persuasive—but they're unlikely to feel alarmed by a photograph of a tiny crack in a distant glacier. They need more intense stimulation to get them to listen. Which is why Gore finally got his message across when he teamed up with whiz-bang Hollywood types who could package his warning into the special-effects-laden show that became *An Inconvenient Truth*.

Gore also drew on his own strengths, using his natural focus and diligence to tirelessly promote the movie. He visited dozens of movie theaters across the country to meet with viewers, and gave innumerable TV and radio interviews. On the subject of global warming, Gore has a clarity of voice that eluded him as a politician. For Gore, immersing himself in a complicated scientific puzzle comes naturally. Focusing on a single passion rather than tap dancing from subject to subject comes naturally. Even talking to crowds comes naturally when the topic is climate change: Gore on global warming has an easy charisma and connection with audience members that eluded him as a political candidate. That's because this mission, for him, is not about politics or personality. It's about the call of his conscience. "It's about the survival of the planet," he says. "Nobody is going to care who won or lost any election when the earth is uninhabitable."

If you're a sensitive sort, then you may be in the habit of pretending to be more of a politician and less cautious or single-mindedly focused than you actually are. But in this chapter I'm asking you to rethink this view. Without people like you, we will, quite literally, drown.

~

Back here at Walker Creek Ranch and the gathering for sensitive people, the Extrovert Ideal and its primacy of cool is turned upside down. If "cool" is low reactivity that predisposes a person to boldness or nonchalance, then the crowd that has come to meet Elaine Aron is deeply uncool.

The atmosphere is startling simply because it's so unusual. It's something you might find at a yoga class or in a Buddhist monastery, except that here there's no unifying religion or worldview, only a shared temperament. It's easy to see this when Aron delivers her speech. She has long observed that when she speaks to groups of highly sensitive people the room is more hushed and respectful than would be usual in a public gathering place, and this is true throughout her presentation. But it carries over all weekend.

I've never heard so many "after you's" and "thank you's" as I do here. During meals, which are held at long communal tables in a summer-camp style, open-air cafeteria, people plunge hungrily into searching conversations. There's a lot of one-on-one discussion about intimate topics like childhood experiences and adult love lives, and social issues like health care and climate change; there's not much in the way of storytelling intended to entertain. People listen carefully to each other and respond thoughtfully; Aron has noted that sensitive people tend to speak softly because that's how they prefer others to communicate with them.

"In the rest of the world," observes Michelle, a web designer who leans forward as if bracing herself against an imaginary blast of wind, "you make a statement and people may or may not discuss it. Here you make a statement and someone says, 'What does that *mean?*' And if you ask that question of someone else, they actually answer."

It's not that there's no small talk, observes Strickland, the leader of the gathering. It's that it comes not at the beginning of conversations but at the end. In most settings, people use small talk as a way of relaxing into a new relationship, and only once they're comfortable do they connect more seriously. Sensitive people seem to do the reverse. They "enjoy small talk only after they've gone deep," says Strickland. "When sensitive people are in environments that nurture their authenticity, they laugh and chitchat just as much as anyone else."

On the first night we drift to our bedrooms, housed in a dormlike building. I brace myself instinctively: now's the time when I'll want to read or sleep, but will instead be called upon to have a pillow fight (summer camp) or play a loud and boring drinking game (college). But at Walker Creek Ranch, my roommate, a twenty-seven-year-old secretary with huge, doe-like eyes and the ambition to become an author, is happy to spend the evening writing peacefully in her journal. I do the same.

Of course, the weekend is not completely without tension. Some people are reserved to the point of appearing sullen. Sometimes the do-your-own-thing policy threatens to devolve into mutual loneliness as everyone goes their own separate ways. In fact, there is such a deficit of the social behavior we call "cool" that I begin thinking someone *should* be cracking jokes, stirring things up, handing out rum-and-Cokes. Shouldn't they?

The truth is, as much as I crave breathing room for sensitive types, I enjoy hail-fellows-well-met, too. I'm glad for the "cool" among us, and I miss them this weekend. I'm starting to speak so softly that I feel like I'm putting myself to sleep. I wonder if deep down the others feel this way, too.

Tom, the software engineer and Abraham Lincoln look-alike, tells me of a former girlfriend who was always throwing open the doors of her house to friends and strangers. She was adventurous in every way: she loved new food, new sexual experiences, new people. It didn't work out between them—Tom eventually craved the company of a partner who would focus more on their relationship and less on the outside world, and he's happily married now to just such a woman—but he's glad for the time with his ex-girlfriend.

As Tom talks, I think of how much I miss my husband, Ken, who's back home in New York and not a sensitive type either, far from it. Sometimes this is frustrating: if something moves me to tears of empathy or anxiety, he'll be touched, but grow impatient if I stay that way too long. But I also know that his tougher attitude is good for me, and I find his company endlessly delightful. I love his effortless charm. I love that he never runs out of interesting things to say. I love how he pours his heart and soul into everything he does, and everyone he loves, especially our family.

But most of all I love his way of expressing compassion. Ken may be aggressive, more aggressive in a week than I'll be in a lifetime, but he uses it on behalf of others. Before we met, he worked for the UN in war zones all over the world, where, among other things, he conducted prisoner-of-war and detainee release negotiations. He would march into fetid jails and face down camp commanders with machine guns strapped to their chests until they agreed to release young girls who'd committed no crime other than to be female and victims of rape. After many years on the job, he went home and wrote down what he'd witnessed, in books and articles that bristled with rage. He didn't write in the style of a sensitive person, and he made a lot of people angry. But he wrote like a person who cares, desperately.

I thought that Walker Creek Ranch would make me long for a world of the highly sensitive, a world in which everyone speaks softly and no one carries a big stick. But instead it reinforced my deeper yearning for balance. This balance, I think, is what Elaine Aron would say is our natural state of being, at least in Indo-European cultures like ours, which she observes have long been divided into "warrior kings" and "priestly advisers," into the executive branch and the judicial branch, into bold and easy FDRs and sensitive, conscientious Eleanor Roosevelts.

WHY DID WALL STREET CRASH AND WARREN BUFFETT PROSPER?

How Introverts and Extroverts Think (and Process Dopamine) Differently

Tocqueville saw that the life of constant action and decision which was entailed by the democratic and businesslike character of American life put a premium upon rough and ready habits of mind, quick decision, and the prompt seizure of opportunities—and that all this activity was not propitious for deliberation, elaboration, or precision in thought.

— RICHARD HOFSTADTER, IN *Anti-Intellectualism in America*

Just after 7:30 a.m. on December 11, 2008, the year of the great stock market crash, Dr. Janice Dorn's phone rang. The markets had opened on the East Coast to another session of carnage. Housing prices were plummeting, credit markets were frozen, and GM teetered on the brink of bankruptcy.

Dorn took the call from her bedroom, as she often does, wearing a headset and perched atop her green duvet. The room was decorated sparely. The most colorful thing in it was Dorn herself, who, with her flowing red hair, ivory skin, and trim frame, looks like a mature version of Lady Godiva. Dorn has a PhD in neuroscience, with a specialty in brain anatomy. She's also an MD trained in psychiatry, an active trader in the gold futures market, and a "financial psychiatrist" who has counseled an estimated six hundred traders.

"Hi, Janice!" said the caller that morning, a confident-sounding man named Alan. "Do you have time to talk?"

Dr. Dorn did not have time. A day trader who prides herself on being in and out of trading positions every half hour, she was eager to start trading. But Dorn heard a desperate note in Alan's voice. She agreed to take the call.

Alan was a sixty-year-old midwesterner who struck Dorn as a salt-of-the-earth type, hardworking and loyal. He had the jovial and assertive manner of an extrovert, and he maintained his good cheer despite the story of disaster he proceeded to tell. Alan and his wife had worked all their lives, and managed to sock away a million dollars for retirement. But four months earlier he'd gotten the idea that, despite having no experience in the markets, he should buy a hundred thousand dollars' worth of GM stock, based on reports that the U.S. government might bail out the auto industry. He was convinced it was a no-lose investment.

After his trade went through, the media reported that the bailout might not happen after all. The market sold off GM and the stock price fell. But Alan imagined the thrill of winning big. It felt so real he could taste it. He held firm. The stock fell again, and again, and kept dropping until finally Alan decided to sell, at a big loss.

There was worse to come. When the next news cycle suggested that the bailout would happen after all, Alan got excited all over again and invested another hundred thousand dollars, buying more stock at the lower price. But the same thing happened: the bailout started looking uncertain.

Alan "reasoned" (this word is in quotation marks because, according to Dorn, conscious reasoning had little to do with Alan's behavior) that the price couldn't go much lower. He held on, savoring the idea of how much fun he and his wife would have spending all the money he stood to make. Again the stock went lower. When finally it hit seven dollars per share, Alan sold. And bought yet again, in a flush of exhilaration, when he heard that the bailout might happen after all . . .

By the time GM's stock price fell to two dollars a share, Alan had lost *seven hundred thousand dollars*, or 70 percent of his family nest egg.

He was devastated. He asked Dorn if she could help recoup his losses. She could not. "It's gone," she told him. "You are never going to make that money back."

He asked what he'd done wrong.

Dorn had many ideas about that. As an amateur, Alan shouldn't have been trading in the first place. And he'd risked far too much money; he should have limited his exposure to 5 percent of his net worth, or $50,000. But the biggest problem may have been beyond Alan's control: Dorn believed he was experiencing an excess of something psychologists call *reward sensitivity*.

A reward-sensitive person is highly motivated to seek rewards—from a promotion to a lottery jackpot to an enjoyable evening out with friends. Reward sensitivity motivates us to pursue goals like sex and money, social status and influence. It prompts us to climb ladders and reach for faraway branches in order to gather life's choicest fruits.

But sometimes we're *too* sensitive to rewards. Reward sensitivity on overdrive gets people into all kinds of trouble. We can get so excited by the prospect of juicy prizes, like winning big in the stock market, that we take outsized risks and ignore obvious warning signals.

Alan was presented with plenty of these signals, but was so animated by the prospect of winning big that he couldn't see them. Indeed, he fell into a classic pattern of reward sensitivity run amok: at exactly the moments when the warning signs suggested slowing down, *he sped up*— dumping money he couldn't afford to lose into a speculative series of trades.

Financial history is full of examples of players accelerating when they should be braking. Behavioral economists have long observed that executives buying companies can get so excited about beating out their competitors that they ignore signs that they're overpaying. This happens so frequently that it has a name: "deal fever," followed by "the winner's curse." The AOL–Time Warner merger, which wiped out $200 billion of Time Warner shareholder value, is a classic example. There were plenty of warnings that AOL's stock, which was the currency for the merger, was wildly overvalued, yet Time Warner's directors approved the deal unanimously.

"I did it with as much or more excitement and enthusiasm as I did when I first made love some forty-two years ago," exclaimed Ted Turner, one of those directors and the largest individual shareholder in the company. "TED TURNER: IT'S BETTER THAN SEX," announced the *New York Post* the day after the deal was struck, a headline to which we'll return for its power to explain why smart people can sometimes be too reward-sensitive.

~

You may be wondering what all this has to do with introversion and extroversion. Don't we all get a little carried away sometimes?

The answer is yes, except that some of us do so more than others. Dorn has observed that her extroverted clients are more likely to be highly reward-sensitive, while the introverts are more likely to pay attention to warning signals. They're more successful at regulating their feelings of desire or excitement. They protect themselves better from the downside. "My introvert traders are much more able to say, 'OK, Janice, I do feel these excited emotions coming up in me, but I understand that I can't act on them.' The introverts are much better at making a plan, staying with a plan, being very disciplined."

To understand why introverts and extroverts might react differently to the prospect of rewards, says Dorn, you have to know a little about brain structure. As we saw in chapter 4, our limbic system, which we share with the most primitive mammals and which Dorn calls the "old brain," is emotional and instinctive. It comprises various structures, including the amygdala, and it's highly interconnected with the nucleus accumbens, sometimes called the brain's "pleasure center." We examined the anxious side of the old brain when we explored the role of the amygdala in high reactivity and introversion. Now we're about to see its greedy side.

The old brain, according to Dorn, is constantly telling us, "Yes, yes, yes! Eat more, drink more, have more sex, take lots of risk, go for all the gusto you can get, and above all, do not think!" The reward-seeking, pleasure-loving part of the old brain is what Dorn believes spurred Alan to treat his life savings like chips at the casino.

We also have a "new brain" called the neocortex, which evolved many thousands of years after the limbic system. The new brain is responsible for thinking, planning, language, and decision-making—some of the very faculties that make us human. Although the new brain also plays a significant role in our emotional lives, it's the seat of rationality. Its job, according to Dorn, includes saying, "No, no, no! Don't do that, because it's dangerous, makes no sense, and is not in your best interests, or those of your family, or of society."

So where was Alan's neocortex when he was chasing stock market gains?

The old brain and the new brain do work together, but not always efficiently. Sometimes they're actually in conflict, and then our decisions are a function of which one is sending out stronger signals. So when Alan's old brain sent its breathless messages up to his new brain, it probably responded as a neocortex should: it told his old brain to slow down. It said, *Watch out!* But it lost the ensuing tug-of-war.

We all have old brains, of course. But just as the amygdala of a high-reactive person is more sensitive than average to novelty, so do extroverts seem to be more susceptible than introverts to the reward-seeking cravings of the old brain. In fact, some scientists are starting to explore the idea that reward-sensitivity is not only an interesting feature of extroversion; it is what *makes* an extrovert an extrovert. Extroverts, in other words, are characterized by their tendency to seek rewards, from top dog status to sexual highs to cold cash. They've been found to have greater economic, political, and hedonistic ambitions than introverts; even their sociability is a function of reward-sensitivity, according to this view—extroverts socialize because human connection is inherently gratifying.

What underlies all this reward-seeking? The key seems to be positive emotion. Extroverts tend to experience more pleasure and excitement than introverts do—emotions that are activated, explains the psychologist Daniel Nettle in his illuminating book on personality, "in response to the pursuit or capture of some resource that is valued. Excitement builds towards the anticipated capture of that resource. Joy follows its capture." Extroverts, in other words, often find themselves in an emotional state we might call "buzz"—a rush of energized, enthusiastic feelings. This is a sensation we all know and like, but not necessarily to the same degree or with the same frequency: extroverts seem to get an extra buzz from the pursuit and attainment of their goals.

The basis of buzz appears to be a high degree of activity in a network of structures in the brain—often called the "reward system"—including the orbitofrontal cortex, the nucleus accumbens, and the amygdala. The job of the reward system is to get us excited about potential goodies; fMRI experiments have shown that the system is activated by any number of possible delights, from anticipation of a squirt of Kool-Aid on the tongue, to money, to pictures of attractive people.

The neurons that transmit information in the reward network operate in part through a neurotransmitter—a chemical that carries information between brain cells—called dopamine. Dopamine is the "reward chemical" released in response to anticipated pleasures. The more responsive your brain is to dopamine, or the higher the level of dopamine you have available to release, some scientists believe, the more likely you are to go after rewards like sex, chocolate, money, and status. Stimulating mid-brain dopamine activity in mice gets them to run around excitedly in an empty cage until they drop dead of starvation. Cocaine and heroin, which stimulate dopamine-releasing neurons in humans, make people euphoric.

Extroverts' dopamine pathways appear to be more active than those of introverts. Although the exact relationship between extroversion, dopamine, and the brain's reward system has not been conclusively established, early findings have been intriguing. In one experiment, Richard Depue, a neurobiologist at Cornell University, gave an amphetamine that activates the dopamine system to a group of introverts and extroverts, and found that the extroverts had a stronger response. Another study found that extroverts who win gambling games have more activity in the reward-sensitive regions of their brains than victorious introverts do. Still other research has shown that the medial orbitofrontal cortex, a key component of the brain's dopamine-driven reward system, is larger in extroverts than in introverts.

By contrast, introverts "have a smaller response" in the reward system, writes psychologist Nettle, "and so go less out of their way to follow up [reward] cues." They will, "like anyone, be drawn from time to time to sex, and parties, and status, but the kick they get will be relatively small, so they are not going to break a leg to get there." In short, introverts just don't buzz as easily.

~

In some ways, extroverts are lucky; buzz has a delightful champagne-bubble quality. It fires us up to work and play hard. It gives us the courage to take chances. Buzz also gets us to do things that would otherwise seem too difficult, like giving speeches. Imagine you work hard to prepare a talk on a subject you care about. You get your message across, and when you finish the audience rises to its feet, its clapping sustained and sincere. One person might leave the room feeling, "I'm glad I got my message across, but I'm also happy it's over; now I can get back to the rest of my life." Another person, more sensitive to buzz, might walk away feeling, "What a trip! Did you hear that applause? Did you see the expression on their faces when I made that life-changing point? This is *great!*"

But buzz also has considerable downsides. "Everyone assumes that it's good to accentuate positive emotions, but that isn't correct," the psychology professor Richard Howard told me, pointing to the example of soccer victories that end in violence and property damage. "A lot of antisocial and self-defeating behavior results from people who amplify positive emotions."

Another disadvantage of buzz may be its connection to risk— sometimes outsized risk. Buzz can cause us to ignore warning signs we should be heeding. When Ted Turner (who appears to be an extreme extrovert) compared the AOL–Time Warner deal to his first sexual experience, he may have been telling us that he was in the same buzzy state of mind as an adolescent who's so excited about spending the night with his new girlfriend that he's not thinking much about the consequences. This blindness to danger may explain why extroverts are more likely than introverts to be killed while driving, be hospitalized as a result of accident or injury, smoke, have risky sex, participate in high-risk sports, have affairs, and remarry. It also helps explain why extroverts are more prone than introverts to overconfidence—defined as greater confidence unmatched by greater ability. Buzz is JFK's Camelot, but it's also the Kennedy Curse.

~

This theory of extroversion is still young, and it is not absolute. We can't say that all extroverts constantly crave rewards or that all introverts always brake for trouble. Still, the theory suggests that we should rethink the roles that introverts and extroverts play in their own lives, and in organizations. It suggests that when it comes time to make group decisions, extroverts would do well to listen to introverts—especially when they see problems ahead.

In the wake of the 2008 crash, a financial catastrophe caused in part by uncalculated risk-taking and blindness to threat, it became fashionable to speculate whether we'd have been better off with more women and fewer men—or less testosterone—on Wall Street. But maybe we should also ask what might have happened with a few more introverts at the helm—and a lot less dopamine.

Several studies answer this question implicitly. Kellogg School of Management Professor Camelia Kuhnen has found that the variation of a dopamine-regulating gene (DRD4) associated with a particularly thrill-seeking version of extroversion is a strong predictor of financial risk-taking. By contrast, people with a variant of a serotonin-regulating gene linked to introversion and sensitivity take 28 percent *less* financial risk than others. They have also been found to outperform their peers when playing gambling games calling for sophisticated decision-making. (When faced with a low probability of winning, people with this gene variant tend to be risk-averse; when they have a high probability of winning, they become relatively risk-seeking.) Another study, of sixty-four traders at an investment bank, found that the highest-performing traders tended to be emotionally stable introverts.

Introverts also seem to be better than extroverts at delaying gratification, a crucial life skill associated with everything from higher SAT scores and income to lower body mass index. In one study, scientists gave participants the choice of a small reward immediately (a gift certificate from Amazon) or a bigger gift certificate in two to four weeks. Objectively, the bigger reward in the near but not immediate future was the more desirable option. But many people went for the "I want it now" choice—and when they did, a brain scanner revealed that their reward network was activated. Those who held out for the larger reward two weeks hence showed more activity in the prefrontal cortex—the part of the new brain that talks us out of sending ill-considered e-mails and eating too much chocolate cake. (A similar study suggests that the former group tended to be extroverts and the latter group introverts.)

Back in the 1990s, when I was a junior associate at a Wall Street law firm, I found myself on a team of lawyers representing a bank considering buying a portfolio of subprime mortgage loans made by other lenders. My job was to perform due diligence—to review the documentation to see whether the loans had been made with the proper paperwork. Had the borrowers been notified of the interest rates they were slated to pay? That the rates would go up over time?

The papers turned out to be chock-full of irregularities. If I'd been in the bankers' shoes, this would have made me nervous, very nervous. But when our legal team summarized the risks in a caution-filled conference call, the bankers seemed utterly untroubled. They saw the potential profits of buying those loans at a discount, and they wanted to go ahead with the deal. Yet it was just this kind of risk-reward miscalculation that contributed to the failure of many banks during the Great Recession of 2008.

At about the same time I evaluated that portfolio of loans, I heard a story circulating on Wall Street about a competition among investment banks for a prestigious piece of business. Each of the major banks sent a squad of their top employees to pitch the client. Each team deployed the usual tools: spread sheets, "pitch books," and PowerPoint presentations. But the winning team added its own piece of theatrics: they ran into the room wearing matching baseball caps and T-shirts emblazoned with the letters FUD, an acronym for *Fear, Uncertainty, and Doubt*. In this case FUD had been crossed out with an emphatic red X; FUD was an unholy trinity. That team, the vanquishers of FUD, won the contest.

Disdain for FUD—and for the type of person who tends to experience it—is what helped cause the crash, says Boykin Curry, a managing director of the investment firm Eagle Capital, who had front-row seats to the 2008 meltdown. Too much power was concentrated in the hands of aggressive risk-takers. "For twenty years, the DNA of nearly every financial institution . . . morphed dangerously," he told *Newsweek* magazine at the height of the crash. "Each time someone at the table pressed for more leverage and more risk, the next few years proved them 'right.' These people were emboldened, they were promoted and they gained control of ever more capital. Meanwhile, anyone in power who hesitated, who argued for caution, was proved 'wrong.' The cautious types were increasingly intimidated, passed over for promotion. They lost their hold on capital. This happened every day in almost every financial institution, over and over, until we ended up with a very specific kind of person running things."

Curry is a Harvard Business School grad and, with his wife, Celerie Kemble, a Palm Beach–born designer, a prominent fixture on New York political and social scenes. Which is to say that he would seem to be a card-carrying member of what he calls the "go-go aggressive" crowd, and an unlikely advocate for the importance of introverts. But one thing he's not shy about is his thesis that it was forceful extroverts who caused the global financial crash.

"People with certain personality types got control of capital and institutions and power," Curry told me. "And people who are congenitally more cautious and introverted and statistical in their thinking became discredited and pushed aside."

Vincent Kaminski, a Rice University business school professor who once served as managing director of research for Enron, the company that famously filed for bankruptcy in 2001 as a result of reckless business practices, told the *Washington Post* a similar story of a business culture in which aggressive risk-takers enjoyed too high a status relative to cautious introverts. Kaminski, a soft-spoken and careful man, was one of the few heroes of the Enron scandal. He repeatedly tried to sound the alarm with senior management that the company had entered into business deals risky enough to threaten its survival. When the top brass wouldn't listen, he refused to sign off on these dangerous transactions and ordered his team not to work on them. The company stripped him of his power to review company-wide deals.

"There have been some complaints, Vince, that you're not helping people to do transactions," the president of Enron told him, according to *Conspiracy of Fools*, a book about the Enron scandal. "Instead, you're spending all your time acting like cops. We don't need cops, Vince."

But they did need them, and still do. When the credit crisis threatened the viability of some of Wall Street's biggest banks in 2007, Kaminski saw the same thing happening all over again. "Let's just say that all the demons of Enron have not been exorcised," he told the *Post* in November of that year. The problem, he explained, was not only that many had failed to understand the risks the banks were taking. It was also that those who *did* understand were consistently ignored—in part because they had the wrong personality style: "Many times I have been sitting across the table from an energy trader and I would say, 'Your portfolio will implode if this specific situation happens.' And the trader would start yelling at me and telling me I'm an idiot, that such a situation would never happen. The problem is that, on one side, you have a rainmaker who is making lots of money for the company and is treated like a superstar, and on the other side you have an introverted nerd. So who do you think wins?"

~

But what exactly is the mechanism by which buzz clouds good judgment? How did Janice Dorn's client, Alan, dismiss the danger signs screaming that he might lose 70 percent of his life savings? What prompts some people to act as if FUD doesn't exist?

One answer comes from an intriguing line of research conducted by the University of Wisconsin psychologist Joseph Newman. Imagine that you've been invited to Newman's lab to participate in one of his studies. You're there to play a game: the more points you get, the more money you win. Twelve different numbers flash across a computer screen, one at a time, in no particular order. You're given a button, as if you were a game-show contestant, which you can press or not as each number appears. If you press the button for a "good" number, you win points; if you press for a "bad" number, you lose points; and if you don't press at all, nothing happens. Through trial and error you learn that four is a nice number and nine is not. So the next time the number nine flashes across your screen, you know not to press that button.

Except that sometimes people press the button for the bad numbers, even when they should know better. Extroverts, especially highly impulsive extroverts, are more likely than introverts to make this mistake. Why? Well, in the words of psychologists John Brebner and Chris Cooper, who have shown that extroverts think less and act faster on such tasks: introverts are "geared to inspect" and extroverts "geared to respond."

But the more interesting aspect of this puzzling behavior is not what the extroverts do *before* they've hit the wrong button, but what they do *after*. When introverts hit the number nine button and find they've lost a point, they slow down before moving on to the next number, as if to reflect on what went wrong. But extroverts not only fail to slow down, *they actually speed up.*

This seems strange; why would anyone do this? Newman explains that it makes perfect sense. If you focus on achieving your goals, as reward-sensitive extroverts do, you don't want anything to get in your way—neither naysayers nor the number nine. You speed up in an attempt to knock these roadblocks down.

Yet this is a crucially important misstep, because the longer you pause to process surprising or negative feedback, the more likely you are to learn from it. If you *force* extroverts to pause, says Newman, they'll do just as well as introverts at the numbers game. But, left to their own devices, they don't stop. And so they don't learn to avoid the trouble staring them in the face. Newman says that this is exactly what might happen to extroverts like Ted Turner when bidding for a company on auction. "When a person bids up too high," he told me, "that's because they didn't inhibit a response they should have inhibited. They didn't consider information that should have been weighing on their decision."

Introverts, in contrast, are constitutionally programmed to down-play reward—to kill their buzz, you might say—and scan for problems. "As soon they get excited," says Newman, "they'll put the brakes on and think about peripheral issues that may be more important. Introverts seem to be specifically wired or trained so when they catch themselves getting excited and focused on a goal, their vigilance increases."

Introverts also tend to compare new information with their expec-tations, he says. They ask themselves, "Is this what I thought would happen? Is it how it should be?" And when the situation falls short of expectations, they form associations between the moment of disappoint-ment (losing points) and whatever was going on in their environment at the time of the disappointment (hitting the number nine.) These asso-ciations let them make accurate predictions about how to react to warn-ing signals in the future.

~

Introverts' disinclination to charge ahead is not only a hedge against risk; it also pays off on intellectual tasks. Here are some of the things we know about the relative performance of introverts and extroverts at com-plex problem-solving. Extroverts get better grades than introverts during elementary school, but introverts outperform extroverts in high school and college. At the university level, introversion predicts academic per-formance better than cognitive ability. One study tested 141 college stu-dents' knowledge of twenty different subjects, from art to astronomy to statistics, and found that introverts knew more than the extroverts about every single one of them. Introverts receive disproportionate numbers of graduate degrees, National Merit Scholarship finalist positions, and Phi Beta Kappa keys. They outperform extroverts on the Watson-Glaser Criti-cal Thinking Appraisal test, an assessment of critical thinking widely used by businesses for hiring and promotion. They've been shown to excel at something psychologists call "insightful problem solving."

The question is: Why?

Introverts are not smarter than extroverts. According to IQ scores, the two types are equally intelligent. And on many kinds of tasks, particularly those performed under time or social pressure or involving multitasking, extroverts do better. Extroverts are better than introverts at handling information overload. Introverts' reflectiveness uses up a lot of cognitive capacity, according to Joseph Newman. On any given task, he says, "if we have 100 percent cognitive capacity, an introvert may have only 75 percent on task and 25 percent off task, whereas an extrovert may have 90 percent on task." This is because most tasks are goal-directed. Extroverts appear to allocate most of their cognitive capacity to the goal at hand, while introverts use up capacity by monitoring how the task is going.

But introverts seem to think more carefully than extroverts, as the psychologist Gerald Matthews describes in his work. Extroverts are more likely to take a quick-and-dirty approach to problem-solving, trading accuracy for speed, making increasing numbers of mistakes as they go, and abandoning ship altogether when the problem seems too difficult or frustrating. Introverts think before they act, digest information thoroughly, stay on task longer, give up less easily, and work more accurately. Introverts and extroverts also direct their attention differently: if you leave them to their own devices, the introverts tend to sit around wondering about things, imagining things, recalling events from their past, and making plans for the future. The extroverts are more likely to focus on what's happening around them. It's as if extroverts are seeing "what is" while their introverted peers are asking "what if."

Introverts' and extroverts' contrasting problem-solving styles have been observed in many different contexts. In one experiment, psychologists gave fifty people a difficult jigsaw puzzle to solve, and found that the extroverts were more likely than the introverts to quit midway. In another, Professor Richard Howard gave introverts and extroverts a complicated series of printed mazes, and found not only that the introverts tended to solve more mazes correctly, but also that they spent a much greater percentage of their allotted time inspecting the maze *before* entering it. A similar thing happened when groups of introverts and extroverts were given the Raven Standard Progressive Matrices, an intelligence test that consists of five sets of problems of increasing difficulty. The extroverts tended to do better on the first two sets, presumably because of their ability to orient quickly to their goal. But on the three more difficult sets, where persistence pays, the introverts significantly outperformed them. By the final, most complicated set, the extroverts were much more likely than the introverts to abandon the task altogether.

Introverts sometimes outperform extroverts even on *social* tasks that require persistence. Wharton management professor Adam Grant (who conducted the leadership studies described in chapter 2) once studied the personality traits of effective call-center employees. Grant predicted that the extroverts would be better telemarketers, but it turned out that there was zero correlation between extroversion levels and cold-calling prowess.

"The extroverts would make these wonderful calls," Grant told me, "but then a shiny object of some kind would cross their paths and they'd lose focus." The introverts, in contrast, "would talk very quietly, but boom, boom, boom, they were making those calls. They were focused and determined." The only extroverts to outperform them were those who also happened to be unusually high scorers for a separate personality trait measuring conscientiousness. Introvert persistence was more than a match for extrovert buzz, in other words, even at a task where social skills might be considered at a premium.

Persistence isn't very glamorous. If genius is one percent inspiration and ninety-nine percent perspiration, then as a culture we tend to lionize the one percent. We love its flash and dazzle. But great power lies in the other ninety-nine percent.

"It's not that I'm so smart," said Einstein, who was a consummate introvert. "It's that I stay with problems longer."

~

None of this is to denigrate those who forge ahead quickly, or to blindly glorify the reflective and careful. The point is that we tend to overvalue buzz and discount the risks of reward-sensitivity: we need to find a balance between action and reflection.

For example, if you were staffing an investment bank, management professor Kuhnen told me, you'd want to hire not only reward-sensitive types, who are likely to profit from bull markets, but also those who remain emotionally more neutral. You'd want to make sure that important corporate decisions reflect the input of both kinds of people, not just one type. And you'd want to know that individuals on all points of the reward-sensitivity spectrum understand their own emotional preferences and can temper them to match market conditions.

But it's not just employers who benefit from taking a closer look at their employees. We also need to take a closer look at ourselves. Understanding where we fall on the reward-sensitivity spectrum gives us the power to live our lives well.

If you're a buzz-prone extrovert, then you're lucky to enjoy lots of invigorating emotions. Make the most of them: build things, inspire others, think big. Start a company, launch a website, build an elaborate tree house for your kids. But also know that you're operating with an Achilles' heel that you must learn to protect. Train yourself to spend energy on what's truly meaningful to you instead of on activities that look like they'll deliver a quick buzz of money or status or excitement. Teach yourself to pause and reflect when warning signs appear that things aren't working out as you'd hoped. Learn from your mistakes. Seek out counterparts (from spouses to friends to business partners) who can help rein you in and compensate for your blind spots.

And when it comes time to invest, or to do anything that involves a sage balance of risk and reward, keep yourself in check. One good way to do this is to make sure that you're not surrounding yourself with images of reward at the crucial moment of decision. Kuhnen and Brian Knutson have found that men who are shown erotic pictures just before they gamble take more risks than those shown neutral images like desks and chairs. This is because anticipating rewards—*any* rewards, whether or not related to the subject at hand—excites our dopamine-driven reward networks and makes us act more rashly. (This may be the single best argument yet for banning pornography from workplaces.)

And if you're an introvert who's relatively immune to the excesses of reward sensitivity? At first blush, the research on dopamine and buzz seems to imply that extroverts, and extroverts alone, are happily motivated to work hard by the excitement they get from pursuing their goals. As an introvert, I was puzzled by this idea when I first came across it. It didn't reflect my own experience. I'm in love with my work and always have been. I wake up in the morning excited to get started. So what drives people like me?

One answer is that even if the reward-sensitivity theory of extroversion turns out to be correct, we can't say that all extroverts are always more sensitive to rewards and blasé about risk, or that all introverts are constantly unmoved by incentives and vigilant about threats. Since the days of Aristotle, philosophers have observed that these two modes— approaching things that appear to give pleasure and avoiding others that seem to cause pain—lie at the heart of all human activity. As a group, extroverts tend to be reward-seeking, but every human being has her own mix of approach and avoidance tendencies, and sometimes the combination differs depending on the situation. Indeed, many contemporary personality psychologists would say that threat-vigilance is more characteristic of a trait known as "neuroticism" than of introversion. The body's reward and threat systems also seem to work independently of each other, so that the same person can be generally sensitive, or insensitive, to both reward *and* threat.

If you want to determine whether you are reward-oriented, threat-oriented, or both, try asking yourself whether the following groups of statements are true of you.

If you are reward-oriented:

1. When I get something I want, I feel excited and energized.
2. When I want something, I usually go all out to get it.
3. When I see an opportunity for something I like, I get excited right away.
4. When good things happen to me, it affects me strongly.
5. I have very few fears compared to my friends.

If you are threat-oriented:
1. Criticism or scolding hurts me quite a bit.
2. I feel pretty worried or upset when I think or know some-body is angry at me.
3. If I think something unpleasant is going to happen, I usu-ally get pretty "worked up."
4. I feel worried when I think I have done poorly at something important.
5. I worry about making mistakes.

But I believe that another important explanation for introverts who love their work may come from a very different line of research by the influential psychologist Mihaly Csikszentmihalyi on the state of being he calls "flow." Flow is an optimal state in which you feel totally engaged in an activity—whether long-distance swimming or songwriting, sumo wrestling or sex. In a state of flow, you're neither bored nor anxious, and you don't question your own adequacy. Hours pass without your noticing.

The key to flow is to pursue an activity for its own sake, *not for the rewards it brings*. Although flow does not depend on being an introvert or an extrovert, many of the flow experiences that Csikszentmihalyi writes about are solitary pursuits that have nothing to do with reward-seeking: reading, tending an orchard, solo ocean cruising. Flow often occurs, he writes, in conditions in which people "become independent of the social environment to the degree that they no longer respond exclusively in terms of its rewards and punishments. To achieve such autonomy, a person has to learn to provide rewards to herself."

In a sense, Csikszentmihalyi transcends Aristotle; he is telling us that there are some activities that are not about approach or avoidance, but about something deeper: the fulfillment that comes from absorption in an activity outside yourself. "Psychological theories usually assume that we are motivated either by the need to eliminate an unpleasant condition like hunger or fear," Csikszentmihalyi writes, "or by the expectation of some future reward such as money, status, or prestige." But in flow, "a person could work around the clock for days on end, for no better reason than to keep on working."

If you're an introvert, find your flow by using your gifts. You have the power of persistence, the tenacity to solve complex problems, and the clear-sightedness to avoid pitfalls that trip others up. You enjoy relative freedom from the temptations of superficial prizes like money and status. Indeed, your biggest challenge may be to fully harness your strengths. You may be so busy trying to appear like a zestful, reward-sensitive extrovert that you undervalue your own talents, or feel underestimated by those around you. But when you're focused on a project that you care about, you probably find that your energy is boundless.

So stay true to your own nature. If you like to do things in a slow and steady way, don't let others make you feel as if you have to race. If you enjoy depth, don't force yourself to seek breadth. If you prefer single-tasking to multitasking, stick to your guns. Being relatively unmoved by rewards gives you the incalculable power to go your own way. It's up to you to use that independence to good effect.

Of course, that isn't always easy. While writing this chapter, I corresponded with Jack Welch, the former chairman of General Electric. He had just published a *BusinessWeek* online column called "Release Your Inner Extrovert," in which he called for introverts to act more extroverted on the job. I suggested that extroverts sometimes need to act more introverted, too, and shared with him some of the ideas you've just read about how Wall Street might have benefited from having more introverts at the helm. Welch was intrigued. But, he said, "the extroverts would argue that they never heard from the introverts."

Welch makes a fair point. Introverts need to trust their gut and share their ideas as powerfully as they can. This does not mean aping extroverts; ideas can be shared quietly, they can be communicated in writing, they can be packaged into highly produced lectures, they can be advanced by allies. The trick for introverts is to honor their own styles instead of allowing themselves to be swept up by prevailing norms. The story of the lead-up to the Great Recession of 2008 is peppered, alas, with careful types who took inappropriate risks, like the former chief executive of Citigroup, Chuck Prince, a former lawyer who made risky loans into a falling market because, he said, "as long as the music is playing, you've got to get up and dance."

"People who are initially cautious become more aggressive," observes Boykin Curry of this phenomenon. "They say, 'Hey, the more aggressive people are getting promoted and I'm not, so I'm going to be more aggressive too.'"

~

But stories of financial crises often contain subplots about people who famously (and profitably) saw them coming—and such tales tend to feature just the kinds of people who embrace FUD, or who like to close the blinds to their offices, insulate themselves from mass opinion and peer pressure, and focus in solitude. One of the few investors who managed to flourish during the crash of 2008 was Seth Klarman, president of a hedge fund called the Baupost Group. Klarman is known for consistently outperforming the market while steadfastly avoiding risk, and for keeping a significant percentage of his assets in cash. In the two years since the crash of 2008, when most investors were fleeing hedge funds in droves, Klarman almost doubled Baupost's assets under management to $22 billion.

Klarman achieved this with an investment strategy based explicitly on FUD. "At Baupost, we are big fans of fear, and in investing, it is clearly better to be scared than sorry," he once wrote in a letter to investors. Klarman is a "world-class worrier," observes the *New York Times*, in a 2007 article called "Manager Frets Over the Market, But Still Outdoes It." He owns a racehorse called "Read the Footnotes."

During the years leading up to the 2008 crash, Klarman "was one of the few people to stick to a cautious and seemingly paranoid message," says Boykin Curry. "When everyone else was celebrating, he was probably storing cans of tuna in his basement, to prepare for the end of civilization. Then, when everyone else panicked, he started buying. It's not just analysis; it's his emotional makeup. The same wiring that helps Seth find opportunities that no one else sees can make him seem aloof or blunt. If you're the kind of person who frets every time the quarter is good, you may have trouble rising to the top of a corporate pyramid. Seth probably wouldn't have made it as a sales manager. But he is one of the great investors of our time."

Similarly, in his book on the run-up to the 2008 crash, *The Big Short*, Michael Lewis introduces three of the few people who were astute enough to forecast the coming disaster. One was a solitary hedge-fund manager named Michael Burry who describes himself as "happy in my own head" and who spent the years prior to the crash alone in his office in San Jose, California, combing through financial documents and developing his own contrarian views of market risk. The others were a pair of socially awkward investors named Charlie Ledley and Jamie Mai, whose entire investment strategy was based on FUD: they placed bets that had limited downside, but would pay off handsomely if dramatic but unexpected changes occurred in the market. It was not an investment strategy so much as a life philosophy—a belief that most situations were not as stable as they appeared to be.

This "suited the two men's personalities," writes Lewis. "They never had to be sure of anything. Both were predisposed to feel that people, and by extension markets, were too certain about inherently uncertain things." Even after being proven right with their 2006 and 2007 bets against the subprime mortgage market, and earning $100 million in the process, "they actually spent time wondering how people who had been so sensationally right (i.e., they themselves) could preserve the capacity for diffidence and doubt and uncertainty that had enabled them to be right."

Ledley and Mai understood the value of their constitutional diffidence, but others were so spooked by it that they gave up the chance to invest money with the two—in effect, sacrificing millions of dollars to their prejudice against FUD. "What's amazing with Charlie Ledley," says Boykin Curry, who knows him well, "is that here you had a brilliant investor who was exceedingly conservative. If you were concerned about risk, there was no one better to go to. But he was terrible at raising capital because he seemed so tentative about everything. Potential clients would walk out of Charlie's office scared to give him money because they thought he lacked conviction. Meanwhile, they poured money into funds run by managers who exuded confidence and certainty. Of course, when the economy turned, the confident group lost half their clients' money, while Charlie and Jamie made a fortune. Anyone who used conventional social cues to evaluate money managers was led to exactly the wrong conclusion."

~

Another example, this one from the 2000 crash of the dot-com bubble, concerns a self-described introvert based in Omaha, Nebraska, where he's well known for shutting himself inside his office for hours at a time.

Warren Buffett, the legendary investor and one of the wealthiest men in the world, has used exactly the attributes we've explored in this chapter—intellectual persistence, prudent thinking, and the ability to see and act on warning signs—to make billions of dollars for himself and the shareholders in his company, Berkshire Hathaway. Buffett is known for thinking carefully when those around him lose their heads. "Success in investing doesn't correlate with IQ," he has said. "Once you have ordinary intelligence, what you need is the temperament to control the urges that get other people into trouble in investing."

Every summer since 1983, the boutique investment bank Allen & Co. has hosted a weeklong conference in Sun Valley, Idaho. This isn't just any conference. It's an extravaganza, with lavish parties, river-rafting trips, ice-skating, mountain biking, fly fishing, horseback riding, and a fleet of babysitters to care for guests' children. The hosts service the media industry, and past guest lists have included newspaper moguls, Hollywood celebrities, and Silicon Valley stars, with marquee names such as Tom Hanks, Candice Bergen, Barry Diller, Rupert Murdoch, Steve Jobs, Diane Sawyer, and Tom Brokaw.

In July 1999, according to Alice Schroeder's excellent biography of Buffett, *The Snowball*, he was one of those guests. He had attended year after year with his entire family in tow, arriving by Gulfstream jet and staying with the other VIP attendees in a select group of condos overlooking the golf course. Buffett loved his annual vacation at Sun Valley, regarding it as a great place for his family to gather and for him to catch up with old friends.

But this year the mood was different. It was the height of the technology boom, and there were new faces at the table—the heads of technology companies that had grown rich and powerful almost overnight, and the venture capitalists who had fed them cash. These people were riding high. When the celebrity photographer Annie Leibovitz showed up to shoot "the Media All-Star Team" for *Vanity Fair*, some of them lobbied to get in the photo. They were the future, they believed.

Buffett was decidedly not a part of this group. He was an old-school investor who didn't get caught up in speculative frenzy around companies with unclear earnings prospects. Some dismissed him as a relic of the past. But Buffett was still powerful enough to give the keynote address on the final day of the conference.

He thought long and hard about that speech and spent weeks preparing for it. After warming up the crowd with a charmingly self-deprecating story—Buffett used to dread public speaking until he took a Dale Carnegie course—he told the crowd, in painstaking, brilliantly analyzed detail, why the tech-fueled bull market wouldn't last. Buffett had studied the data, noted the danger signals, and then paused and reflected on what they meant. It was the first public forecast he had made in thirty years.

The audience wasn't thrilled, according to Schroeder. Buffett was raining on their parade. They gave him a standing ovation, but in private, many dismissed his ideas. "Good old Warren," they said. "Smart man, but this time he missed the boat."

Later that evening, the conference wrapped up with a glorious display of fireworks. As always, it had been a blazing success. But the most important aspect of the gathering—Warren Buffett alerting the crowd to the market's warning signs—wouldn't be revealed until the following year, when the dot-com bubble burst, just as he said it would.

Buffett takes pride not only in his track record, but also in following his own "inner scorecard." He divides the world into people who focus on their own instincts and those who follow the herd. "I feel like I'm on my back," says Buffett about his life as an investor, "and there's the Sistine Chapel, and I'm painting away. I like it when people say, 'Gee, that's a pretty good-looking painting.' But it's my painting, and when somebody says, 'Why don't you use more red instead of blue?' Good-bye. It's my painting. And I don't care what they sell it for. The painting itself will never be finished. That's one of the great things about it."

Part

Three

DO ALL CULTURES HAVE AN

EXTROVERT IDEAL?

8

SOFT POWER

Asian-Americans and the Extrovert Ideal

In a gentle way, you can shake the world.
—MAHATMA GANDHI

It's a sunny spring day in 2006, and Mike Wei, a seventeen-year-old Chinese-born senior at Lynbrook High School near Cupertino, California, is telling me about his experiences as an Asian-American student. Mike is dressed in sporty all-American attire of khakis, windbreaker, and baseball cap, but his sweet, serious face and wispy mustache give him the aura of a budding philosopher, and he speaks so softly that I have to lean forward to hear him.

"At school," says Mike, "I'm a lot more interested in listening to what the teacher says and being the good student, rather than the class clown or interacting with other kids in the class. If being outgoing, shouting, or acting out in class is gonna affect the education I receive, it's better if I go for education."

Mike relates this view matter-of-factly, but he seems to know how unusual it is by American standards. His attitude comes from his parents, he explains. "If I have a choice between doing something for myself, like going out with my friends, or staying home and studying, I think of my parents. That gives me the strength to keep studying. My father tells me that his job is computer programming, and my job is to study."

Mike's mother taught the same lesson by example. A former math teacher who worked as a maid when the family immigrated to North America, she memorized English vocabulary words while washing dishes. She is very quiet, says Mike, and very resolute. "It's really Chinese to pursue your own education like that. My mother has the kind of strength that not everyone can see."

By all indications, Mike has made his parents proud. His e-mail username is "A-student," and he's just won a coveted spot in Stanford University's freshman class. He's the kind of thoughtful, dedicated student that any community would be proud to call its own. And yet, according to an article called "The New White Flight" that ran in the *Wall Street Journal* just six months previously, white families are leaving Cupertino in droves, precisely because of kids like Mike. They are fleeing the sky-high test scores and awe-inspiring study habits of many Asian-American students. The article said that white parents feared that their kids couldn't keep up academically. It quoted a student from a local high school: "If you were Asian, you had to confirm you were smart. If you were white, you had to prove it."

But the article didn't explore what lay behind this stellar academic performance. I was curious whether the town's scholarly bent reflected a culture insulated from the worst excesses of the Extrovert Ideal—and if so, what that would feel like. I decided to visit and find out.

At first blush, Cupertino seems like the embodiment of the American Dream. Many first- and second-generation Asian immigrants live here and work at the local high-tech office parks. Apple Computer's headquarters at 1 Infinite Loop is in town. Google's Mountain View headquarters is just down the road. Meticulously maintained cars glide along the boulevards; the few pedestrians are crisply dressed in bright colors and cheerful whites. Unprepossessing ranch houses are pricey, but buyers think the cost is worth it to get their kids into the town's famed public school system, with its ranks of Ivy-bound kids. Of the 615 students in the graduating class of 2010 at Cupertino's Monta Vista High School (77 percent of whom are Asian-American, according to the school's website, some of which is accessible in Chinese), 53 were National Merit Scholarship semifinalists. The average combined score of Monta Vista students who took the SAT in 2009 was 1916 out of 2400, 27 percent higher than the nationwide average.

Respected kids at Monta Vista High School are not necessarily athletic or vivacious, according to the students I meet here. Rather, they're studious and sometimes quiet. "Being smart is actually admired, even if you're weird," a Korean-American high school sophomore named Chris tells me. Chris describes the experience of his friend, whose family left to spend two years in a Tennessee town where few Asian-Americans lived. The friend enjoyed it, but suffered culture shock. In Tennessee "there were insanely smart people, but they were always by themselves. Here, the really smart people usually have a lot of friends, because they can help people out with their work."

The library is to Cupertino what the mall or soccer field is to other towns: an unofficial center of village life. High school kids cheerfully refer to studying as "going nerding." Football and cheerleading aren't particularly respected activities. "Our football team sucks," Chris says good-naturedly. Though the team's recent stats are more impressive than Chris suggests, having a lousy football team seems to hold symbolic significance for him. "You couldn't really even tell they're football players," he explains. "They don't wear their jackets and travel in big groups. When one of my friends graduated, they played a video and my friend was like, 'I can't believe they're showing football players and cheerleaders in this video.' That's not what drives this town."

Ted Shinta, a teacher and adviser to the Robotics Team at Monta Vista High School, tells me something similar. "When I was in high school," he says, "you were discouraged from voting in student elections unless you were wearing a varsity jacket. At most high schools you have a popular group that tyrannizes the others. But here the kids in that group don't hold any power over the other students. The student body is too academically oriented for that."

A local college counselor named Purvi Modi agrees. "Introversion is not looked down upon," she tells me. "It is accepted. In some cases it is even highly respected and admired. It is cool to be a Master Chess Champion and play in the band." There's an introvert-extrovert spectrum here, as everywhere, but it's as if the population is distributed a few extra degrees toward the introverted end of the scale. One young woman, a Chinese-American about to begin her freshman year at an elite East Coast college, noticed this phenomenon after meeting some of her future classmates online, and worries what the post-Cupertino future might hold. "I met a couple of people on Facebook," she says, "and they're just so different. I'm really quiet. I'm not that much of a partier or socializer, but everyone there seems to be very social and stuff. It's just very different from my friends. I'm not even sure if I'm gonna *have* friends when I get there."

One of her Facebook correspondents lives in nearby Palo Alto, and I ask how she'll respond if that person invites her to get together over the summer.

"I probably wouldn't do it," she says. "It would be interesting to meet them and stuff, but my mom doesn't want me going out that much, because I have to study."

I'm struck by the young woman's sense of filial obligation, and its connection to prioritizing study over social life. But this is not unusual in Cupertino. Many Asian-American kids here tell me that they study all summer at their parents' request, even declining invitations to July birthday parties so they can get ahead on the following October's calculus curriculum.

"I think it's our culture," explains Tiffany Liao, a poised Swarthmore-bound high school senior whose parents are from Taiwan. "Study, do well, don't create waves. It's inbred in us to be more quiet. When I was a kid and would go to my parents' friends' house and didn't want to talk, I would bring a book. It was like this shield, and they would be like, 'She's so studious!' And that was praise."

It's hard to imagine other American moms and dads outside Cupertino smiling on a child who reads in public while everyone else is gathered around the barbecue. But parents schooled a generation ago in Asian countries were likely taught this quieter style as children. In many East Asian classrooms, the traditional curriculum emphasizes listening, writing, reading, and memorization. Talking is simply not a focus, and is even discouraged.

"The teaching back home is very different from here," says Hung Wei Chien, a Cupertino mom who came to the United States from Taiwan in 1979 to attend graduate school at UCLA. "There, you learn the subject, and they test you. At least when I grew up, they don't go off subject a lot, and they don't allow the students to ramble. If you stand up and talk nonsense, you'll be reprimanded."

Hung is one of the most jolly, extroverted people I've ever met, given to large, expansive gestures and frequent belly laughs. Dressed in running shorts, sneakers, and amber jewelry, she greets me with a bear hug and drives us to a bakery for breakfast. We dig into our pastries, chatting companionably.

So it's telling that even Hung recalls her culture shock upon entering her first American-style classroom. She considered it rude to participate in class because she didn't want to waste her classmates' time. And sure enough, she says, laughing, "I was the quiet person there. At UCLA, the professor would start class, saying, 'Let's discuss!' I would look at my peers while they were talking nonsense, and the professors were so patient, just listening to everyone." She nods her head comically, mimicking the overly respectful professors.

"I remember being amazed. It was a linguistics class, and that's not even linguistics the students are talking about! I thought, 'Oh, in the U.S., as soon as you start talking, you're fine.'"

If Hung was bewildered by the American style of class participation, it's likely that her teachers were equally perplexed by her unwillingness to speak. A full twenty years after Hung moved to the United States, the *San Jose Mercury News* ran an article called "East, West Teaching Traditions Collide," exploring professors' dismay at the reluctance of Asian-born students like Hung to participate in California university classrooms. One professor noted a "deference barrier" created by Asian students' reverence for their teachers. Another vowed to make class participation part of the grade in order to prod Asian students to speak in class. "You're supposed to downgrade yourself in Chinese learning because other thinkers are so much greater than you," said a third. "This is a perennial problem in classes with predominantly Asian-American students."

The article generated a passionate reaction in the Asian-American community. Some said the universities were right that Asian students need to adapt to Western educational norms. "Asian-Americans have let people walk all over them because of their silence," posted a reader of the sardonically titled website ModelMinority.com. Others felt that Asian students shouldn't be forced to speak up and conform to the Western mode. "Perhaps instead of trying to change their ways, colleges can learn to listen to their sound of silence," wrote Heejung Kim, a Stanford University cultural psychologist, in a paper arguing that talking is not always a positive act.

~

How is it that Asians and Westerners can look at the exact same classroom interactions, and one group will label it "class participation" and the other "talking nonsense"? The *Journal of Research in Personality* has published an answer to this question in the form of a map of the world drawn by research psychologist Robert McCrae. McCrae's map looks like something you'd see in a geography textbook, but it's based, he says, "not on rainfall or population density, but on personality trait levels," and its shadings of dark and light grays—dark for extroversion, light for introversion—reveal a picture that "is quite clear: Asia . . . is introverted, Europe extroverted." Had the map also included the United States, it would be colored dark gray. Americans are some of the most extroverted people on earth.

McCrae's map might seem like a grand exercise in cultural stereotyping. To group entire continents by personality type is an act of gross generalization: you can find loud people in mainland China just as easily as in Atlanta, Georgia. Nor does the map account for subtleties of cultural difference within a country or region. People in Beijing have different styles from those in Shanghai, and both are different still from the citizens of Seoul or Tokyo. Similarly, describing Asians as a "model minority"—even when meant as a compliment—is just as confining and condescending as any description that reduces individuals to a set of perceived group characteristics. Perhaps it is also problematic to characterize Cupertino as an incubator for scholarly stand-outs, no matter how flattering this might sound to some.

But although I don't want to encourage rigid national or ethnic typecasting, to avoid entirely the topic of cultural difference and introversion would be a shame: there are too many aspects of Asian cultural and personality styles that the rest of the world could and should learn from. Scholars have for decades studied cultural differences in personality type, especially between East and West, and especially the dimension of introversion-extroversion, the one pair of traits that psychologists, who agree on practically nothing when it comes to cataloging human personality, believe is salient and measurable all over the world.

Much of this research yields the same results as McCrae's map. One study comparing eight- to ten-year-old children in Shanghai and southern Ontario, Canada, for example, found that shy and sensitive children are shunned by their peers in Canada but make sought-after playmates in China, where they are also more likely than other children to be considered for leadership roles. Chinese children who are sensitive and reticent are said to be *dongshi* (understanding), a common term of praise.

Similarly, Chinese high school students tell researchers that they prefer friends who are "humble" and "altruistic," "honest" and "hard-working," while American high school students seek out the "cheerful," "enthusiastic," and "sociable." "The contrast is striking," writes Michael Harris Bond, a cross-cultural psychologist who focuses on China. "The Americans emphasize sociability and prize those attributes that make for easy, cheerful association. The Chinese emphasize deeper attributes, focusing on moral virtues and achievement."

Another study asked Asian-Americans and European-Americans to think out loud while solving reasoning problems, and found that the Asians did much better when they were allowed to be quiet, compared to the Caucasians, who performed well when vocalizing their problem-solving.

These results would not surprise anyone familiar with traditional Asian attitudes to the spoken word: talk is for communicating need-to-know information; quiet and introspection are signs of deep thought and higher truth. Words are potentially dangerous weapons that reveal things better left unsaid. They hurt other people; they can get their speaker into trouble. Consider, for example, these proverbs from the East:

The wind howls, but the mountain remains still.
—JAPANESE PROVERB

Those who know do not speak.
Those who speak do not know.
—LAO ZI, *The Way of Lao Zi*

Even though I make no special attempt to observe the discipline of silence, living alone automatically makes me refrain from the sins of speech.
—KAMO NO CHOMEI, *12th Century Japanese recluse*

And compare them to proverbs from the West:

Be a craftsman in speech that thou mayest be strong, for the strength of one is the tongue, and speech is mightier than all fighting.
—MAXIMS OF PTAHHOTEP, *2400 B.C.E.*

Speech is civilization itself. The word, even the most contradictory word, preserves contact—it is silence which isolates.
—THOMAS MANN, *The Magic Mountain*

The squeaky wheel gets the grease.

What lies behind these starkly different attitudes? One answer is the widespread reverence for education among Asians, particularly those from "Confucian belt" countries like China, Japan, Korea, and Vietnam. To this day, some Chinese villages display statues of students who passed the grueling Ming dynasty–era *jinshi* exam hundreds of years ago. It's a lot easier to achieve that kind of distinction if—like some of the kids from Cupertino—you spend your summers studying.

Another explanation is group identity. Many Asian cultures are team-oriented, but not in the way that Westerners think of teams. Individuals in Asia see themselves as part of a greater whole—whether family, corporation, or community—and place tremendous value on harmony within their group. They often subordinate their own desires to the group's interests, accepting their place in its hierarchy.

Western culture, by contrast, is organized around the individual. We see ourselves as self-contained units; our destiny is to express ourselves, to follow our bliss, to be free of undue restraint, to achieve the one thing that we, and we alone, were brought into this world to do. We may be gregarious, but we don't submit to group will, or at least we don't like to think we do. We love and respect our parents, but bridle at notions like filial piety, with their implications of subordination and restraint. When we get together with others, we do so as self-contained units having fun with, competing with, standing out from, jockeying for position with, and, yes, loving, other self-contained units. Even the Western God is assertive, vocal, and dominant; his son Jesus is kind and tender, but also a charismatic, crowd-pleasing man of influence (*Jesus Christ Superstar*).

It makes sense, then, that Westerners value boldness and verbal skill, traits that promote individuality, while Asians prize quiet, humility, and sensitivity, which foster group cohesion. If you live in a collective, then things will go a lot more smoothly if you behave with restraint, even submission.

This preference was vividly demonstrated in a recent fMRI study in which researchers showed seventeen Americans and seventeen Japanese pictures of men in dominance poses (arms crossed, muscles bulging, legs planted squarely on the ground) and subordinate positions (shoulders bent, hands interlocked protectively over groin, legs squeezed together tight). They found that the dominant pictures activated pleasure centers in the American brains, while the submissive pictures did the same for the Japanese.

From a Western perspective, it can be hard to see what's so attractive about submitting to the will of others. But what looks to a Westerner like subordination can seem like basic politeness to many Asians. Don Chen, the Chinese-American Harvard Business School student you met in chapter 2, told me about the time he shared an apartment with a group of Asian friends plus his close Caucasian friend, a gentle, easygoing guy Don felt would fit right in.

Conflicts arose when the Caucasian friend noticed dishes piling up in the sink and asked his Asian roommates to do their fair share of the washing up. It wasn't an unreasonable complaint, says Don, and his friend thought he phrased his request politely and respectfully. But his Asian roommates saw it differently. To them, he came across as harsh and angry. An Asian in that situation, said Don, would be more careful with his tone of voice. He would phrase his displeasure in the form of a question, not a request or command. Or he might not bring it up at all. It wouldn't be worth upsetting the group over a few dirty dishes.

What looks to Westerners like Asian deference, in other words, is actually a deeply felt concern for the sensibilities of others. As the psychologist Harris Bond observes, "It is only those from an explicit tradition who would label [the Asian] mode of discourse 'self-effacement.' Within this indirect tradition it might be labeled 'relationship honouring.'" And relationship honoring leads to social dynamics that can seem remarkable from a Western perspective.

It's because of relationship honoring, for example, that social anxiety disorder in Japan, known as *taijin kyofusho*, takes the form not of excessive worry about embarrassing oneself, as it does in the United States, but of embarrassing *others*. It's because of relationship-honoring that Tibetan Buddhist monks find inner peace (and off-the-chart happiness levels, as measured in brain scans) by meditating quietly on compassion. And it's because of relationship-honoring that Hiroshima victims apologized to each other for surviving. "Their civility has been well documented but still stays the heart," writes the essayist Lydia Millet. "'I am sorry,' said one of them, bowing, with the skin of his arms peeling off in strips. 'I regret I am still alive while your baby is not.' 'I am sorry,' another said earnestly, with lips swollen to the size of oranges, as he spoke to a child weeping beside her dead mother. 'I am so sorry that I was not taken instead.'"

Though Eastern relationship-honoring is admirable and beautiful, so is Western respect for individual freedom, self-expression, and personal destiny. The point is not that one is superior to the other, but that a profound difference in cultural values has a powerful impact on the personality styles favored by each culture. In the West, we subscribe to the Extrovert Ideal, while in much of Asia (at least before the Westernization of the past several decades), silence is golden. These contrasting outlooks affect the things we say when our roommates' dishes pile up in the sink—and the things we don't say in a university classroom.

Moreover, they tell us that the Extrovert Ideal is not as sacrosanct as we may have thought. So if, deep down, you've been thinking that it's only natural for the bold and sociable to dominate the reserved and sensitive, and that the Extrovert Ideal is innate to humanity, Robert McCrae's personality map suggests a different truth: that each way of being—quiet and talkative, careful and audacious, inhibited and unrestrained—is characteristic of its own mighty civilization.

~

Ironically, some of the people who have the most trouble holding on to this truth are Asian-American kids from Cupertino. Once they emerge from adolescence and leave the confines of their hometown, they find a world in which loudness and speaking out are the tickets to popularity and financial success. They come to live with a double-consciousness—part Asian and part American—with each side calling the other into question. Mike Wei, the high school senior who told me he'd rather study than socialize, is a perfect example of this ambivalence. When we first met, he was a high school senior, still nestled in the Cupertino cocoon. "Because we put so much emphasis on education," Mike told me then, referring to Asians in general, "socializing is not a big part of our selves."

When I caught up with Mike the following autumn, in his freshman year at Stanford, only a twenty-minute drive from Cupertino but a world away demographically, he seemed unsettled. We met at an outdoor café, where we sat next to a coed group of athletes erupting regularly in laughter. Mike nodded at the athletes, all of whom were white. Caucasians, he said, seem to be "less afraid of other people thinking that what they said was too loud or too stupid." Mike was frustrated by the superficiality of dining-hall conversation, and by the "bullshitting" that often substituted for class participation in freshman seminars. He was spending his free time mostly with other Asians, partly because they had "the same level of outgoingness" he did. The non-Asians tended to make him feel as if he had to "be really hyped up or excited, even though that might not be true to who I am."

"My dorm has four Asians in it, out of fifty kids," he told me. "So I feel more comfortable around them. There's this one guy called Brian, and he's pretty quiet. I can tell he has that Asian quality where you're kind of shy, and I feel comfortable around him for that reason. I feel like I can be myself around him. I don't have to do something just to look cool, whereas around a big group of people that aren't Asian or are just really loud, I feel like I have to play a role."

Mike sounded dismissive of Western communication styles, but he admitted that he sometimes wished he could be noisy and uninhibited himself. "They're more comfortable with their own character," he said of his Caucasian classmates. Asians are "not uncomfortable with who they are, but are uncomfortable with *expressing* who they are. In a group, there's always that pressure to be outgoing. When they don't live up to it, you can see it in their faces."

Mike told me about a freshman icebreaking event he'd participated in, a scavenger hunt in San Francisco that was supposed to encourage students to step out of their comfort zones. Mike was the only Asian assigned to a rowdy group, some of whom streaked naked down a San Francisco street and cross-dressed in a local department store during the hunt. One girl went to a Victoria's Secret display and stripped down to her underwear. As Mike recounted these details, I thought he was going to tell me that his group had been over the top, inappropriate. But he wasn't critical of the other students. He was critical of himself.

"When people do things like that, there's a moment where I feel uncomfortable with it. It shows my own limits. Sometimes I feel like they're better than I am."

Mike was getting similar messages from his professors. A few weeks after the orientation event, his freshman adviser—a professor at Stanford's medical school—invited a group of students to her house. Mike hoped to make a good impression, but he couldn't think of anything to say. The other students seemed to have no problem joking around and asking intelligent questions. "Mike, you were so loud today," the professor teased him when finally he said good-bye. "You just blew me away." He left her house feeling bad about himself. "People who don't talk are seen as weak or lacking," he concluded ruefully.

To be sure, these feelings were not totally new to Mike. He'd experienced glimmers of them back in high school. Cupertino may have an almost Confucian ethic of quiet, study, and relationship-honoring, but it's subject to the mores of the Extrovert Ideal all the same. At the local shopping center on a weekday afternoon, cocky Asian-American teenage guys with spiky haircuts call out to eye-rolling, wise-cracking girls in spaghetti-strap tank tops. On a Saturday morning at the library, some teens study intently in corners, but others congregate at boisterous tables. Few of the Asian-American kids I spoke to in Cupertino wanted to identify themselves with the word *introvert*, even if they effectively described themselves that way. While deeply committed to their parents' values, they seemed to divide the world into "traditional" Asians versus "Asian superstars." The traditionals keep their heads down and get their homework done. The superstars do well academically but also joke around in class, challenge their teachers, and get themselves noticed.

Many students deliberately try to be more outgoing than their parents, Mike told me. "They think their parents are too quiet and they try to overcompensate by being flauntingly outgoing." Some of the parents have started to shift their values too. "Asian parents are starting to see that it doesn't pay to be quiet, so they encourage their kids to take speech and debate," Mike said. "Our speech and debate program was the second largest in California, to give kids exposure to speaking loudly and convincingly."

Still, when I first met Mike in Cupertino, his sense of himself and his values was pretty much intact. He knew that he wasn't one of the Asian superstars—he rated himself a 4 on a popularity scale of 1 to 10—but seemed comfortable in his own skin. "I'd rather hang out with people whose personalities are more genuine," he told me then, "and that tends to lead me toward more quiet people. It's hard to be gleeful when at the same time I'm trying to be wise."

Indeed, Mike was probably lucky to enjoy the Cupertino cocoon for as long as he did. Asian-American kids who grow up in more typical American communities often face the issues that Mike confronted as a Stanford freshman much earlier in their lives. One study comparing European-American and second-generation Chinese-American teens over a five-year period found that the Chinese-Americans were sig-nificantly more introverted than their American peers throughout adolescence—and paid the price with their self-esteem. While intro-verted Chinese-American twelve-year-olds felt perfectly fine about themselves—presumably because they still measured themselves accord-ing to their parents' traditional value systems—by the time they got to be seventeen and had been more exposed to America's Extrovert Ideal, their self-regard had taken a nosedive.

~

For Asian-American kids, the cost of failing to fit in is social unease. But as they grow up, they may pay the price with their paychecks. The jour-nalist Nicholas Lemann once interviewed a group of Asian-Americans on the subject of meritocracy for his book *The Big Test*. "A sentiment that emerges consistently," he wrote, "is that meritocracy ends on gradu-ation day, and that afterward, Asians start to fall behind because they don't have quite the right cultural style for getting ahead: too passive, not hail-fellow-well-met enough."

I met many professionals in Cupertino who were struggling with this issue. A well-heeled housewife confided that all the husbands in her social circle had recently accepted jobs in China, and were now com-muting between Cupertino and Shanghai, partly because their quiet styles prevented them from advancing locally. The American companies "think they can't handle business," she said, "because of presentation. In business, you have to put a lot of nonsense together and present it. My husband always just makes his point and that's the end of it. When you look at big companies, almost none of the top executives are Asians. They hire someone who doesn't know anything about the business, but maybe he can make a good presentation."

A software engineer told me how overlooked he felt at work in com-parison to other people, "especially people from European origin, who speak without thinking." In China, he said, "If you're quiet, you're seen as being wise. It's completely different here. Here people like to speak out. Even if they have an idea, not completely mature yet, people still speak out. If I could be better in communication, my work would be much more recognized. Even though my manager appreciates me, he still doesn't know I have done work so wonderful."

The engineer then confided that he had sought training in American-style extroversion from a Taiwanese-born communications professor named Preston Ni. At Foothill College, just outside Cupertino, Ni conducts daylong seminars called "Communication Success for Foreign-Born Professionals." The class is advertised online through a local group called the Silicon Valley SpeakUp Association, whose mission is to "help foreign-born professionals to succeed in life through enhancement in soft skills." ("Speak you [sic] mind!" reads the organization's home page. "Together everyone achieve [sic] more at SVSpeakup.")

Curious about what speaking one's mind looks like from an Asian perspective, I signed up for the class and, a few Saturday mornings later, found myself sitting at a desk in a starkly modern classroom, the Northern California mountain sun streaming through its plate-glass windows. There were about fifteen students in all, many from Asian countries but some from Eastern Europe and South America, too.

Professor Ni, a friendly-looking man wearing a Western-style suit, a gold-colored tie with a Chinese drawing of a waterfall, and a shy smile, began the class with an overview of American business culture. In the United States, he warned, you need style as well as substance if you want to get ahead. It may not be fair, and it might not be the best way of judging a person's contribution to the bottom line, "but if you don't have charisma you can be the most brilliant person in the world and you'll still be disrespected."

This is different from many other cultures, said Ni. When a Chinese Communist leader makes a speech, he reads it, not even from a teleprompter but from a paper. "If he's the leader, everyone has to listen."

Ni asked for volunteers and brought Raj, a twentysomething Indian software engineer at a Fortune 500 company, to the front of the room. Raj was dressed in the Silicon Valley uniform of casual button-down shirt and chinos, but his body language was defensive. He stood with his arms crossed protectively over his chest, scuffing at the ground with his hiking boots. Earlier that morning, when we'd gone around the room introducing ourselves, he'd told us, in a tremulous voice from his seat in the back row, that he wanted to learn "how to make more conversation" and "to be more open."

Professor Ni asked Raj to tell the class about his plans for the rest of the weekend.

"I'm going to dinner with a friend," replied Raj, looking fixedly at Ni, his voice barely audible, "and then perhaps tomorrow I'll go hiking."

Professor Ni asked him to try it again.

"I'm going to dinner with a friend," said Raj, "and then, *mumble, mumble, mumble,* I'll go hiking."

"My impression of you," Professor Ni told Raj gently, "is that I can give you a lot of work to do, but I don't have to pay much attention to you. Remember, in Silicon Valley, you can be the smartest, most capable person, but if you can't express yourself aside from showing your work, you'll be underappreciated. Many foreign-born professionals experience this; you're a glorified laborer instead of a leader."

The class nodded sympathetically.

"But there's a way to be yourself," continued Ni, "and to let more of you come out through your voice. Many Asians use only a narrow set of muscles when they speak. So we'll start with breathing."

With that, he directed Raj to lie on his back and vocalize the five American English vowels. "A . . . E . . . U . . . O . . . I . . ." intoned Raj, his voice floating up from the classroom floor. "A . . . E . . . U . . . O . . . I . . . A . . . E . . . U . . . O . . . I . . ."

Finally Professor Ni deemed Raj ready to stand up again.

"Now, what interesting things do you have planned for after class?" he asked, clapping his hands encouragingly.

"Tonight I'm going to a friend's place for dinner, and tomorrow I'm going hiking with another friend." Raj's voice was louder than before, and the class applauded with gusto.

The professor himself is a role model for what can happen when you work at it. After class, I visited him in his office, and he told me how shy he'd been when he first came to the United States—how he put himself in situations, like summer camp and business school, where he could practice acting extroverted until it came more naturally. These days he has a successful consulting practice, with clients that include Yahoo!,

Chevron, and Microsoft, teaching some of the same skills he labored to acquire himself.

But when we began talking about Asian concepts of "soft power"—what Ni calls leadership "by water rather than by fire"—I started to see a side of him that was less impressed by Western styles of communication. "In Asian cultures," Ni said, "there's often a subtle way to get what you want. It's not always aggressive, but it can be very determined and very skillful. In the end, much is achieved because of it. Aggressive power beats you up; soft power wins you over."

I asked the professor for real-life examples of soft power, and his eyes shone as he told me of clients whose strength lay in their ideas and heart. Many of these people were organizers of employee groups—women's groups, diversity groups—who had managed to rally people to their cause through conviction rather than dynamism. He also talked about groups like Mothers Against Drunk Driving—clusters of people who change lives through the power not of their charisma but of their caring. Their communication skills are sufficient to convey their message, but their real strength comes from substance.

"In the long run," said Ni, "if the idea is good, people shift. If the cause is just and you put heart into it, it's almost a universal law: you will attract people who want to share your cause. Soft power is quiet persistence. The people I'm thinking of are very persistent in their day-to-day, person-to-person interactions. Eventually they build up a team." Soft power, said Ni, was wielded by people we've admired throughout history: Mother Teresa, the Buddha, Gandhi.

I was struck when Ni mentioned Gandhi. I had asked almost all the Cupertino high school students I met to name a leader they admired, and many had named Gandhi. What was it about him that inspired them so?

~

Gandhi was, according to his autobiography, a constitutionally shy and quiet man. As a child, he was afraid of everything: thieves, ghosts, snakes, the dark, and especially other people. He buried himself in books and ran home from school as soon as it was over, for fear of having to talk to anybody. Even as a young man, when he was elected to his first leadership position as a member of the Executive Committee of the Vegetarian Society, he attended every meeting, but was too shy to speak.

"You talk to me quite all right," one of the members asked him, confused, "but why is it that you never open your lips at a committee meeting? You are a drone." When a political struggle occurred on the committee, Gandhi had firm opinions, but was too scared to voice them. He wrote his thoughts down, intending to read them aloud at a meeting. But in the end he was too cowed even to do that.

Gandhi learned over time to manage his shyness, but he never really overcame it. He couldn't speak extemporaneously; he avoided making speeches whenever possible. Even in his later years, he wrote, "I do not think I could or would even be inclined to keep a meeting of friends engaged in talk."

But with his shyness came his unique brand of strength—a form of restraint best understood by examining little known corners of Gandhi's life story. As a young man he decided to travel to England to study law, against the wishes of the leaders of his Modhi Bania subcaste. Caste members were forbidden to eat meat, and the leaders believed that vegetarianism was impossible in England. But Gandhi had already vowed to his beloved mother to abstain from meat, so he saw no danger in the trip. He said as much to the Sheth, the headman of the community.

"Will you disregard the orders of the caste?" demanded the Sheth.

"I am really helpless," replied Gandhi. "I think the caste should not interfere in the matter."

Boom! He was excommunicated—a judgment that remained in force even when he returned from England several years later with the promise of success that attended a young, English-speaking lawyer. The community was divided over how to handle him. One camp embraced him; the other cast him out. This meant that Gandhi was not allowed even to eat or drink at the homes of fellow subcaste members, including his own sister and his mother- and father-in-law.

Another man, Gandhi knew, would protest for readmission. But he couldn't see the point. He knew that fighting would only generate retaliation. Instead he followed the Sheth's wishes and kept at a distance, even from his own family. His sister and in-laws were prepared to host him at their homes in secret, but he turned them down.

The result of this compliance? The subcaste not only stopped bothering him, but its members—including those who had excommunicated him—helped in his later political work, without expecting anything in return. They treated him with affection and generosity. "It is my conviction," Gandhi wrote later, "that all these good things are due to my non-resistance. Had I agitated for being admitted to the caste, had I attempted to divide it into more camps, had I provoked the castemen, they would surely have retaliated, and instead of steering clear of the storm, I should, on arrival from England, have found myself in a whirlpool of agitation."

This pattern—the decision to accept what another man would challenge—occurred again and again in Gandhi's life. As a young lawyer in South Africa, he applied for admission to the local bar. The Law Society didn't want Indian members, and tried to thwart his application by requiring an original copy of a certificate that was on file in the Bombay High Court and therefore inaccessible. Gandhi was enraged; he knew well that the true reason for these barriers was discrimination. But he didn't let his feelings show. Instead he negotiated patiently, until the Law Society agreed to accept an affidavit from a local dignitary.

The day arrived when he stood to take the oath, at which point the chief justice ordered him to take off his turban. Gandhi saw his true limitations then. He knew that resistance would be justified, but believed in picking his battles, so he took off his headgear. His friends were upset. They said he was weak, that he should have stood up for his beliefs. But Gandhi felt that he had learned "to appreciate the beauty of compromise."

If I told you these stories without mentioning Gandhi's name and later achievements, you might view him as a deeply passive man. And in the West, passivity is a transgression. To be "passive," according to the Merriam-Webster Dictionary, means to be "acted upon by an external agency." It also means to be "submissive." Gandhi himself ultimately rejected the phrase "passive resistance," which he associated with weakness, preferring *satyagraha*, the term he coined to mean "firmness in pursuit of truth."

But as the word *satyagraha* implies, Gandhi's passivity was not weakness at all. It meant focusing on an ultimate goal and refusing to divert energy to unnecessary skirmishes along the way. Restraint, Gandhi believed, was one of his greatest assets. And it was born of his shyness:

> I have naturally formed the habit of restraining my thoughts. A thoughtless word hardly ever escaped my tongue or pen. Experience has taught me that silence is part of the spiritual discipline of a votary of truth. We find so many people impatient to talk. All this talking can hardly be said to be of any benefit to the world. It is so much waste of time. My shyness has been in reality my shield and buckler. It has allowed me to grow. It has helped me in my discernment of truth.

~

Soft power is not limited to moral exemplars like Mahatma Gandhi. Consider, for example, the much-ballyhooed excellence of Asians in fields like math and science. Professor Ni defines soft power as "quiet persistence," and this trait lies at the heart of academic excellence as surely as it does in Gandhi's political triumphs. Quiet persistence requires sustained attention—in effect restraining one's reactions to external stimuli.

The TIMSS exam (Trends in International Mathematics and Science Study) is a standardized math and science test given every four years to kids around the world. After each test, researchers slice and dice the results, comparing the performance of students from different countries; Asian countries such as Korea, Singapore, Japan, and Taiwan consistently rank at the top of the list. In 1995, for example, the first year the TIMSS was given, Korea, Singapore, and Japan had the world's highest average middle-school math scores and were among the top four worldwide in science. In 2007, when researchers measured how many students in a given country reached the Advanced International Benchmark—a kind of superstar status for math students—they found that most of the standouts were clustered in just a few Asian countries. About 40 percent of fourth graders in Singapore and Hong Kong reached or surpassed the Advanced Benchmark, and about 40 to 45 percent of eighth graders in Taiwan, Korea, and Singapore pulled it off. Worldwide, the median percentage of students reaching the Advanced Benchmark was only 5 percent at the fourth grade and 2 percent at the eighth grade.

How to explain these sensational performance gaps between Asia and the rest of the world? Consider this interesting wrinkle in the TIMSS exam. Students taking the test are also asked to answer a tedious series of questions about themselves, ranging from how much they enjoy science to whether there are enough books in their home to fill three or more bookcases. The questionnaire takes a long time to complete, and since it doesn't count toward the final grade, many students leave a lot of questions blank. You'd have to be pretty persistent to answer every single one. But it turns out, according to a study by education professor Erling Boe, that the nations whose students fill out more of the questionnaire also tend to have students who do well on the TIMSS test. In other words, excellent students seem not only to possess the cognitive ability to solve math and science problems, but also to have a useful personality characteristic: quiet persistence.

Other studies have also found unusual levels of persistence in even very young Asian children. For example, the cross-cultural psychologist Priscilla Blinco gave Japanese and American first graders an unsolvable puzzle to work on in solitude, without the help of other children or a teacher, and compared how long they tried before giving up. The Japanese children spent an average of 13.93 minutes on the puzzle before calling it quits, whereas the American kids spent only 9.47 minutes. Fewer than 27 percent of the American students persisted as long as the average Japanese student—and only 10 percent of the Japanese students gave up as quickly as the average American. Blinco attributes these results to the Japanese quality of persistence.

The quiet persistence shown by many Asians, and Asian-Americans, is not limited to the fields of math and science. Several years after my first trip to Cupertino, I caught up with Tiffany Liao, the Swarthmore-bound high school student whose parents had praised her so highly for loving to read, even in public, when she was a young girl. When we first met, Tiffany was a baby-faced seventeen-year-old on her way to college. She told me then that she was excited to travel to the East Coast and meet new people, but was also afraid of living in a place where no one else would drink bubble tea, the popular drink invented in Taiwan.

Now Tiffany was a worldly and sophisticated college senior. She had studied abroad in Spain. She signed her notes with a continental touch: "Abrazos, Tiffany." In her Facebook picture, the childlike look was gone, replaced with a smile that was still soft and friendly but also knowing.

Tiffany was on her way to realizing her dream of becoming a journalist, having just been elected editor-in-chief of the college newspaper. She still described herself as shy—she feels a heat rush on her face when she first speaks in public or picks up the phone to call a stranger—but had become more comfortable speaking up. She believed that her "quiet traits," as she called them, had *helped* her become editor-in-chief. For Tiffany, soft power meant listening attentively, taking thorough notes, and doing deep research on her interview subjects before meeting them face-to-face. "This process has contributed to my success as a journalist," she wrote to me. Tiffany had come to embrace the power of quiet.

~

When I first met Mike Wei, the Stanford student who wished he was as uninhibited as his classmates, he said that there was no such thing as a quiet leader. "How can you let people know you have conviction if you're quiet about it?" he asked. I reassured him that this wasn't so, but Mike had so much quiet conviction about the inability of quiet people to convey conviction that deep down I'd wondered whether he had a point.

But that was before I heard Professor Ni talk about Asian-style soft power, before I read Gandhi on *satyagraha*, before I contemplated Tiffany's bright future as a journalist. Conviction is conviction, the kids from Cupertino taught me, at whatever decibel level it's expressed.

Part

Four

HOW TO LOVE, HOW TO WORK

WHEN SHOULD YOU ACT MORE EXTROVERTED THAN YOU REALLY ARE?

A man has as many social selves as there are distinct groups of persons about whose opinion he cares. He generally shows a different side of himself to each of these different groups.

—WILLIAM JAMES

Meet Professor Brian Little, former Harvard University psychology lecturer and winner of the 3M Teaching Fellowship, sometimes referred to as the Nobel Prize of university teaching. Short, sturdy, bespectacled, and endearing, Professor Little has a booming baritone, a habit of breaking into song and twirling about onstage, and an old-school actor's way of emphasizing consonants and elongating vowels. He's been described as a cross between Robin Williams and Albert Einstein, and when he makes a joke that pleases his audience, which happens a lot, he looks even more delighted than they do. His classes at Harvard were always oversubscribed and often ended with standing ovations.

In contrast, the man I'm about to describe seems a very different breed: he lives with his wife in a tucked-away house on more than two acres of remote Canadian woods, visited occasionally by his children and grandchildren, but otherwise keeping to himself. He spends his free time scoring music, reading and writing books and articles, and e-mailing friends long notes he calls "e-pistles." When he does socialize, he favors one-on-one encounters. At parties, he pairs off into quiet conversations as soon as he can or excuses himself "for a breath of fresh air." When he's forced to spend too much time out and about or in any situation involving conflict, he can literally become ill.

Would you be surprised if I told you that the vaudevillean professor and the recluse who prefers a life of the mind are one and the same man? Maybe not, when you consider that we all behave differently depending on the situation. But if we're capable of such flexibility, does it even make sense to chart the differences between introverts and extroverts? Is the very notion of introversion-extroversion too pat a dichotomy: the introvert as sage philosopher, the extrovert as fearless leader? The introvert as poet or science nerd, the extrovert as jock or cheerleader? Aren't we all a little of both?

Psychologists call this the "person-situation" debate: Do fixed personality traits really exist, or do they shift according to the situation in which people find themselves? If you talk to Professor Little, he'll tell you that despite his public persona and his teaching accolades, he's a true blue, off-the-charts introvert, not only behaviorally but also neurophysiologically (he took the lemon juice test I described in chapter 4 and salivated right on cue). This would seem to place him squarely on the "person" side of the debate: Little believes that personality traits exist, that they shape our lives in profound ways, that they're based on physiological mechanisms, and that they're relatively stable across a lifespan. Those who take this view stand on broad shoulders: Hippocrates, Milton, Schopenhauer, Jung, and more recently the prophets of fMRI machines and skin conductance tests.

On the other side of the debate are a group of psychologists known as the Situationists. Situationism posits that our generalizations about people, including the words we use to describe one another—shy, aggressive, conscientious, agreeable—are misleading. There is no core self; there are only the various selves of Situations X, Y, and Z. The Situationist view rose to prominence in 1968 when the psychologist Walter Mischel published *Personality and Assessment*, challenging the idea of fixed personality traits. Mischel argued that situational factors predict the behavior of people like Brian Little much better than supposed personality traits.

For the next few decades, Situationism prevailed. The postmodern view of self that emerged around this time, influenced by theorists like Erving Goffman, author of *The Presentation of Self in Everyday Life*, suggested that social life is performance and social masks are our true selves. Many researchers doubted whether personality traits even existed in any meaningful sense. Personality researchers had trouble finding jobs.

But just as the nature-nurture debate was replaced with interactionism—the insight that both factors contribute to who we are, and indeed influence each other—so has the person-situation debate been superseded by a more nuanced understanding. Personality psychologists acknowledge that we can feel sociable at 6:00 p.m. and solitary at 10:00 p.m., and that these fluctuations are real and situation-dependent. But they also emphasize how much evidence has emerged to support the premise that notwithstanding these variations, there truly is such a thing as a fixed personality.

These days, even Mischel admits that personality traits exist, but he believes they tend to occur in patterns. For example, some people are aggressive with peers and subordinates but docile with authority figures; others are just the opposite. People who are "rejection-sensitive" are warm and loving when they feel secure, hostile and controlling when they feel rejected.

But this comfortable compromise raises a variation on the problem of free will that we explored in chapter 5. We know that there are physiological limits on who we are and how we act. But should we attempt to manipulate our behavior within the range available to us, or should we simply be true to ourselves? At what point does controlling our behavior become futile, or exhausting?

If you're an introvert in corporate America, should you try to save your true self for quiet weekends and spend your weekdays striving to "get out there, mix, speak more often, and connect with your team and others, deploying all the energy and personality you can muster," as Jack Welch advised in a *BusinessWeek* online column? If you're an extroverted university student, should you save your true self for rowdy weekends and spend your weekdays focusing and studying? *Can* people fine-tune their own personalities this way?

The only good answer I've heard to these questions comes from Professor Brian Little.

~

On the morning of October 12, 1979, Little visited the Royal Military College Saint-Jean on the Richelieu River, forty kilometers south of Montreal, to address a group of senior military officers. As an introvert might be expected to do, he'd prepared thoroughly for the speech, not only rehearsing his remarks but also making sure he could cite the latest research. Even while delivering his talk, he was in what he calls classic introvert mode, continually scanning the room for audience displeasure and making adjustments as needed—a statistical reference here, a dollop of humor there.

The speech was a success (so much so that he would be invited to make it every year). But the next invitation the college extended horrified him: to join the top brass for lunch. Little had to deliver another lecture that afternoon, and he knew that making small talk for an hour and a half would wipe him out. He needed to recharge for his afternoon performance.

Thinking quickly, he announced that he had a passion for ship design and asked his hosts if he might instead take the opportunity of his visit to admire the boats passing by on the Richelieu River. He then spent his lunch hour strolling up and down the river pathway with an appreciative expression on his face.

For years Little returned to lecture at the college, and for years, at lunchtime, he walked the banks of the Richelieu River indulging his imaginary hobby—until the day the college moved its campus to a land-locked location. Stripped of his cover story, Professor Little resorted to the only escape hatch he could find—the men's room. After each lecture, he would race to the restroom and hide inside a stall. One time, a military man spotted Little's shoes under the door and began a hearty conversation, so Little took to keeping his feet propped up on the bathroom walls, where they would be hidden from view. (Taking shelter in bathrooms is a surprisingly common phenomenon, as you probably know if you're an introvert. "After a talk, I'm in bathroom stall number nine," Little once told Peter Gzowski, one of Canada's most eminent talk-show hosts. "After a show, I'm in stall number eight," replied Gzowski, not missing a beat.)

You might wonder how a strong introvert like Professor Little manages to speak in public so effectively. The answer, he says, is simple, and it has to do with a new field of psychology that he created almost singlehandedly, called Free Trait Theory. Little believes that fixed traits and free traits coexist. According to Free Trait Theory, we are born and culturally endowed with certain personality traits—introversion, for example—but we can and do act out of character in the service of "core personal projects."

In other words, introverts are capable of acting like extroverts for the sake of work they consider important, people they love, or anything they value highly. Free Trait Theory explains why an introvert might throw his extroverted wife a surprise party or join the PTA at his daughter's school. It explains how it's possible for an extroverted scientist to behave with reserve in her laboratory, for an agreeable person to act hard-nosed during a business negotiation, and for a cantankerous uncle to treat his niece tenderly when he takes her out for ice cream. As these examples suggest, Free Trait Theory applies in many different contexts, but it's especially relevant for introverts living under the Extrovert Ideal.

According to Little, our lives are dramatically enhanced when we're involved in core personal projects that we consider meaningful, manageable, and not unduly stressful, and that are supported by others. When someone asks us "How are things?" we may give a throwaway answer, but our true response is a function of how well our core personal projects are going.

That's why Professor Little, the consummate introvert, lectures with such passion. Like a modern-day Socrates, he loves his students deeply; opening their minds and attending to their well-being are two of his core personal projects. When Little held office hours at Harvard, the students lined up in the hallway as if he were giving out free tickets to a rock concert. For more than twenty years his students asked him to write several hundred letters of recommendation *a year*. "Brian Little is the most engaging, entertaining, and caring professor I have ever encountered," wrote one student about him. "I cannot even begin to explain the myriad ways in which he has positively affected my life." So, for Brian Little, the additional effort required to stretch his natural boundaries is justified by seeing his core personal project—igniting all those minds—come to fruition.

At first blush, Free Trait Theory seems to run counter to a cherished piece of our cultural heritage. Shakespeare's oft-quoted advice, "To thine own self be true," runs deep in our philosophical DNA. Many of us are uncomfortable with the idea of taking on a "false" persona for any length of time. And if we act out of character by convincing ourselves that our pseudo-self is real, we can eventually burn out without even knowing why. The genius of Little's theory is how neatly it resolves this discomfort. Yes, we are only pretending to be extroverts, and yes, such inauthenticity can be morally ambiguous (not to mention exhausting), but if it's in the service of love or a professional calling, then we're doing just as Shakespeare advised.

~

When people are skilled at adopting free traits, it can be hard to believe that they're acting out of character. Professor Little's students are usually incredulous when he claims to be an introvert. But Little is far from unique; many people, especially those in leadership roles, engage in a certain level of pretend-extroversion. Consider, for example, my friend Alex, the socially adept head of a financial services company, who agreed to give a candid interview on the condition of sealed-in-blood anonymity. Alex told me that pretend-extroversion was something he taught himself in the seventh grade, when he decid 1 that other kids were taking advantage of him.

"I was the nicest person you'd ever want to know," Alex recalls, "but the world wasn't that way. The problem was that if you were just a nice person, you'd get crushed. I refused to live a life where people could do that stuff to me. I was like, OK, what's the policy prescription here? And there really was only one. I needed to have every person in my pocket. If I wanted to be a nice person, I needed to run the school."

But how to get from A to B? "I studied social dynamics, I guarantee more than anyone you've ever met," Alex told me. He observed the way people talked, the way they walked—especially male dominance poses. He adjusted his own persona, which allowed him to go on being a fundamentally shy, sweet kid, but without being taken advantage of. "Any hard thing where you can get crushed, I was like, 'I need to learn how to do this.' So by now I'm built for war. Because then people don't screw you."

Alex also took advantage of his natural strengths. "I learned that boys basically do only one thing: they chase girls. They get them, they lose them, they talk about them. I was like, 'That's completely circuitous. I really *like* girls.' That's where intimacy comes from. So rather than sitting around and *talking* about girls, I got to know them. I used having relationships with girls, plus being good at sports, to have the guys in my pocket. Oh, and every once in a while, you have to punch people. I did that, too."

Today Alex has a folksy, affable, whistle-while-you-work demeanor. I've never seen him in a bad mood. But you'll see his self-taught bellicose side if you ever try to cross him in a negotiation. And you'll see his introverted self if you ever try to make dinner plans with him.

"I could literally go years without having any friends except for my wife and kids," he says. "Look at you and me. You're one of my best friends, and how many times do we actually talk—when you call me! I don't like socializing. My dream is to live off the land on a thousand acres with my family. You never see a team of friends in that dream. So notwithstanding whatever you might see in my public persona, I am an introvert. I think that fundamentally I'm the same person I always was. Massively shy, but I compensate for it."

~

But how many of us are really capable of acting out of character to this degree (putting aside, for the moment, the question of whether we want to)? Professor Little happens to be a great performer, and so are many CEOs. What about the rest of us?

Some years ago, a research psychologist named Richard Lippa set out to answer this question. He called a group of introverts to his lab and asked them to act like extroverts while pretending to teach a math class. Then he and his team, video cameras in hand, measured the length of their strides, the amount of eye contact they made with their "students," the percentage of time they spent talking, the pace and volume of their speech, and the total length of each teaching session. They also rated how generally extroverted the subjects appeared, based on their recorded voices and body language.

Then Lippa did the same thing with actual extroverts and compared the results. He found that although the latter group came across as more extroverted, some of the pseudo-extroverts were surprisingly convincing. It seems that most of us know how to fake it to some extent. Whether or not we're aware that the length of our strides and the amount of time we spend talking and smiling mark us as introverts and extroverts, we know it unconsciously.

Still, there's a limit to how much we can control our self-presentation. This is partly because of a phenomenon called behavioral leakage, in which our true selves seep out via unconscious body language: a subtle look away at a moment when an extrovert would have made eye contact, or a skillful turn of the conversation by a lecturer that places the burden of talking on the audience when an extroverted speaker would have held the floor a little longer.

How was it that some of Lippa's pseudo-extroverts came so close to the scores of *true* extroverts? It turned out that the introverts who were especially good at acting like extroverts tended to score high for a trait that psychologists call "self-monitoring." Self-monitors are highly skilled at modifying their behavior to the social demands of a situation. They look for cues to tell them how to act. When in Rome, they do as the Romans do, according to the psychologist Mark Snyder, author of *Public Appearances, Private Realities*, and creator of the Self-Monitoring Scale.

One of the most effective self-monitors I've ever met is a man named Edgar, a well-known and much-beloved fixture on the New York social circuit. He and his wife host or attend fund-raisers and other social events seemingly every weeknight. He's the kind of *enfant terrible* whose latest antics are a favorite topic of conversation. But Edgar is an avowed introvert. "I'd much rather sit and read and think about things than talk to people," he says.

Yet talk to people he does. Edgar was raised in a highly social family that expected him to self-monitor, and he's motivated to do so. "I love politics," he says. "I love policy, I love making things happen, I want to change the world in my own way. So I do stuff that's artificial. I don't really like being the guest at someone else's party, because then I have to be entertaining. But I'll host parties because it puts you at the center of things without actually being a social person."

When he does find himself at other people's parties, Edgar goes to great lengths to play his role. "All through college, and recently even, before I ever went to a dinner or cocktail party, I would have an index card with three to five relevant, amusing anecdotes. I'd come up with them during the day—if something struck me I'd jot it down. Then, at dinner, I'd wait for the right opening and launch in. Sometimes I'd have to go to the bathroom and pull out my cards to remember what my little stories were."

Over time, though, Edgar stopped bringing index cards to dinner parties. He still considers himself an introvert, but he grew so deeply into his extroverted role that telling anecdotes started to come naturally to him. Indeed, the highest self-monitors not only tend to be good at producing the desired effect and emotion in a given social situation— they also experience less stress while doing so.

In contrast to the Edgars of the world, low self-monitors base their behavior on their own internal compass. They have a smaller repertoire of social behaviors and masks at their disposal. They're less sensitive to situational cues, like how many anecdotes you're expected to share at a dinner party, and less interested in role-playing, even when they know what the cues are. It's as if low self-monitors (LSMs) and high self-monitors (HSMs) play to different audiences, Snyder has said: one inner, the other outer.

If you want to know how strong a self-monitor you are, here are a few questions from Snyder's Self-Monitoring Scale:

- When you're uncertain how to act in a social situation, do you look to the behavior of others for cues?
- Do you often seek the advice of your friends to choose movies, books, or music?
- In different situations and with different people, do you often act like very different people?
- Do you find it easy to imitate other people?
- Can you look someone in the eye and tell a lie with a straight face if for a right end?
- Do you ever deceive people by being friendly when really you dislike them?
- Do you put on a show to impress or entertain people?
- Do you sometimes appear to others to be experiencing deeper emotions than you actually are?

The more times you answered "yes" to these questions, the more of a high self-monitor you are.

Now ask yourself these questions:

- Is your behavior usually an expression of your true inner feelings, attitudes, and beliefs?
- Do you find that you can only argue for ideas that you already believe?
- Would you refuse to change your opinions, or the way you do things, in order to please someone else or win their favor?
- Do you dislike games like charades or improvisational acting?
- Do you have trouble changing your behavior to suit different people and different situations?

The more you tended to answer "yes" to this second set of questions, the more of a *low* self-monitor you are.

When Professor Little introduced the concept of self-monitoring to his personality psychology classes, some students got very worked up about whether it was ethical to be a high self-monitor. A few "mixed" couples—HSMs and LSMs in love—even broke up over it, he was told. To high self-monitors, low self-monitors can seem rigid and socially awkward. To low self-monitors, high self-monitors can come across as conformist and deceptive—"more pragmatic than principled," in Mark Snyder's words. Indeed, HSMs have been found to be better liars than LSMs, which would seem to support the moralistic stance taken by low self-monitors.

But Little, an ethical and sympathetic man who happens to be an extremely high self-monitor, sees things differently. He views self-monitoring as an act of modesty. It's about accommodating oneself to situational norms, rather than "grinding down everything to one's own needs and concerns." Not all self-monitoring is based on acting, he says, or on working the room. A more introverted version may be less concerned with spotlight-seeking and more with the avoidance of social faux pas. When Professor Little makes a great speech, it's partly because he's self-monitoring every moment, continually checking his audience for subtle signs of pleasure or boredom and adjusting his presentation to meet its needs.

~

So if you *can* fake it, if you master the acting skills, the attention to social nuance, and the willingness to submit to social norms that self-monitoring requires, *should* you? The answer is that a Free Trait strategy can be effective when used judiciously, but disastrous if overdone.

Recently I spoke on a panel at Harvard Law School. The occasion was the fifty-fifth anniversary of women being admitted to the law school. Alumnae from all over the country gathered on campus to celebrate. The subject of the panel was "In a Different Voice: Strategies for Powerful Self-Presentation." There were four speakers: a trial lawyer, a judge, a public-speaking coach, and me. I'd prepared my remarks carefully; I knew the role I wanted to play.

The public-speaking coach went first. She talked about how to give a talk that knocks people's socks off. The judge, who happened to be Korean-American, spoke of how frustrating it is when people assume that all Asians are quiet and studious when in fact she's outgoing and assertive. The litigator, who was petite and blond and feisty as hell, talked about the time she conducted a cross-examination only to be admonished by a judge to "Back down, tiger!"

When my turn came, I aimed my remarks at the women in the audience who didn't see themselves as tigers, myth-busters, or sock-knocker-offers. I said that the ability to negotiate is not inborn, like blond hair or straight teeth, and it does not belong exclusively to the table-pounders of the world. Anyone can be a great negotiator, I told them, and in fact it often pays to be quiet and gracious, to listen more than talk, and to have an instinct for harmony rather than conflict. With this style, you can take aggressive positions without inflaming your counterpart's ego. And by listening, you can learn what's truly motivating the person you're negotiating with and come up with creative solutions that satisfy both parties.

I also shared some psychological tricks for feeling calm and secure during intimidating situations, such as paying attention to how your face and body arrange themselves when you're feeling genuinely confident, and adopting those same positions when it comes time to fake it. Studies show that taking simple physical steps—like smiling—makes us feel stronger and happier, while frowning makes us feel worse.

Naturally, when the panel was over and the audience member came around to chat with the panelists, it was the introverts and pseudo-extroverts who sought me out. Two of those women stand out in my mind.

The first was Alison, a trial lawyer. Alison was slim and meticulously groomed, but her face was pale, pinched, and unhappy-looking. She'd been a litigator at the same corporate law firm for over a decade. Now she was applying for general counsel positions at various companies, which seemed a logical next step, except that her heart clearly wasn't in it. And sure enough, she hadn't gotten a single job offer. On the strength of her credentials, she was advancing to the final round of interviews, only to be weeded out at the last minute. And she knew why, because the head-hunter who'd coordinated her interviews gave the same feedback each time: she lacked the right personality for the job. Alison, a self-described introvert, looked pained as she related this damning judgment.

The second alumna, Jillian, held a senior position at an environmental advocacy organization that she loved. Jillian came across as kind, cheerful, and down-to-earth. She was fortunate to spend much of her time researching and writing policy papers on topics she cared about. Sometimes, though, she had to chair meetings and make presentations. Although she felt deep satisfaction after these meetings, she didn't enjoy the spotlight, and wanted my advice on staying cool when she felt scared.

So what was the difference between Alison and Jillian? Both were pseudo-extroverts, and you might say that Alison was trying and failing where Jillian was succeeding. But Alison's problem was actually that she was acting out of character in the service of a project she didn't care about. She didn't love the law. She'd chosen to become a Wall Street litigator because it seemed to her that this was what powerful and successful lawyers did, so her pseudo-extroversion was not supported by deeper values. She was not telling herself, *I'm doing this to advance work I care about deeply, and when the work is done I'll settle back into my true self.* Instead, her interior monologue was *The route to success is to be the sort of person I am not.* This is not self-monitoring; it is self-negation. Where Jillian acts out of character for the sake of worthy tasks that temporarily require a different orientation, Alison believes that there is something fundamentally wrong with who she is.

It's not always so easy, it turns out, to identify your core personal projects. And it can be especially tough for introverts, who have spent so much of their lives conforming to extroverted norms that by the time they choose a career, or a calling, it feels perfectly normal to ignore their own preferences. They may be uncomfortable in law school or nursing school or in the marketing department, but no more so than they were back in middle school or summer camp.

I, too, was once in this position. I enjoyed practicing corporate law, and for a while I convinced myself that I was an attorney at heart. I badly wanted to believe it, since I had already invested years in law school and on-the-job training, and much about Wall Street law was alluring. My colleagues were intellectual, kind, and considerate (mostly). I made a good living. I had an office on the forty-second floor of a skyscraper with views of the Statue of Liberty. I enjoyed the idea that I could flourish in such a high-powered environment. And I was pretty good at asking the "but" and "what if" questions that are central to the thought processes of most lawyers.

It took me almost a decade to understand that the law was never my personal project, not even close. Today I can tell you unhesitatingly what is: my husband and sons; writing; promoting the values of this book. Once I realized this, I had to make a change. I look back on my years as a Wall Street lawyer as time spent in a foreign country. It was absorbing, it was exciting, and I got to meet a lot of interesting people whom I never would have known otherwise. But I was always an expatriate.

Having spent so much time navigating my own career transition and counseling others through theirs, I have found that there are three key steps to identifying your own core personal projects.

First, think back to what you loved to do when you were a child. How did you answer the question of what you wanted to be when you grew up? The specific answer you gave may have been off the mark, but the under-lying impulse was not. If you wanted to be a fireman, what did a fireman mean to you? A good man who rescued people in distress? A daredevil? Or the simple pleasure of operating a truck? If you wanted to be a dancer, was it because you got to wear a costume, or because you craved applause, or was it the pure joy of twirling around at lightning speed? You may have known more about who you were then than you do now.

Second, pay attention to the work you gravitate to. At my law firm I never once volunteered to take on an extra corporate legal assignment, but I did spend a lot of time doing pro bono work for a nonprofit wom-en's leadership organization. I also sat on several law firm committees dedicated to mentoring, training, and personal development for young lawyers in the firm. Now, as you can probably tell from this book, I am not the committee type. But the goals of those committees lit me up, so that's what I did.

Finally, pay attention to what you envy. Jealousy is an ugly emotion, but it tells the truth. You mostly envy those who have what you desire. I met my own envy after some of my former law school classmates got together and compared notes on alumni career tracks. They spoke with admiration and, yes, jealousy, of a classmate who argued regularly before the Supreme Court. At first I felt critical. More power to that classmate! I thought, congratulating myself on my magnanimity. Then I realized that my largesse came cheap, because I didn't aspire to argue a case be-fore the Supreme Court, or to any of the other accolades of lawyering. When I asked myself whom I *did* envy, the answer came back instantly.

My college classmates who'd grown up to be writers or psychologists. Today I'm pursuing my own version of both those roles.

~

But even if you're stretching yourself in the service of a core personal project, you don't want to act out of character too much, or for too long. Remember those trips Professor Little made to the restroom in between speeches? Those hideout sessions tell us that, paradoxically, the best way to act out of character is to stay as true to yourself as you possibly can—starting by creating as many "restorative niches" as possible in your daily life.

"Restorative niche" is Professor Little's term for the place you go when you want to return to your true self. It can be a physical place, like the path beside the Richelieu River, or a temporal one, like the quiet breaks you plan between sales calls. It can mean canceling your social plans on the weekend before a big meeting at work, practicing yoga or meditation, or choosing e-mail over an in-person meeting. (Even Victorian ladies, whose job effectively was to be available to friends and family, were expected to withdraw for a rest each afternoon.)

You choose a restorative niche when you close the door to your private office (if you're lucky enough to have one) in between meetings. You can even create a restorative niche *during* a meeting, by carefully selecting where you sit, and when and how you participate. In his memoir *In an Uncertain World*, Robert Rubin, the treasury secretary under President Clinton, describes how he "always liked to be away from the center, whether in the Oval Office or the chief of staff's office, where my regular seat became the foot of the table. That little bit of physical distance felt more comfortable to me, and let me read the room and comment from a perspective ever so slightly removed. I didn't worry about being overlooked. No matter how far away you were sitting or standing, you could always just say, 'Mr. President, I think this, that, or the other.'"

We would all be better off if, before accepting a new job, we evaluated the presence or absence of restorative niches as carefully as we consider the family leave policy or health insurance plans. Introverts should ask themselves: Will this job allow me to spend time on in-character activities like, for example, reading, strategizing, writing, and researching? Will I have a private workspace or be subject to the constant demands of an open office plan? If the job doesn't give me enough restorative niches, will I have enough free time on evenings and weekends to grant them to myself?

Extroverts will want to look for restorative niches, too. Does the job involve talking, traveling, and meeting new people? Is the office space stimulating enough? If the job isn't a perfect fit, are the hours flexible enough that I can blow off steam after work? Think through the job description carefully. One highly extroverted woman I interviewed was excited about a position as the "community organizer" for a parenting website, until she realized that she'd be sitting by herself behind a computer every day from nine to five.

Sometimes people find restorative niches in professions where you'd least expect them. One of my former colleagues is a trial lawyer who spends most of her time in splendid solitude, researching and writing legal briefs. Because most of her cases settle, she goes to court rarely enough that she doesn't mind exercising her pseudo-extroversion skills when she has to. An introverted administrative assistant I interviewed parlayed her office experience into a work-from-home Internet business that serves as a clearinghouse and coaching service for "virtual assistants." And in the next chapter we'll meet a superstar salesman who broke his company's sales records year after year by insisting on staying true to his introverted self. All three of these people have taken decidedly extroverted fields and reinvented them in their own image, so that they're acting in character most of the time, effectively turning their workdays into one giant restorative niche.

Finding restorative niches isn't always easy. You might want to read quietly by the fire on Saturday nights, but if your spouse wishes you'd spend those evenings out with her large circle of friends, then what? You might want to retreat to the oasis of your private office in between sales calls, but what if your company just switched over to an open office plan? If you plan to exercise free traits, you'll need the help of friends, family, and colleagues. Which is why Professor Little calls, with great passion, for each of us to enter into "a Free Trait Agreement."

This is the final piece of Free Trait Theory. A Free Trait Agreement acknowledges that we'll each act out of character some of the time—in exchange for being ourselves the rest of the time. It's a Free Trait Agreement when a wife who wants to go out every Saturday night and a husband who wants to relax by the fire work out a schedule: *half the time we'll go out, and half the time we'll stay home*. It's a Free Trait Agreement when you attend your extroverted best friend's wedding shower, engagement celebration, and bachelorette party, but she understands when you skip out on the three days' worth of group activities leading up to the wedding itself.

It's often possible to negotiate Free Trait Agreements with friends and lovers, whom you want to please and who love your true, in-character self. Your work life is a little trickier, since most businesses still don't think in these terms. For now, you may have to proceed indirectly. Career counselor Shoya Zichy told me the story of one of her clients, an introverted financial analyst who worked in an environment where she was either presenting to clients or talking to colleagues who continually cycled in and out of her office. She was so burned out that she planned to quit her job—until Zichy suggested that she negotiate for downtime.

Now, this woman worked for a Wall Street bank, not a culture conducive to a frank discussion about the needs of the highly introverted. So she carefully considered how to frame her request. She told her boss that the very nature of her work—strategic analysis—required quiet time in which to concentrate. Once she made her case empirically, it was easier to ask for what she needed psychologically: two days a week of working from home. Her boss said yes.

But the person with whom you can best strike a Free Trait Agreement—after overcoming his or her resistance—is yourself.

Let's say you're single. You dislike the bar scene, but you crave intimacy, and you want to be in a long-term relationship in which you can share cozy evenings and long conversations with your partner and a small circle of friends. In order to achieve this goal, you make an agreement with yourself that you will push yourself to go to social events, because only in this way can you hope to meet a mate and reduce the number of gatherings you attend over the long term. But while you pursue this goal, you will attend only as many events as you can comfortably stand. You decide in advance what that amount is—once a week, once a month, once a quarter. And once you've met your quota, you've earned the right to stay home without feeling guilty.

Or perhaps you've always dreamed of building your own small company, working from home so you can spend more time with your spouse and children. You know you'll need to do a certain amount of networking, so you make the following Free Trait Agreement with yourself: you will go to one schmooze-fest per week. At each event you will have at least one genuine conversation (since this comes easier to you than "working the room") and follow up with that person the next day. After that, you get to go home and not feel bad when you turn down other networking opportunities that come your way.

~

Professor Little knows all too well what happens when you lack a Free Trait Agreement with yourself. Apart from occasional excursions to the Richelieu River or the restroom, he once followed a schedule that combined the most energy-zapping elements of both introversion and extroversion. On the extroverted side, his days consisted of nonstop lectures, meetings with students, monitoring a student discussion group, and writing all those letters of recommendation. On the introverted side, he took those responsibilities very, very seriously.

"One way of looking at this," he says now, "is to say that I was heavily engaged in extrovert-like behaviors, but, of course, had I been a real extrovert I would have done quicker, less nuanced letters of recommendation, would not have invested the time in preparation of lectures, and the social events would not have drained me." He also suffered from a certain amount of what he calls "reputational confusion," in which he became known for being over-the-top effervescent, and the reputation fed on itself. This was the persona that others knew, so it was the persona he felt obliged to serve up.

Naturally, Professor Little started to burn out, not only mentally but also physically. Never mind. He loved his students, he loved his field, he loved it all. Until the day that he ended up in the doctor's office with a case of double pneumonia that he'd been too busy to notice. His wife had dragged him there against his will, and a good thing too. According to the doctors, if she had waited much longer, he would have died.

Double pneumonia and an overscheduled life can happen to anyone, of course, but for Little, it was the result of acting out of character for too long and without enough restorative niches. When your conscientiousness impels you to take on more than you can handle, you begin to lose interest, even in tasks that normally engage you. You also risk your physical health. "Emotional labor," which is the effort we make to control and change our own emotions, is associated with stress, burnout, and even physical symptoms like an increase in cardiovascular disease. Professor Little believes that prolonged acting out of character may also increase autonomic nervous system activity, which can, in turn, compromise immune functioning.

One noteworthy study suggests that people who suppress negative emotions tend to leak those emotions later in unexpected ways. The psychologist Judith Grob asked people to hide their emotions as she showed them disgusting images. She even had them hold pens in their mouths to prevent them from frowning. She found that this group reported feeling less disgusted by the pictures than did those who'd been allowed to react naturally. Later, however, the people who hid their emotions suffered side effects. Their memory was impaired, and the negative emotions they'd suppressed seemed to color their outlook. When Grob had them fill in the missing letter to the word "gr_ss," for example, they were more likely than others to offer "gross" rather than "grass." "People who tend to [suppress their negative emotions] regularly," concludes Grob, "might start to see the world in a more negative light."

That's why these days Professor Little is in restorative mode, retired from the university and reveling in his wife's company in their house in the Canadian countryside. Little says that his wife, Sue Phillips, the director of the School of Public Policy and Administration at Carleton University, is so much like him that they don't need a Free Trait Agreement to govern their relationship. But his Free Trait Agreement with *himself* provides that he do his remaining "scholarly and professional deeds with good grace," but not "hang around longer than necessary."

Then he goes home and snuggles by the fire with Sue.

10

THE COMMUNICATION GAP

How to Talk to Members of the Opposite Type

The meeting of two personalities is like the contact of two chemical substances; if there is any reaction, both are transformed.
—CARL JUNG

If introverts and extroverts are the north and south of temperament—opposite ends of a single spectrum—then how can they possibly get along? Yet the two types are often drawn to each other—in friendship, business, and especially romance. These pairs can enjoy great excitement and mutual admiration, a sense that each completes the other. One tends to listen, the other to talk; one is sensitive to beauty, but also to slings and arrows, while the other barrels cheerfully through his days; one pays the bills and the other arranges the children's play dates. But it can also cause problems when members of these unions pull in opposite directions.

Greg and Emily are an example of an introvert-extrovert couple who love and madden each other in equal measure. Greg, who just turned thirty, has a bounding gait, a mop of dark hair continually falling over his eyes, and an easy laugh. Most people would describe him as gregarious. Emily, a mature twenty-seven, is as self-contained as Greg is expansive. Graceful and soft-spoken, she keeps her auburn hair tied in a chignon, and often gazes at people from under lowered lashes.

Greg and Emily complement each other beautifully. Without Greg,

Emily might forget to leave the house, except to go to work. But without Emily, Greg would feel—paradoxically for such a social creature—alone.

Before they met, most of Greg's girlfriends were extroverts. He says he enjoyed those relationships, but never got to know his girlfriends well, because they were always "plotting how to be with groups of people." He speaks of Emily with a kind of awe, as if she has access to a deeper state of being. He also describes her as "the anchor" around which his world revolves.

Emily, for her part, treasures Greg's ebullient nature; he makes her feel happy and alive. She has always been attracted to extroverts, who she says "do all the work of making conversation. For them, it's not work at all."

The trouble is that for most of the five years they've been together, Greg and Emily have been having one version or another of the same fight. Greg, a music promoter with a large circle of friends, wants to host dinner parties every Friday—casual, animated get-togethers with heaping bowls of pasta and flowing bottles of wine. He's been giving Friday-night dinners since he was a senior in college, and they've become a highlight of his week and a treasured piece of his identity.

Emily has come to dread these weekly events. A hardworking staff attorney for an art museum and a very private person, the last thing she wants to do when she gets home from work is entertain. Her idea of a perfect start to the weekend is a quiet evening at the movies, just her and Greg.

It seems an irreconcilable difference: Greg wants fifty-two dinner parties a year, Emily wants zero.

Greg says that Emily should make more of an effort. He accuses her of being antisocial. "I *am* social," she says. "I love you, I love my family, I love my close friends. I just don't love dinner parties. People don't really *relate* at those parties—they just *socialize*. You're lucky because I devote all my energy to you. You spread yours around to everyone."

But Emily soon backs off, partly because she hates fighting, but also because she doubts herself. *Maybe I am antisocial*, she thinks. *Maybe there is something wrong with me*. Whenever she and Greg argue about this, she's flooded with childhood memories: how school was tougher for her than for her emotionally hardier younger sister; how she seemed to worry more than other people did about social issues, like how to say no when someone asked her to get together after school and she preferred to stay home. Emily had plenty of friends—she's always had a talent for friendship—but she never traveled in packs.

Emily has suggested a compromise: What if Greg gives his dinner parties whenever she's out of town visiting her sister? But Greg doesn't want to host dinners by himself. He loves Emily and wants to be with her, and so does everyone else, once they get to know her. So why does Emily withdraw?

This question, for Greg, is more than mere pique. Being alone for him is a kind of Kryptonite; it makes him feel weak. He had looked forward to a married life of shared adventures. He'd imagined being part of a couple at the center of things. And he'd never admitted it to himself, but for him being married meant never having to be by himself. But now Emily is saying that he should socialize without her. He feels as if she's backing out of a fundamental part of their marriage contract. And he believes that something is indeed wrong with his wife.

~

Is something wrong with me? It's not surprising that Emily asks herself this question, or that Greg aims this charge at her. Probably the most common—and damaging—misunderstanding about personality type is that introverts are antisocial and extroverts are pro-social. But as we've seen, neither formulation is correct; introverts and extroverts are *differently* social. What psychologists call "the need for intimacy" is present in introverts and extroverts alike. In fact, people who value intimacy highly don't tend to be, as the noted psychologist David Buss puts it, "the loud, outgoing, life-of-the-party extrovert." They are more likely to be someone with a select group of close friends, who prefers "sincere and meaningful conversations over wild parties." They are more likely to be someone like Emily.

Conversely, extroverts do not necessarily seek closeness from their socializing. "Extroverts seem to need people as a forum to fill needs for social impact, just as a general needs soldiers to fill his or her need to lead," the psychologist William Graziano told me. "When extroverts show up at a party, everyone knows they are present."

Your degree of extroversion seems to influence how many friends you have, in other words, but not how good a friend you are. In a study of 132 college students at Humboldt University in Berlin, the psychologists Jens Aspendorf and Susanne Wilpers set out to understand the effect of different personality traits on students' relationships with their peers and families. They focused on the so-called Big Five traits: Introversion-Extroversion; Agreeableness; Openness to Experience; Conscientiousness; and Emotional Stability. (Many personality psychologists believe that human personality can be boiled down to these five characteristics.)

Aspendorf and Wilpers predicted that the extroverted students would have an easier time striking up new friendships than the introverts, and this was indeed the case. But if the introverts were truly antisocial and extroverts pro-social, then you'd suppose that the students with the most harmonious relationships would also be highest in extroversion. And this was not the case at all. Instead, the students whose relationships were freest of conflict had high scores for agreeableness. Agreeable people are warm, supportive, and loving; personality psychologists have found that if you sit them down in front of a computer screen of words, they focus longer than others do on words like *caring, console,* and *help,* and a shorter time on words like *abduct, assault,* and *harass.* Introverts and extroverts are equally likely to be agreeable; there is no correlation between extroversion and agreeableness. This explains why some extroverts love the stimulation of socializing but don't get along particularly well with those closest to them.

It also helps explain why some introverts—like Emily, whose talent for friendship suggests that she's a highly agreeable type herself—lavish attention on their family and close friends but dislike small talk. So when Greg labels Emily "antisocial," he's off base. Emily nurtures her marriage in just the way that you'd expect an agreeable introvert to do, making Greg the center of her social universe.

Except when she doesn't. Emily has a demanding job, and sometimes when she gets home at night she has little energy left. She's always happy to see Greg, but sometimes she'd rather sit next to him reading than go out for dinner or make animated conversation. Simply to be in his company is enough. For Emily, this is perfectly natural, but Greg feels hurt that she makes an effort for her colleagues and not for him.

This was a painfully common dynamic in the introvert-extrovert couples I interviewed: the introverts desperately craving downtime and understanding from their partners, the extroverts longing for company, and resentful that others seemed to benefit from their partners' "best" selves.

It can be hard for extroverts to understand how badly introverts need to recharge at the end of a busy day. We all empathize with a sleep-deprived mate who comes home from work too tired to talk, but it's harder to grasp that social overstimulation can be just as exhausting.

It's also hard for introverts to understand just how hurtful their silence can be. I interviewed a woman named Sarah, a bubbly and dynamic high school English teacher married to Bob, an introverted law school dean who spends his days fund-raising, then collapses when he gets home. Sarah cried tears of frustration and loneliness as she told me about her marriage.

"When he's on the job, he's amazingly engaging," she said. "Everyone tells me that he's so funny and I'm so lucky to be married to him. And I want to throttle them. Every night, as soon as we're done eating, he jumps up and cleans the kitchen. Then he wants to read the paper alone and work on his photography by himself. At around nine, he comes into the bedroom and wants to watch TV and be with me. But he's not really with me even then. He wants me to lay my head on his shoulder while we stare at the TV. It's a grownup version of parallel play." Sarah is trying to convince Bob to make a career change. "I think we'd have a great life if he had a job where he could sit at the computer all day, but he's consistently fund-raising," she says.

In couples where the man is introverted and the woman extroverted, as with Sarah and Bob, we often mistake personality conflicts for gender difference, then trot out the conventional wisdom that "Mars" needs to retreat to his cave while "Venus" prefers to interact. But whatever the reason for these differences in social needs—whether gender or temperament—what's important is that it's possible to work through them. In *The Audacity of Hope*, for example, President Obama confides that early in his marriage to Michelle, he was working on his first book and "would often spend the evening holed up in my office in the back of our railroad apartment; what I considered normal often left Michelle feeling lonely." He attributes his own style to the demands of writing and to having been raised mostly as an only child, and then says that he and Michelle have learned over the years to meet each other's needs, and to see them as legitimate.

~

It can also be hard for introverts and extroverts to understand each other's ways of resolving differences. One of my clients was an immaculately dressed lawyer named Celia. Celia wanted a divorce, but dreaded letting her husband know. She had good reasons for her decision but anticipated that he would beg her to stay and that she would crumple with guilt. Above all, Celia wanted to deliver her news compassionately.

We decided to role-play their discussion, with me acting as her husband.

"I want to end this marriage," said Celia. "I mean it this time."

"I've been doing everything I can to hold things together," I pleaded. "How can you do this to me?"

Celia thought for a minute.

"I've spent a lot of time thinking this through, and I believe this is the right decision," she replied in a wooden voice.

"What can I do to change your mind?" I asked.

"Nothing," said Celia flatly.

Feeling for a minute what her husband would feel, I was dumbstruck. She was so rote, so dispassionate. She was about to divorce me—me, her husband of eleven years! *Didn't she care?*

I asked Celia to try again, this time with emotion in her voice.

"I can't," she said. "I can't do it."

But she did. "I want to end this marriage," she repeated, her voice choked with sadness. She began to weep uncontrollably.

Celia's problem was not lack of feeling. It was how to *show* her emotions without losing control. Reaching for a tissue, she quickly gathered herself, and went back into crisp, dispassionate lawyer mode. These were the two gears to which she had ready access—overwhelming feelings or detached self-possession.

I tell you Celia's story because in many ways she's a lot like Emily and many introverts I've interviewed. Emily is talking to Greg about dinner parties, not divorce, but her communication style echoes Celia's. When she and Greg disagree, her voice gets quiet and flat, her manner slightly distant. What she's trying to do is minimize aggression—Emily is uncomfortable with anger—but she *appears* to be receding emotionally. Meanwhile, Greg does just the opposite, raising his voice and sounding belligerent as he gets ever more engaged in working out their problem. The more Emily seems to withdraw, the more alone, then hurt, then enraged Greg becomes; the angrier he gets, the more hurt and distaste Emily feels, and the deeper she retreats. Pretty soon they're locked in a destructive cycle from which they can't escape, partly because both spouses believe they're arguing in an appropriate manner.

This dynamic shouldn't surprise anyone familiar with the relationship between personality and conflict resolution style. Just as men and women often have different ways of resolving conflict, so do introverts and extroverts; studies suggest that the former tend to be conflict-avoiders, while the latter are "confrontive copers," at ease with an up-front, even argumentative style of disagreement.

These are diametrically opposite approaches, so they're bound to create friction. If Emily didn't mind conflict so much, she might not react so strongly to Greg's head-on approach; if Greg were milder-mannered, he might appreciate Emily's attempt to keep a lid on things. When people have compatible styles of conflict, a disagreement can be an occasion for each partner to affirm the other's point of view. But Greg and Emily seem to understand each other a little *less* each time they argue in a way that the other disapproves of.

Do they also *like* each other a little less, at least for the duration of the fight? An illuminating study by the psychologist William Graziano suggests that the answer to this question might be yes. Graziano divided a group of sixty-one male students into teams to play a simulated football game. Half the participants were assigned to a cooperative game, in which they were told, "Football is useful to us because to be successful in football, *team members have to work well together*." The other half were assigned to a game emphasizing competition between teams. Each student was then shown slides and fabricated biographical information about his teammates and his competitors on the other team, and asked to rate how he felt about the other players.

The differences between introverts and extroverts were remarkable. The introverts assigned to the cooperative game rated all players—not just their competitors, but also their teammates—more positively than the introverts who played the competitive game. The extroverts did just the opposite: they rated all players more positively when they played the competitive version of the game. These findings suggest something very important: introverts like people they meet in friendly contexts; extroverts prefer those they compete with.

A very different study, in which robots interacted with stroke patients during physical rehabilitation exercises, yielded strikingly similar results. Introverted patients responded better and interacted longer with robots that were designed to speak in a soothing, gentle manner: "I know it is hard, but remember that it's for your own good," and, "Very nice, keep up the good work." Extroverts, on the other hand, worked harder for robots that used more bracing, aggressive language: "You can do more than that, I know it!" and "Concentrate on your exercise!"

These findings suggest that Greg and Emily face an interesting challenge. If Greg likes people more when they're behaving forcefully or competitively, and if Emily feels the same way about nurturing, cooperative people, then how can they reach a compromise about their dinner-party impasse—and get there in a loving way?

An intriguing answer comes from a University of Michigan business school study, not of married couples with opposite personality styles, but of negotiators from different cultures—in this case, Asians and Israelis. Seventy-six MBA students from Hong Kong and Israel were asked to imagine they were getting married in a few months and had to finalize arrangements with a catering company for the wedding reception. This "meeting" took place by video.

Some of the students were shown a video in which the business manager was friendly and smiley; the others saw a video featuring an irritable and antagonistic manager. But the caterer's message was the same in both cases. Another couple was interested in the same wedding date. The price had gone up. Take it or leave it.

The students from Hong Kong reacted very differently from the Israeli students. The Asians were far more likely to accept a proposal from the friendly business manager than from the hostile one; only 14 percent were willing to work with the difficult manager, while 71 percent accepted the deal from the smiling caterer. But the Israelis were just as likely to accept the deal from *either* manager. In other words, for the Asian negotiators, style counted as well as substance, while the Israelis were more focused on the information being conveyed. They were unmoved by a display of either sympathetic *or* hostile emotions.

The explanation for this stark difference has to do with how the two cultures define respect. As we saw in chapter 8, many Asian people show esteem by minimizing conflict. But Israelis, say the researchers, "are not likely to view [disagreement] as a sign of disrespect, but as a signal that the opposing party is concerned and is passionately engaged in the task."

We might say the same of Greg and Emily. When Emily lowers her voice and flattens her affect during fights with Greg, she thinks she's being respectful by taking the trouble not to let her negative emotions show. But Greg thinks she's checking out or, worse, that she doesn't give a damn. Similarly, when Greg lets his anger fly, he assumes that Emily feels, as he does, that this is a healthy and honest expression of their deeply committed relationship. But to Emily, it's as if Greg has suddenly turned on her.

~

In her book *Anger: The Misunderstood Emotion*, Carol Tavris recounts a story about a Bengali cobra that liked to bite passing villagers. One day a swami—a man who has achieved self-mastery—convinces the snake that biting is wrong. The cobra vows to stop immediately, and does. Before long, the village boys grow unafraid of the snake and start to abuse him. Battered and bloodied, the snake complains to the swami that this is what came of keeping his promise.

"I told you not to bite," said the swami, "but I did not tell you not to hiss."

"Many people, like the swami's cobra, confuse the hiss with the bite," writes Tavris.

Many people—like Greg and Emily. Both have much to learn from the swami's story: Greg to stop biting, Emily that it's OK for him—and for her—to hiss.

Greg can start by changing his assumptions about anger. He believes, as most of us do, that venting anger lets off steam. The "catharsis hypothesis"—that aggression builds up inside us until it's healthily released—dates back to the Greeks, was revived by Freud, and gained steam during the "let it all hang out" 1960s of punching bags and primal screams. But the catharsis hypothesis is a myth—a plausible one, an elegant one, but a myth nonetheless. Scores of studies have shown that venting doesn't soothe anger; *it fuels it*.

We're best off when we don't allow ourselves to go to our angry place. Amazingly, neuroscientists have even found that people who use Botox, which prevents them from making angry faces, seem to be less anger-prone than those who don't, because the very act of frowning triggers the amygdala to process negative emotions. And anger is not just damaging in the moment; for days afterward, venters have repair work to do with their partners. Despite the popular fantasy of fabulous sex after fighting, many couples say that it takes time to feel loving again.

What can Greg do to calm down when he feels his fury mounting? He can take a deep breath. He can take a ten-minute break. And he can ask himself whether the thing that's making him so angry is really that important. If not, he might let it go. But if it is, then he'll want to phrase his needs not as personal attacks but as neutral discussion items. "You're so antisocial!" can become "Can we figure out a way to organize our weekends that works for us both?"

This advice would hold even if Emily weren't a sensitive introvert (no one likes to feel dominated or disrespected), but it so happens that Greg's married to a woman who is *especially* put off by anger. So he needs to respond to the conflict-avoidant wife he has, not the confrontational one that he wishes, at least in the heat of the moment, he were married to.

Now let's look at Emily's side of the equation. What could she be doing differently? She's right to protest when Greg bites—when he attacks unfairly—but what about when he hisses? Emily might address her own counterproductive reactions to anger, among them her tendency to slip into a cycle of guilt and defensiveness. We know from chapter 6 that many introverts are prone from earliest childhood to strong guilt feelings; we also know that we all tend to project our own reactions onto others. Because conflict-avoidant Emily would never "bite" or even hiss unless Greg had done something truly horrible, on some level she processes *his* bite to mean that she's terribly guilty—of something, anything, who knows what? Emily's guilt feels so intolerable that she tends to deny the validity of all of Greg's claims—the legitimate ones along with those exaggerated by anger. This, of course, leads to a vicious cycle in which she shuts down her natural empathy and Greg feels unheard.

So Emily needs to accept that it's OK to be in the wrong. At first she may have trouble puzzling out when she is and when she isn't; the fact that Greg expresses his grievances with such passion makes it hard to sort this out. But Emily must try not to get dragged into this morass. When Greg makes legitimate points, she should acknowledge them, not only to be a good partner to her husband, but also to teach herself that it's OK to have transgressed. This will make it easier for her not to feel hurt—and to fight back—when Greg's claims *are* unjustified.

Fight back? But Emily hates fighting.

That's OK. She needs to become more comfortable with the sound of her own hiss. Introverts may be hesitant to cause disharmony, but, like the passive snake, they should be equally worried about encouraging vitriol from their partners. And fighting back may not invite retaliation, as Emily fears; instead it may encourage Greg to back off. She need not put on a huge display. Often, a firm "that's not OK with me" will do.

Every once in a while, Emily might also want to step outside her usual comfort zone and let her own anger fly. Remember, for Greg, heat means connection. In the same way that the extroverted players in the football game study felt warmly toward their fellow competitors, so Greg may feel closer to Emily if she can take on just a little of the coloration of a pumped-up player, ready to take the field.

Emily can also overcome her own distaste for Greg's behavior by reminding herself that he's not really as aggressive as he seems. John, an introvert I interviewed who has a great relationship with his fiery wife, describes how he learned to do this after twenty-five years of marriage:

> When Jennifer's after me about something, she's really after me. If I went to bed without tidying the kitchen, the next morning she'll shout at me, "This kitchen is filthy!" I come in and look around the kitchen. There are three or four cups out; it's not filthy. But the drama with which she imbues such moments is natural to her. That's her way of saying, *Gee, when you get a chance I'd appreciate it if you could just tidy up the kitchen a little more.* If she did say it that way to me, I would say, *I'd be happy to, and I'm sorry that I didn't do it sooner.* But because she comes at me with that two-hundred-mile-per-hour freight-train energy, I want to bridle and say, *Too bad.* The reason I don't is because we've been married for twenty-five years, and I've come to understand that Jennifer didn't put me in a life-threatening situation when she spoke that way.

So what's John's secret for relating to his forceful wife? He lets her know that her words were unacceptable, but he also tries to listen to their meaning. "I try to tap into my empathy," he says. "I take her tone out of the equation. I take out the assault on my senses, and I try to get to what she's trying to say."

And what Jennifer is trying to say, underneath her freight-train words, is often quite simple: Respect me. Pay attention to me. Love me.

Greg and Emily now have valuable insights about how to talk through their differences. But there's one more question they need to answer: Why exactly do they experience those Friday-night dinner parties so differently? We know that Emily's nervous system probably goes into overdrive when she enters a room full of people. And we know that Greg feels the opposite: propelled toward people, conversations, events, anything that gives him that dopamine-fueled, go-for-it sensation that extroverts crave. But let's dig a little deeper into the anatomy of cocktail-hour chatter. The key to bridging Greg and Emily's differences lies in the details.

~

Some years ago, thirty-two pairs of introverts and extroverts, all of them strangers to each other, chatted on the phone for a few minutes as part of an experiment conducted by a neuroscientist named Dr. Matthew Lieberman, then a graduate student at Harvard. When they hung up, they were asked to fill out detailed questionnaires, rating how they'd felt and behaved during the conversation. How much did you like your conversational partner? How friendly were you? How much would you like to interact with this person again? They were also asked to put themselves in the shoes of their conversational partners: How much did your partner like you? How sensitive was she to you? How encouraging?

Lieberman and his team compared the answers and also listened in on the conversations and made their own judgments about how the parties felt about each other. They found that the extroverts were a lot more accurate than the introverts in assessing whether their partner liked talking to them. These findings suggest that extroverts are better at decoding social cues than introverts. At first, this seems unsurprising, writes Lieberman; it echoes the popular assumption that extroverts are better at reading social situations. The only problem, as Lieberman showed through a further twist to his experiment, is that this assumption is not quite right.

Lieberman and his team asked a select group of participants to listen to a tape of the conversations they'd just had—*before* filling out the questionnaire. In this group, he found, there was no difference between introverts and extroverts in their ability to read social cues. Why?

The answer is that the subjects who listened to the tape recording were able to decode social cues *without having to do anything else at the same time*. And introverts are pretty fine decoders, according to several studies predating the Lieberman experiments. One of these studies actually found that introverts were better decoders than extroverts.

But these studies measured how well introverts *observe* social dynamics, not how well they participate in them. Participation places a very different set of demands on the brain than observing does. It requires a kind of mental multitasking: the ability to process a lot of short-term information at once without becoming distracted or overly stressed. This is just the sort of brain functioning that extroverts tend to be well suited for. In other words, extroverts are sociable because their brains are good at handling competing demands on their attention—which is just what dinner-party conversation involves. In contrast, introverts often feel repelled by social events that force them to attend to many people at once.

Consider that the simplest social interaction between two people requires performing an astonishing array of tasks: interpreting what the other person is saying; reading body language and facial expressions; smoothly taking turns talking and listening; responding to what the other person said; assessing whether you're being understood; determining whether you're well received, and, if not, figuring out how to improve or remove yourself from the situation. Think of what it takes to juggle all this at once! And that's just a one-on-one conversation. Now imagine the multitasking required in a group setting like a dinner party.

So when introverts assume the observer role, as when they write novels, or contemplate unified field theory—or fall quiet at dinner parties—they're not demonstrating a failure of will or a lack of energy. They're simply doing what they're constitutionally suited for.

~

The Lieberman experiment helps us understand what trips up introverts socially. It doesn't show us how they can shine.

Consider the case of an unassuming-looking fellow named Jon Berghoff. Jon is a stereotypical introvert, right down to his physical appearance: lean, wiry body; sharply etched nose and cheekbones; thoughtful expression on his bespectacled face. He's not much of a talker, but what he says is carefully considered, especially when he's in a group: "If I'm in a room with ten people and I have a choice between talking and not talking," he says, "I'm the one not talking. When people ask, 'Why aren't you saying anything?' I'm the guy they're saying it to."

Jon is also a standout salesman, and has been ever since he was a teenager. In the summer of 1999, when he was still a junior in high school, he started working as an entry-level distributor, selling Cutco kitchen products. The job had him going into customers' homes, selling knives. It was one of the most intimate sales situations imaginable, not in a boardroom or a car dealership, but inside a potential client's kitchen, selling them a product they'd use daily to help put food on the table.

Within Jon's first eight weeks on the job, he sold $50,000 worth of knives. He went on to be the company's top representative from over 40,000 new recruits that year. By the year 2000, when he was still a high school senior, Jon had generated more than $135,000 in commissions and had broken more than twenty-five national and regional sales records. Meanwhile, back in high school, he was still a socially awkward guy who hid inside the library at lunchtime. But by 2002 he'd recruited, hired, and trained ninety other sales reps, and increased territory sales 500 percent over the previous year. Since then, Jon has launched Global Empowerment Coaching, his own personal coaching and sales training business. To date he's given hundreds of speeches, training seminars, and private consultations to more than 30,000 salespeople and managers.

What's the secret of Jon's success? One important clue comes from an experiment by the developmental psychologist Avril Thorne, now a professor at the University of California, Santa Cruz. Thorne gathered fifty-two young women—twenty-six introverts and twenty-six extroverts—and assigned them to two different conversational pairings. Each person had one ten-minute conversation with a partner of her own type and a second conversation of equal length with her "dispositional opposite." Thorne's team taped the conversations and asked the participants to listen to a playback tape.

This process revealed some surprising findings. The introverts and extroverts participated about equally, giving the lie to the idea that introverts always talk less. But the introvert pairs tended to focus on one or two serious subjects of conversation, while the extrovert pairs chose lighter-hearted and wider-ranging topics. Often the introverts discussed problems or conflicts in their lives: school, work, friendships, and so on.

Perhaps because of this fondness for "problem talk," they tended to adopt the role of adviser, taking turns counseling each other on the problem at hand. The extroverts, by contrast, were more likely to offer casual information about themselves that established commonality with the other person: *You have a new dog? That's great. A friend of mine has an amazing tank of saltwater fish!*

But the most interesting part of Thorne's experiment was how much the two types appreciated each other. Introverts talking to extroverts chose cheerier topics, reported making conversation more easily, and described conversing with extroverts as a "breath of fresh air." In contrast, the extroverts felt that they could relax more with introvert partners and were freer to confide their problems. They didn't feel pressure to be falsely upbeat.

These are useful pieces of social information. Introverts and extroverts sometimes feel mutually put off, but Thorne's research suggests how much each has to offer the other. Extroverts need to know that introverts—who often seem to disdain the superficial—may be only too happy to be tugged along to a more lighthearted place; and introverts, who sometimes feel as if their propensity for problem talk makes them a drag, should know that they make it safe for others to get serious.

Thorne's research also helps us to understand Jon Berghoff's astonishing success at sales. He has turned his affinity for serious conversation, and for adopting an advisory role rather than a persuasive one, into a kind of therapy for his prospects. "I discovered early on that people don't buy from me because they understand what I'm selling," explains Jon. "They buy because they feel understood."

Jon also benefits from his natural tendency to ask a lot of questions and to listen closely to the answers. "I got to the point where I could walk into someone's house and instead of trying to sell them some knives, I'd ask a hundred questions in a row. I could manage the entire conversation just by asking the right questions." Today, in his coaching business, Jon does the same thing. "I try to tune in to the radio station of the person I'm working with. I pay attention to the energy they exude. It's easy for me to do that because I'm in my head a lot, anyways."

But doesn't salesmanship require the ability to get excited, to pump people up? Not according to Jon. "A lot of people believe that selling requires being a fast talker, or knowing how to use charisma to persuade. Those things do require an extroverted way of communicating. But in sales there's a truism that 'we have two ears and one mouth and we should use them proportionately.' I believe that's what makes someone really good at selling or consulting—the number-one thing is they've got to really listen well. When I look at the top salespeople in my organization, none of those extroverted qualities are the key to their success."

~

And now back to Greg and Emily's impasse. We've just acquired two crucial pieces of information: first, Emily's distaste for conversational multitasking is real and explicable; and second, when introverts are able to experience conversations in their own way, they make deep and enjoyable connections with others.

It was only once they accepted these two realities that Greg and Emily found a way to break their stalemate. Instead of focusing on the *number* of dinner parties they'd give, they started talking about the *format* of the parties. Instead of seating everyone around a big table, which would require the kind of all-hands conversational multitasking Emily dislikes so much, why not serve dinner buffet style, with people eating in small, casual conversational groupings on the sofas and floor pillows? This would allow Greg to gravitate to his usual spot at the center of the room and Emily to hers on the outskirts, where she could have the kind of intimate, one-on-one conversations she enjoys.

This issue solved, the couple was now free to address the thornier question of how many parties to give. After some back-and-forth, they agreed on two evenings a month—twenty-four dinners a year—instead of fifty-two. Emily still doesn't look forward to these events. But she sometimes enjoys them in spite of herself. And Greg gets to host the evenings he enjoys so much, to hold on to his identity, and to be with the person he most adores—all at the same time.

ON COBBLERS AND GENERALS

How to Cultivate Quiet Kids in a
World That Can't Hear Them

*With anything young and tender the most important part of the task is the
beginning of it; for that is the time at which the character is being formed
and the desired impression more readily taken.*

— PLATO, *THE REPUBLIC*

Mark Twain once told a story about a man who scoured the planet looking for the greatest general who ever lived. When the man was informed
that the person he sought had already died and gone to heaven, he
made a trip to the Pearly Gates to look for him. Saint Peter pointed at a
regular-looking Joe.

"That isn't the greatest of all generals," protested the man. "I knew
that person when he lived on Earth, and he was only a cobbler."

"I know that," said Saint Peter, "but if he *had* been a general, he
would have been the greatest of them all."

We should all look out for cobblers who might have been great generals. Which means focusing on introverted children, whose talents are
too often stifled, whether at home, at school, or on the playground.

Consider this cautionary tale, told to me by Dr. Jerry Miller, a child
psychologist and the director of the Center for the Child and the Family at
the University of Michigan. Dr. Miller had a patient named Ethan, whose

parents brought him for treatment on four separate occasions. Each time, the parents voiced the same fears that something was wrong with their child. Each time, Dr. Miller assured them that Ethan was perfectly fine.

The reason for their initial concern was simple enough. Ethan was seven, and his four-year-old brother had beaten him up several times. Ethan didn't fight back. His parents —both of them outgoing, take-charge types with high-powered corporate jobs and a passion for competitive golf and tennis—were OK with their younger son's aggression, but worried that Ethan's passivity was "going to be the story of his life."

As Ethan grew older, his parents tried in vain to instill "fighting spirit" in him. They sent him onto the baseball diamond and the soccer field, but Ethan just wanted to go home and read. He wasn't even competitive at school. Though very bright, he was a B student. He could have done better, but preferred to focus on his hobbies, especially building model cars. He had a few close friends, but was never in the thick of classroom social life. Unable to account for his puzzling behavior, Ethan's parents thought he might be depressed.

But Ethan's problem, says Dr. Miller, was not depression but a classic case of poor "parent-child fit." Ethan was tall, skinny, and unathletic; he looked like a stereotypical nerd. His parents were sociable, assertive people, who were "always smiling, always talking to people while dragging Ethan along behind them."

Compare their worries about Ethan to Dr. Miller's assessment: "He was like the classic Harry Potter kid—he was always reading," says Dr. Miller enthusiastically. "He enjoyed any form of imaginative play. He loved to build things. He had so many things he wanted to tell you about. He had more acceptance of his parents than they had of him. He didn't define them as pathological, just as different from himself. That same kid in a different home would be a model child."

But Ethan's own parents never found a way to see him in that light. The last thing Dr. Miller heard was that his parents finally consulted with another psychologist who agreed to "treat" their son. And now Dr. Miller is the one who's worried about Ethan.

"This is a clear case of an 'iatrogenic' problem,'" he says. "That's when the treatment makes you sick. The classic example is when you use treatment to try to make a gay child into a straight one. I worry for that kid. These parents are very caring and well-meaning people. They feel that without treatment, they're not preparing their son for society. That he needs more fire in him. Maybe there's truth to that last part; I don't know. But whether there is or not, I firmly believe that it's impossible to change that kid. I worry that they're taking a perfectly healthy boy and damaging his sense of self."

Of course, it doesn't have to be a bad fit when extroverted parents have an introverted child. With a little mindfulness and understanding, any parent can have a good fit with any kind of child, says Dr. Miller. But parents need to step back from their own preferences and see what the world looks like to their quiet children.

~

Take the case of Joyce and her seven-year-old daughter, Isabel. Isabel is an elfin second grader who likes to wear glittery sandals and colorful rubber bracelets snaking up her skinny arms. She has several best friends with whom she exchanges confidences, and she gets along with most of the kids in her class. She's the type to throw her arms around a classmate who's had a bad day; she even gives her birthday presents away to charity. That's why her mother, Joyce, an attractive, good-natured woman with a wisecracking sense of humor and a bring-it-on demeanor, was so confused by Isabel's problems at school.

In first grade, Isabel often came home consumed with worry over the class bully, who hurled mean comments at anyone sensitive enough to feel bruised by them. Even though the bully usually picked on other kids, Isabel spent hours dissecting the meaning of the bully's words, what her true intentions had been, even what the bully might be suffering at home that could possibly motivate her to behave so dreadfully at school.

By second grade, Isabel started asking her mother not to arrange play dates without checking with her first. Usually she preferred to stay home. When Joyce picked up Isabel from school, she often found the other girls gathered into groups and Isabel off on the playground, shooting baskets by herself. "She just wasn't in the mix. I had to stop doing pickups for a while," recalls Joyce. "It was just too upsetting for me to watch." Joyce couldn't understand why her sweet, loving daughter wanted to spend so much time alone. She worried that something was wrong with Isabel. Despite what she'd always thought about her daughter's empathetic nature, might Isabel lack the ability to relate with others?

It was only when I suggested that Joyce's daughter might be an introvert, and explained what that was, that Joyce started thinking differently about Isabel's experiences at school. And from Isabel's perspective, things didn't sound alarming at all. "I need a break after school," she told me later. "School is hard because a lot of people are in the room, so you get tired. I freak out if my mom plans a play date without telling me, because I don't want to hurt my friends' feelings. But I'd rather stay home. At a friend's house you have to do the things other people want to do. I like hanging out with my mom after school because I can learn from her. She's been alive longer than me. We have thoughtful conversations. I like having thoughtful conversations because they make people happy."*

Isabel is telling us, in all her second-grade wisdom, that introverts relate to other people. Of course they do. They just do it in their own way.

Now that Joyce understands Isabel's needs, mother and daughter brainstorm happily, figuring out strategies to help Isabel navigate her school day. "Before, I would have had Isabel going out and seeing people all the time, packing her time after school full of activities," says Joyce. "Now I understand that it's very stressful for her to be in school, so we figure out together how much socializing makes sense and when it should happen." Joyce doesn't mind when Isabel wants to hang out alone in her room after school or leave a birthday party a little earlier than the other kids. She also understands that since Isabel doesn't see any of this as a problem, there's no reason that she should.

Joyce has also gained insight into how to help her daughter manage playground politics. Once, Isabel was worried about how to divide her time among three friends who didn't get along with each other. "My initial instinct," says Joyce, "would be to say, *Don't worry about it! Just*

---

* Some who read this book before publication commented that the quote from Isabel couldn't possibly be accurate—"no second grader talks that way!" But this is what she said.

play with them all! But now I understand that Isabel's a different kind of person. She has trouble strategizing about how to handle all these people simultaneously on the playground. So we talk about who she's going to play with and when, and we rehearse things she can tell her friends to smooth the situation over."

Another time, when Isabel was a little older, she felt upset because her friends sat at two different tables in the lunch room. One table was populated with her quieter friends, the other with the class extroverts. Isabel described the second group as "loud, talking all the time, sitting on top of each other—*ugh!*" But she was sad because her best friend Amanda loved to sit at the "crazy table," even though she was also friends with the girls at the "more relaxed and chill table." Isabel felt torn. Where should she sit?

Joyce's first thought was that the "crazy table" sounded like more fun. But she asked Isabel what *she* preferred. Isabel thought for a minute and said, "Maybe every now and then I'll sit with Amanda, but I do like being quieter and taking a break at lunch from everything."

Why would you want to do that? thought Joyce. But she caught herself before she said it out loud. "Sounds good to me," she told Isabel. "And Amanda still loves you. She just really likes that other table. But it doesn't mean she doesn't like you. And you should get yourself the peaceful time you need."

Understanding introversion, says Joyce, has changed the way she parents—and she can't believe it took her so long. "When I see Isabel being her wonderful self, I value it even if the world may tell her she should want to be at that other table. In fact, looking at that table through her eyes, it helps me reflect on how I might be perceived by others and how I need to be aware and manage my extroverted 'default' so as not to miss the company of others like my sweet daughter."

Joyce has also come to appreciate Isabel's sensitive ways. "Isabel is an old soul," she says. "You forget that she's only a child. When I talk to her, I'm not tempted to use that special tone of voice that people reserve for children, and I don't adapt my vocabulary. I talk to her the way I would to any adult. She's very sensitive, very caring. She worries about other people's well-being. She can be easily overwhelmed, but all these things go together and I love this about my daughter."

~

Joyce is as caring a mother as I've seen, but she had a steep learning curve as parent to her daughter because of their difference in temperaments. Would she have enjoyed a more natural parent-child fit if she'd been an introvert herself? Not necessarily. Introverted parents can face challenges of their own. Sometimes painful childhood memories can get in the way.

Emily Miller, a clinical social worker in Ann Arbor, Michigan, told me about a little girl she treated, Ava, whose shyness was so extreme that it prevented her from making friends or from concentrating in class. Recently she sobbed when asked to join a group singing in front of the classroom, and her mother, Sarah, decided to seek Miller's help. When Miller asked Sarah, a successful business journalist, to act as a partner in Ava's treatment, Sarah burst into tears. She'd been a shy child, too, and felt guilty that she'd passed on to Ava her terrible burden.

"I hide it better now, but I'm still just like my daughter," she explained. "I can approach anyone, but only as long as I'm behind a journalist's notebook."

Sarah's reaction is not unusual for the pseudo-extrovert parent of a shy child, says Miller. Not only is Sarah reliving her own childhood, but she's projecting onto Ava the worst of her own memories. But Sarah needs to understand that she and Ava are not the same person, even if they do seem to have inherited similar temperaments. For one thing, Ava is influenced by her father, too, and by any number of environmental factors, so her temperament is bound to have a different expression. Sarah's own distress need not be her daughter's, and it does Ava a great disservice to assume that it will be. With the right guidance, Ava may get to the point where her shyness is nothing more than a small and infrequent annoyance.

But even parents who still have work to do on their own self-esteem can be enormously helpful to their kids, according to Miller. Advice from a parent who appreciates how a child feels is inherently validating. If your son is nervous on the first day of school, it helps to tell him that you felt the same way when you started school and still do sometimes at work, but that it gets easier with time. Even if he doesn't believe you, you'll signal that you understand and accept him.

You can also use your empathy to help you judge when to encourage him to face his fears, and when this would be too overwhelming. For example, Sarah might know that singing in front of the classroom really is too big a step to ask Ava to take all at once. But she might also sense that singing in private with a small and *simpatico* group, or with one trusted friend, is a manageable first step, even if Ava protests at first. She can, in other words, sense when to push Ava, and how much.

~

The psychologist Elaine Aron, whose work on sensitivity I described in chapter 6, offers insight into these questions when she writes about Jim, one of the best fathers she knows. Jim is a carefree extrovert with two young daughters. The first daughter, Betsy, is just like him, but the second daughter, Lily, is more sensitive—a keen but anxious observer of her world. Jim is a friend of Aron's, so he knew all about sensitivity and introversion. He embraced Lily's way of being, but at the same time he didn't want her to grow up shy.

So, writes Aron, he "became determined to introduce her to every potentially pleasurable opportunity in life, from ocean waves, tree climbing, and new foods to family reunions, soccer, and varying her clothes rather than wearing one comfortable uniform. In almost every instance, Lily initially thought these novel experiences were not such good ideas, and Jim *always* respected her opinion. He never forced her, although he could be very persuasive. He simply shared his view of a situation with her—the safety and pleasures involved, the similarities to things she already liked. He would wait for that little gleam in her eye that said she wanted to join in with the others, even if she couldn't yet.

"Jim always assessed these situations carefully to ensure that she would not ultimately be frightened, but rather be able to experience pleasure and success. Sometimes he held her back until she was overly ready. Above all, he kept it an internal conflict, not a conflict between him and her. . . . And if she or anyone else comments on her quietness or hesitancy, Jim's prompt reply is, 'That's just your style. Other people have different styles. But this is yours. You like to take your time and be sure.' Jim also knows that part of her style is befriending anyone whom others tease, doing careful work, noticing everything going on in the family, and being the best soccer strategist in her league."

One of the best things you can do for an introverted child is to work with him on his reaction to novelty. Remember that introverts react not only to new people, but also to new places and events. So don't mistake your child's caution in new situations for an inability to relate to others. *He's recoiling from novelty or overstimulation, not from human contact.* As we saw in the last chapter, introversion-extroversion levels are not correlated with either agreeableness or the enjoyment of intimacy. Introverts are just as likely as the next kid to seek others' company, though often in smaller doses.

The key is to expose your child gradually to new situations and people—taking care to respect his limits, even when they seem extreme. This produces more-confident kids than either overprotection or pushing too hard. Let him know that his feelings are normal and natural, but also that there's nothing to be afraid of: "I know it can feel funny to play with someone you've never met, but I bet that boy would love to play trucks with you if you asked him." Go at your child's pace; don't rush him. If he's young, make the initial introductions with the other little boy if you have to. And stick around in the background—or, when he's really little, with a gentle, supportive hand on his back—for as long as he seems to benefit from your presence. When he takes social risks, let him know you admire his efforts: "I saw you go up to those new kids yesterday. I know that can be difficult, and I'm proud of you."

The same goes for new situations. Imagine a child who's more afraid of the ocean than are other kids the same age. Thoughtful parents recognize that this fear is natural and even wise; the ocean is indeed dangerous. But they don't allow her to spend the summer on the safety of the dunes, and neither do they drop her in the water and expect her to swim. Instead they signal that they understand her unease, while urging her to take small steps. Maybe they play in the sand for a few days with the ocean waves crashing at a safe distance. Then one day they approach the water's edge, perhaps with the child riding on a parent's shoulders. They wait for calm weather, or low tide, to immerse a toe, then a foot, then a knee. They don't rush; every small step is a giant stride in a child's world. When ultimately she learns to swim like a fish, she has reached a crucial turning point in her relationship not only with water but also with fear.

Slowly your child will see that it's worth punching through her wall of discomfort to get to the fun on the other side. She'll learn how to do the punching by herself. As Dr. Kenneth Rubin, the director of the Center for Children, Relationships and Culture at the University of Maryland, writes, "If you're consistent in helping your young child learn to regulate his or her emotions and behaviors in soothing and supportive ways, something rather magical will begin to happen: in time, you might watch your daughter seem to be silently reassuring herself: 'Those kids are having fun, I can go over there.' He or she is learning to self-regulate fearfulness and wariness."

If you want your child to learn these skills, don't let her hear you call her "shy": she'll believe the label and experience her nervousness as a fixed trait rather than an emotion she can control. She also knows full well that "shy" is a negative word in our society. Above all, do not shame her for her shyness.

If you can, it's best to teach your child self-coaxing skills while he's still very young, when there's less stigma associated with social hesitancy. Be a role model by greeting strangers in a calm and friendly way, and by getting together with your own friends. Similarly, invite some of his classmates to your house. Let him know gently that when you're together with others, it's not OK to whisper or tug at your pants leg to communicate his needs; he needs to speak up. Make sure that his social encounters are pleasant by selecting kids who aren't overly aggressive and playgroups that have a friendly feel to them. Have your child play with younger kids if this gives him confidence, older kids if they inspire him.

If he's not clicking with a particular child, don't force it; you want most of his early social experiences to be positive. Arrange for him to enter new social situations as gradually as possible. When you're going to a birthday party, for example, talk in advance about what the party will be like and how the child might greet her peers ("First I'll say 'Happy birthday, Joey,' and then I'll say 'Hi, Sabrina.'"). And make sure to get there early. It's much easier to be one of the earlier guests, so your child feels as if other people are joining him in a space that he "owns," rather than having to break into a preexisting group.

Similarly, if your child is nervous before school starts for the year, bring him to see his classroom and, ideally, to meet the teacher one-on-one, as well as other friendly-looking adults, such as principals and guidance counselors, janitors and cafeteria workers. You can be subtle about this: "I've never seen your new classroom, why don't we drive by and take a look?" Figure out together where the bathroom is, what the policy is for going there, the route from the classroom to the cafeteria, and where the school bus will pick him up at day's end. Arrange playdates during the summer with compatible kids from his class.

You can also teach your child simple social strategies to get him through uncomfortable moments. Encourage him to look confident even if he's not feeling it. Three simple reminders go a long way: smile, stand up straight, and make eye contact. Teach him to look for friendly faces in a crowd. Bobby, a three-year-old, didn't like going to his city preschool because at recess the class left the safe confines of the classroom and played on the roof with the bigger kids in the older classes. He felt so intimidated that he wanted to go to school only on rainy days when there was no roof time. His parents helped him figure out which kids he felt comfortable playing with, and to understand that a noisy group of older boys didn't have to spoil his fun.

If you think that you're not up to all this, or that your child could use extra practice, ask a pediatrician for help locating a social skills workshop in your area. These workshops teach kids how to enter groups, introduce themselves to new peers, and read body language and facial expressions. And they can help your child navigate what for many introverted kids is the trickiest part of their social lives: the school day.

~

It's a Tuesday morning in October, and the fifth-grade class at a public school in New York City is settling down for a lesson on the three branches of American government. The kids sit cross-legged on a rug in a brightly lit corner of the room while their teacher, perched on a chair with a textbook in her lap, takes a few minutes to explain the basic concepts. Then it's time for a group activity applying the lesson.

"This classroom gets so messy after lunch," says the teacher. "There's bubble gum under the tables, food wrappers everywhere, and Cheese Nips all over the floor. We don't like our room to be so messy, do we?"

The students shake their heads no.

"Today we're going to do something about this problem—together," says the teacher.

She divides the class into three groups of seven kids each: a legislative group, tasked with enacting a law to regulate lunchtime behavior; an executive group, which must decide how to enforce the law; and a judicial branch, which has to come up with a system for adjudicating messy eaters.

The kids break excitedly into their groups, seating themselves in three large clusters. There's no need to move any furniture. Since so much of the curriculum is designed for group work, the classroom desks are already arranged in pods of seven desks each. The room erupts in a merry din. Some of the kids who'd looked deathly bored during the ten-minute lecture are now chattering with their peers.

But not all of them. When you see the kids as one big mass, they look like a room full of joyfully squirming puppies. But when you focus on individual children—like Maya, a redhead with a ponytail, wire-rimmed glasses, and a dreamy expression on her face—you get a strikingly different picture.

In Maya's group, the "executive branch," everyone is talking at once. Maya hangs back. Samantha, tall and plump in a purple T-shirt, takes charge. She pulls a sandwich bag from her knapsack and announces, "Whoever's holding the plastic bag gets to talk!" The students pass around the bag, each contributing a thought in turn. They remind me of the kids in The Lord of the Flies civic-mindedly passing around their conch shell, at least until all hell breaks loose.

Maya looks overwhelmed when the bag makes its way to her.

"I agree," she says, handing it like a hot potato to the next person.

The bag circles the table several times. Each time Maya passes it to her neighbor, saying nothing. Finally the discussion is done. Maya looks troubled. She's embarrassed, I'm guessing, that she hasn't participated. Samantha reads from her notebook a list of enforcement mechanisms that the group has brainstormed.

"Rule Number 1," she says. "If you break the laws, you miss recess. . . ."

"Wait!" interrupts Maya. "I have an idea!"

"Go ahead," says Samantha, a little impatiently. But Maya, who like many sensitive introverts seems attuned to the subtlest cues for disapproval, notices the sharpness in Samantha's voice. She opens her mouth to speak, but lowers her eyes, only managing something rambling and unintelligible. No one can hear her. No one tries. The cool girl in the group—light-years ahead of the rest in her slinkiness and fashion-forward clothes—sighs dramatically. Maya peters off in confusion, and the cool girl says, "OK, Samantha, you can keep reading the rules now."

The teacher asks the executive branch for a recap of its work. Everyone vies for airtime. Everyone except Maya. Samantha takes charge as usual, her voice carrying over everyone else's, until the rest of the group falls silent. Her report doesn't make a lot of sense, but she's so confident and good-natured that it doesn't seem to matter.

Maya, for her part, sits curled up at the periphery of the group, writing her name over and over again in her notebook, in big block letters, as if to reassert her identity. At least to herself.

Earlier, Maya's teacher had told me that she's an intellectually alive student who shines in her essay-writing. She's a gifted softball player. And she's kind to others, offering to tutor other children who lag behind academically. But none of Maya's positive attributes were evident that morning.

~

Any parent would be dismayed to think that this was their child's experience of learning, of socializing, and of herself. Maya is an introvert; she is out of her element in a noisy and overstimulating classroom where lessons are taught in large groups. Her teacher told me that she'd do much better in a school with a calm atmosphere where she could work with other kids who are "equally hardworking and attentive to detail," and where a larger portion of the day would involve independent work. Maya needs to learn to assert herself in groups, of course, but will experiences like the one I witnessed teach her this skill?

The truth is that many schools are designed for extroverts. Introverts need different kinds of instruction from extroverts, write College of William and Mary education scholars Jill Burruss and Lisa Kaenzig. And too often, "very little is made available to that learner except constant advice on becoming more social and gregarious."

We tend to forget that there's nothing sacrosanct about learning in large group classrooms, and that we organize students this way not because it's the best way to learn but because it's cost-efficient, and what else would we do with our children while the grown-ups are at work? If your child prefers to work autonomously and socialize one-on-one, there's nothing wrong with her; she just happens not to fit the prevailing model. The purpose of school should be to prepare kids for the rest of their lives, but too often what kids need to be prepared for is surviving the school day itself.

The school environment can be highly unnatural, especially from the perspective of an introverted child who loves to work intensely on projects he cares about, and hang out with one or two friends at a time. In the morning, the door to the bus opens and discharges its occupants in a noisy, jostling mass. Academic classes are dominated by group discussions in which a teacher prods him to speak up. He eats lunch in the cacophonous din of the cafeteria, where he has to jockey for a place at a crowded table. Worst of all, there's little time to think or create. The structure of the day is almost guaranteed to sap his energy rather than stimulate it.

Why do we accept this one-size-fits-all situation as a given when we know perfectly well that adults don't organize themselves this way? We often marvel at how introverted, geeky kids "blossom" into secure and happy adults. We liken it to a metamorphosis. However, maybe it's not the children who change but their environments. As adults, they get to select the careers, spouses, and social circles that suit them. They don't have to live in whatever culture they're plunked into. Research from a field known as "person-environment fit" shows that people flourish when, in the words of psychologist Brian Little, they're "engaged in occupations, roles or settings that are concordant with their personalities." The inverse is also true: kids stop learning when they feel emotionally threatened.

No one knows this better than LouAnne Johnson, a tough-talking former marine and schoolteacher widely recognized for educating some of the most troubled teens in the California public school system (Michelle Pfeiffer played her in the movie *Dangerous Minds*). I visited Johnson at her home in Truth or Consequences, New Mexico, to find out more about her experience teaching children of all stripes.

Johnson happens to be skilled at working with very shy children— which is no accident. One of her techniques is to share with her students how timid she herself used to be. Her earliest school memory is of being made to stand on a stool in kindergarten because she preferred to sit in the corner and read books, and the teacher wanted her to "interact." "Many shy children are thrilled to discover that their teacher had been as shy as they were," she told me. "I remember one very shy girl in my high school English class whose mother thanked me for telling her daughter that I believed she would peak much later in life, so not to worry that she didn't shine in high school. She said that one comment had changed her daughter's entire outlook on life. Imagine—one offhand comment made such an impact on a tender child."

When encouraging shy children to speak, says Johnson, it helps to make the topic so compelling that they forget their inhibitions. She advises asking students to discuss hot-button subjects like "Boys have life a lot easier than girls do." Johnson, who is a frequent public speaker on education despite a lifelong public speaking phobia, knows firsthand how well this works. "I haven't overcome my shyness," she says. "It is sitting in the corner, calling to me. But I am passionate about changing our schools, so my passion overcomes my shyness once I get started on a speech. If you find something that arouses your passion or provides a welcome challenge, you forget yourself for a while. It's like an emotional vacation."

But don't risk having children make a speech to the class unless you've provided them with the tools to know with reasonable confidence that it will go well. Have kids practice with a partner and in small groups, and if they're still too terrified, don't force it. Experts believe that negative public speaking experiences in childhood can leave children with a lifelong terror of the podium.

So, what kind of school environment would work best for the Mayas of the world? First, some thoughts for teachers:

- Don't think of introversion as something that needs to be cured. If an introverted child needs help with social skills, teach her or recommend training outside class, just as you'd do for a student who needs extra attention in math or reading. But celebrate these kids for who they are. "The typical comment on many children's report cards is, 'I wish Molly would talk more in class,'" Pat Adams, the former head of the Emerson School for gifted students in Ann Arbor, Michigan, told me. "But here we have an understanding that many kids are introspective. We try to bring them out, but we don't make it a big deal. We think about introverted kids as having a different learning style."

- Studies show that one third to one half of us are introverts. This means that you have more introverted kids in your class than you think. Even at a young age, some introverts become adept at acting like extroverts, making it tough to spot them. Balance teaching methods to serve all the kids in your class. Extroverts tend to like movement, stimulation, collaborative work. Introverts prefer lectures, downtime, and independent projects. Mix it up fairly.

- Introverts often have one or two deep interests that are not necessarily shared by their peers. Sometimes they're made to feel freaky for the force of these passions, when in fact studies show that this sort of intensity is a prerequisite to talent development. Praise these kids for their interests, encourage them, and help them find like-minded friends, if not in the classroom, then outside it.

- Some collaborative work is fine for introverts, even beneficial. But it should take place in small groups—pairs or threesomes—and be carefully structured so that each child knows her role. Roger Johnson, co-director of the Cooperative Learning Center at the University of Minnesota, says that shy or introverted kids benefit especially from well-managed small-group work because "they are usually very comfortable talking with one or two of their class-mates to answer a question or complete a task, but would never think of raising their hand and addressing the whole class. It is very important that these students get a chance to translate their thoughts into language." Imagine how different Maya's experience would have been if her group had been smaller and someone had taken the time to say, "Samantha, you're in charge of keeping the discussion on track. Maya, your job is to take notes and read them back to the group."

- On the other hand, remember Anders Ericsson's research on Deliberate Practice from chapter 3. In many fields, it's impossible to gain mastery without knowing how to work on one's own. Have your extroverted students take a page from their introverted peers' playbooks. Teach all kids to work independently.

- Don't seat quiet kids in "high-interaction" areas of the classroom, says communications professor James McCroskey. They won't talk more in those areas; they'll feel more threatened and will have trouble concentrating. Make it easy for introverted kids to partici-pate in class, but don't insist. "Forcing highly apprehensive young people to perform orally is harmful," writes McCroskey. "It will increase apprehension and reduce self-esteem."

- If your school has a selective admissions policy, think twice be-fore basing your admissions decisions on children's performance in a playgroup setting. Many introverted kids clam up in groups of strangers, and you will not get even a glimpse of what these kids are like once they're relaxed and comfortable.

And here are some thoughts for parents. If you're lucky enough to have control over where your child goes to school, whether by scouting out a magnet school, moving to a neighborhood whose public schools you like, or sending your kids to private or parochial school, you can look for a school that

- prizes independent interests and emphasizes autonomy
- conducts group activities in moderation and in small, carefully managed groups
- values kindness, caring, empathy, good citizenship
- insists on orderly classrooms and hallways
- is organized into small, quiet classes
- chooses teachers who seem to understand the shy/serious/introverted/sensitive temperament
- focuses its academic/athletic/extracurricular activities on subjects that are particularly interesting to your child
- strongly enforces an anti-bullying program
- emphasizes a tolerant, down-to-earth culture
- attracts like-minded peers, for example intellectual kids, or artistic or athletic ones, depending on your child's preference

Handpicking a school may be unrealistic for many families. But whatever the school, there's much you can do to help your introverted child thrive. Figure out which subjects energize him most, and let him run with them, either with outside tutors, or extra programming like science fairs or creative writing classes. As for group activities, coach him to look for comfortable roles within larger groups. One of the advantages of group work, even for introverts, is that it often offers many different niches. Urge your child to take the initiative, and claim for himself the responsibility of note-taker, picture-drawer, or whatever role interests him most. Participation will feel more comfortable when he knows what his contribution is supposed to be.

You can also help him practice speaking up. Let him know that it's OK to take his time to gather his thoughts before he speaks, even if it seems as if everyone else is jumping into the fray. At the same time, advise him that contributing earlier in a discussion is a lot easier than waiting until everyone else has talked and letting the tension build as he waits to take his turn. If he's not sure what to say, or is uncomfortable making assertions, help him play to his strengths. Does he tend to ask thoughtful questions? Praise this quality, and teach him that good questions are often more useful than proposing answers. Does he tend to look at things from his own unique point of view? Teach him how valuable this is, and discuss how he might share his outlook with others.

Explore real-life scenarios: for example, Maya's parents could sit down with her and figure out how she might have handled the executive-group exercise differently. Try role-playing, in situations that are as specific as possible. Maya could rehearse in her own words what it's like to say "I'll be the note-taker!" or "What if we make a rule that anyone who throws wrappers on the floor has to spend the last ten minutes of lunch picking up litter?"

The catch is that this depends on getting Maya to open up and tell you what happened during her school day. Even if they're generally forthcoming, many kids won't share experiences that made them feel ashamed. The younger your child is, the more likely she is to open up, so you should start this process as early in her school career as possible. Ask your child for information in a gentle, nonjudgmental way, with specific, clear questions. Instead of "How was your day?" try "What did you do in math class today?" Instead of "Do you like your teacher?" ask "What do you like about your teacher?" Or "What do you not like so much?" Let her take her time to answer. Try to avoid asking, in the overly bright voice of parents everywhere, "Did you have fun in school today?!" She'll sense how important it is that the answer be yes.

If she still doesn't want to talk, wait for her. Sometimes she'll need to decompress for hours before she's ready. You may find that she'll open up only during cozy, relaxed moments, like bathtime or bedtime. If that's the case, make sure to build these situations into the day. And if she'll talk to others, like a trusted babysitter, aunt, r older sibling, but not to you, swallow your pride and enlist help.

Finally, try not to worry if all signs suggest that your introverted child is not the most popular kid at school. It's critically important for his emotional and social development that he have one or two solid friendships, child development experts tell us, but being popular isn't necessary. Many introverted kids grow up to have excellent social skills, although they tend to join groups in their own way—waiting a while before they plunge in, or participating only for short periods. That's OK. Your child needs to acquire social skills and make friends, not turn into the most gregarious student in school. This doesn't mean that popularity isn't a lot of fun. You'll probably wish it for him, just as you might wish that he have good looks, a quick wit, or athletic talent. But make sure you're not imposing your own longings, and remember that there are many paths to a satisfying life.

~

Many of those paths will be found in passions outside the classroom. While extroverts are more likely to skate from one hobby or activity to another, introverts often stick with their enthusiasms. This gives them a major advantage as they grow, because true self-esteem comes from competence, not the other way around. Researchers have found that intense engagement in and commitment to an activity is a proven route to happiness and well-being. Well-developed talents and interests can be a great source of confidence for your child, no matter how different he might feel from his peers.

For example, Maya, the girl who was such a quiet member of the "executive branch," loves to go home every day after school and read. But she also loves softball, with all of its social and performance pressures. She still recalls the day she made the team after participating in tryouts. Maya was scared stiff, but she also felt strong—capable of hitting the ball with a good, powerful whack. "I guess all those drills finally paid off," she reflected later. "I just kept smiling. I was so excited and proud— and that feeling never went away."

For parents, however, it's not always easy to orchestrate situations where these deep feelings of satisfaction arise. You might feel, for example, that you should encourage your introverted child to play whichever sport is the ticket to friendship and esteem in your town. And that's fine, if he enjoys that sport and is good at it, as Maya is with softball. Team sports can be a great boon for anyone, especially for kids who otherwise feel uncomfortable joining groups. But let your child take the lead in picking the activities he likes best. He may not like any team sports, and that's OK. Help him look for activities where he'll meet other kids, but also have plenty of his own space. Cultivate the strengths of his disposition. If his passions seem too solitary for your taste, remember that even solo activities like painting, engineering, or creative writing can lead to communities of fellow enthusiasts.

"I have known children who found others," says Dr. Miller, "by sharing important interests: chess, elaborate role-playing games, even discussing deep interests like math or history." Rebecca Wallace-Segall, who teaches creative-writing workshops for kids and teens as director of Writopia Lab in New York City, says that the students who sign up for her classes "are often not the kids who are willing to talk for hours about fashion and celebrity. Those kids are less likely to come, perhaps because they're less inclined to analyze and dig deep—that's not their comfort zone. The so-called shy kids are often hungry to brainstorm ideas, deconstruct them, and act on them, and, paradoxically, when they're allowed to interact this way, they're not shy at all. They're connecting with each other, but in a deeper zone, in a place that's considered boring or tiresome by some of their peers." And these kids do "come out" when they're ready; most of the Writopia kids read their works at local bookstores, and a staggering number win prestigious national writing competitions.

If your child is prone to overstimulation, then it's also a good idea for her to pick activities like art or long-distance running, that depend less on performing under pressure. If she's drawn to activities that require performance, though, you can help her thrive.

When I was a kid, I loved figure skating. I could spend hours on the rink, tracing figure eights, spinning happily, or flying through the air. But on the day of my competitions, I was a wreck. I hadn't slept the night before and would often fall during moves that I had sailed through in practice. At first I believed what people told me—that I had the jitters, just like everybody else. But then I saw a TV interview with the Olympic gold medalist Katarina Witt. She said that pre-competition nerves gave her the adrenaline she needed to *win* the gold.

I knew then that Katarina and I were utterly different creatures, but it took me decades to figure out why. Her nerves were so mild that they simply energized her, while mine were constricting enough to make me choke. At the time, my very supportive mother quizzed the other skating moms about how their own daughters handled pre-competition anxiety, and came back with insights that she hoped would make me feel better. *Kristen's nervous too*, she reported. *Renée's mom says she's scared the night before a competition*. But I knew Kristen and Renée well, and I was certain that they weren't as frightened as I was.

I think it might have helped if I'd understood myself better back then. If you're the parent of a would-be figure skater, help her to accept that she has heavy-duty jitters without giving her the idea that they're fatal to success. What she's most afraid of is failing publicly. She needs to desensitize herself to this fear by getting used to competing, and even to failing. Encourage her to enter low-stakes competitions far away from home, where she feels anonymous and no one will know if she falls. Make sure she has rehearsed thoroughly. If she's planning to compete on an unfamiliar rink, try to have her practice there a few times first. Talk about what might go wrong and how to handle it: *OK, so what if you do fall and come in last place, will life still go on?* And help her visualize what it will feel like to perform her moves smoothly.

~

Unleashing a passion can transform a life, not just for the space of time that your child's in elementary or middle or high school, but way beyond. Consider the story of David Weiss, a drummer and music journalist. David is a good example of someone who grew up feeling like Charlie Brown and went on to build a life of creativity, productivity, and meaning. He loves his wife and baby son. He relishes his work. He has a wide and interesting circle of friends, and lives in New York City, which he considers the most vibrant place in the world for a music enthusiast. If you measure a life by the classic barometers of love and work, then David is a blazing success.

But it wasn't always clear, at least not to David, that his life would unfold as well as it did. As a kid, he was shy and awkward. The things that interested him, music and writing, held no value for the people who mattered most back then: his peers. "People would always tell me, 'These are the best years of your life,'" he recalls. "And I would think to myself, *I hope not!* I hated school. I remember thinking, *I've gotta get out of here*. I was in sixth grade when *Revenge of the Nerds* came out, and I looked like I stepped out of the cast. I knew I was intelligent, but I grew up in suburban Detroit, which is like ninety-nine percent of the rest of the country: if you're a good-looking person and an athlete, you're not gonna get hassled. But if you seem too smart, that's not something that kids respect you for. They're more likely to try and beat you down for it. It was my best attribute, and I definitely enjoyed using it, but it was something you also had to try and keep in check."

So how did he get from there to here? The key for David was playing the drums. "At one point," David says, "I totally overcame all my childhood stuff. And I know exactly how: I started playing the drums. Drums are my muse. They're my Yoda. When I was in middle school, the high school jazz band came and performed for us, and I thought that the coolest one by a long shot was the kid playing the drum set. To me, drummers were kind of like athletes, but musical athletes, and I loved music."

At first, for David, drumming was mostly about social validation; he stopped getting kicked out of parties by jocks twice his size. But soon it became something much deeper: "I suddenly realized this was a form of creative expression, and it totally blew my mind. I was fifteen. That's when I became committed to sticking with it. My entire life changed because of my drums, and it hasn't stopped, to this day."

David still remembers acutely what it was like to be his nine-year-old self. "I feel like I'm in touch with that person today," he says. "Whenever I'm doing something that I think is cool, like if I'm in New York City in a room full of people, interviewing Alicia Keys or something, I send a message back to that person and let him know that everything turned out OK. I feel like when I was nine, I was receiving that signal from the future, which is one of the things that gave me the strength to hang in there. I was able to create this loop between who I am now and who I was then."

The other thing that gave David strength was his parents. They focused less on developing his confidence than on making sure that he found ways to be productive. It didn't matter what he was interested in, so long as he pursued it and enjoyed himself. His father was an avid foot-ball fan, David recalls, but "the last person to say, 'How come you're not out on the football field?'" For a while David took up piano, then cello. When he announced that he wanted to switch to drumming, his parents were surprised, but never wavered. They embraced his new passion. It was their way of embracing their son.

~

If David Weiss's tale of transformation resonates for you, there's a good reason. It's a perfect example of what the psychologist Dan McAdams calls a redemptive life story—and a sign of mental health and well-being.

At the Foley Center for the Study of Lives at Northwestern University, McAdams studies the stories that people tell about themselves. We all write our life stories as if we were novelists, McAdams believes, with beginnings, conflicts, turning points, and endings. And the way we characterize our past setbacks profoundly influences how satisfied we are with our current lives. Unhappy people tend to see setbacks as contami-nants that ruined an otherwise good thing ("I was never the same again after my wife left me"), while generative adults see them as blessings in disguise ("The divorce was the most painful thing that ever happened to me, but I'm so much happier with my new wife"). Those who live the most fully realized lives—giving back to their families, societies, and ul-timately themselves—tend to find meaning in their obstacles. In a sense, McAdams has breathed new life into one of the great insights of Western mythology: that where we stumble is where our treasure lies.

For many introverts like David, adolescence is the great stumbling place, the dark and tangled thicket of low self-esteem and social unease. In middle and high school, the main currency is vivacity and gregari-ousness; attributes like depth and sensitivity don't count for much. But many introverts succeed in composing life stories much like David's: our Charlie Brown moments are the price we have to pay to bang our drums happily through the decades.

CONCLUSION

Wonderland

Our culture made a virtue of living only as extroverts. We discouraged the inner journey, the quest for a center. So we lost our center and have to find it again.

—ANAÏS NIN

Whether you're an introvert yourself or an extrovert who loves or works with one, I hope you'll benefit personally from the insights in this book. Here is a blueprint to take with you:

Love is essential; gregariousness is optional. Cherish your nearest and dearest. Work with colleagues you like and respect. Scan new acquaintances for those who might fall into the former categories or whose company you enjoy for its own sake. And don't worry about socializing with everyone else. Relationships make everyone happier, introverts included, but think quality over quantity.

The secret to life is to put yourself in the right lighting. For some it's a Broadway spotlight; for others, a lamplit desk. Use your natural powers—of persistence, concentration, insight, and sensitivity—to do work you love and work that matters. Solve problems, make art, think deeply.

Figure out what you are meant to contribute to the world and make sure you contribute it. If this requires public speaking or networking or other activities that make you uncomfortable, do them anyway. But accept that they're difficult, get the training you need to make them easier, and reward yourself when you're done.

Quit your job as a TV anchor and get a degree in library science. But if TV anchoring is what you love, then create an extroverted persona to get yourself through the day. Here's a rule of thumb for networking events: one new honest-to-goodness relationship is worth ten fistfuls of business cards. Rush home afterward and kick back on your sofa. Carve out restorative niches.

Respect your loved ones' need for socializing and your own for solitude (and vice versa if you're an extrovert).

Spend your free time the way you like, not the way you think you're supposed to. Stay home on New Year's Eve if that's what makes you happy. Skip the committee meeting. Cross the street to avoid making aimless chitchat with random acquaintances. Read. Cook. Run. Write a story. Make a deal with yourself that you'll attend a set number of social events in exchange for not feeling guilty when you beg off.

If your children are quiet, help them make peace with new situations and new people, but otherwise let them be themselves. Delight in the originality of their minds. Take pride in the strength of their consciences and the loyalty of their friendships. Don't expect them to follow the gang. Encourage them to follow their passions instead. Throw confetti when they claim the fruits of those passions, whether it's on the drummer's throne, on the softball field, or on the page.

If you're a teacher, enjoy your gregarious and participatory students. But don't forget to cultivate the shy, the gentle, the autonomous, the ones with single-minded enthusiasms for chemistry sets or parrot taxonomy or nineteenth-century art. They are the artists, engineers, and thinkers of tomorrow.

If you're a manager, remember that one third to one half of your workforce is probably introverted, whether they appear that way or not. Think twice about how you design your organization's office space. Don't expect introverts to get jazzed up about open office plans or, for that matter, lunchtime birthday parties or team-building retreats. Make the most of introverts' strengths—these are the people who can help you think deeply, strategize, solve complex problems, and spot canaries in your coal mine.

Also, remember the dangers of the New Groupthink. If it's creativity you're after, ask your employees to solve problems alone before sharing their ideas. If you want the wisdom of the crowd, gather it electronically, or in writing, and make sure people can't see each other's ideas until everyone's had a chance to contribute. Face-to-face contact is important because it builds trust, but group dynamics contain unavoidable impediments to creative thinking. Arrange for people to interact one-on-one and in small, casual groups. Don't mistake assertiveness or eloquence for good ideas. If you have a proactive work force (and I hope you do), remember that they may perform better under an introverted leader than under an extroverted or charismatic one.

Whoever you are, bear in mind that appearance is not reality. Some people act like extroverts, but the effort costs them in energy, authenticity, and even physical health. Others seem aloof or self-contained, but their inner landscapes are rich and full of drama. So the next time you see a person with a composed face and a soft voice, remember that inside her mind she might be solving an equation, composing a sonnet, designing a hat. She might, that is, be deploying the powers of quiet.

We know from myths and fairy tales that there are many different kinds of powers in this world. One child is given a light saber, another a wizard's education. The trick is not to amass all the different kinds of available power, but to use well the kind you've been granted. Introverts are offered keys to private gardens full of riches. To possess such a key is to tumble like Alice down her rabbit hole. She didn't *choose* to go to Wonderland—but she made of it an adventure that was fresh and fantastic and very much her own.

Lewis Carroll was an introvert, too, by the way. Without him, there would be no *Alice in Wonderland*. And by now, this shouldn't surprise us.

A Note on the Dedication

My grandfather was a soft-spoken man with sympathetic blue eyes, and a passion for books and ideas. He always dressed in a suit, and had a courtly way of exclaiming over whatever was exclaimable in people, especially in children. In the Brooklyn neighborhood where he served as a rabbi, the sidewalks were filled with men in black hats, women in skirts that hid their knees, and improbably well-behaved kids. On his way to synagogue, my grandfather would greet the passersby, gently praising this child's brains, that one's height, the other's command of current events. Kids adored him, businessmen respected him, lost souls clung to him.

But what he loved to do best was read. In his small apartment, where as a widower he'd lived alone for decades, all the furniture had yielded its original function to serve as a surface for piles of books: gold-leafed Hebrew texts jumbled together with Margaret Atwood and Milan Kundera. My grandfather would sit beneath a halo-shaped fluorescent light at his tiny kitchen table, sipping Lipton tea and snacking on marble cake, a book propped open on the white cotton tablecloth. In his sermons, each a tapestry of ancient and humanist thought, he'd share with his congregation the fruits of that week's study. He was a shy person who had trouble making eye contact with the audience, but he was so bold in his spiritual and intellectual explorations that when he spoke the congregation swelled to standing-room-only.

The rest of my family took its cue from him. In our house, reading was the primary group activity. On Saturday afternoons we curled up with our books in the den. It was the best of both worlds: you had the animal warmth of your family right next to you, but you also got to roam around the adventure-land inside your own head.

Yet as a preteen I began to wonder whether all this reading had marked me as "out of it," a suspicion that seemed confirmed when I went away to summer camp at the age of ten and watched as a girl with thick glasses and a high forehead refused to put down her book on the all-important first day of camp and instantly became a pariah, her days and nights a hell of social exclusion. I longed to read, too, but left my own paperbacks untouched in my suitcase (though I felt guilty about this, as if the books needed me and I was forsaking them). I saw that the girl who kept reading was considered bookish and shy, the very things that I was, too, and knew that I must hide.

After that summer, I felt less comfortable about my desire to be alone with a book. In high school, in college, and as a young lawyer, I tried to make myself appear more extroverted and less eggheady than I truly was.

But as I grew older, I drew inspiration from my grandfather's example. He was a quiet man, and a great one. When he died at the age of ninety-four, after sixty-two years at the pulpit, the NYPD had to close the streets of his neighborhood to accommodate the throngs of mourners. He would have been surprised to know this. Today, I think that one of the best things about him was his humility.

This book is dedicated, with love, to my childhood family. To my mother, with her endless enthusiasm for quiet kitchen-table chats; she gave us children the gift of intimacy. I was so lucky to have such a devoted mother. To my father, a dedicated physician who taught by example the joys of sitting for hours at a desk, hunting for knowledge, but who also came up for air to introduce me to his favorite poems and science experiments. To my brother and sister, who share to this day the warmth and affection of having grown up in our small family and household full of literature. To my grandmother, for her pluck, grit, and caring.

And in memory of my grandfather, who spoke so eloquently the language of quiet.

A Note on the Words *Introvert* and *Extrovert*

This book is about introversion as seen from a *cultural* point of view. Its primary concern is the age-old dichotomy between the "man of action" and the "man of contemplation," and how we could improve the world if only there were a greater balance of power between the two types. It focuses on the person who recognizes him- or herself somewhere in the following constellation of attributes: reflective, cerebral, bookish, unassuming, sensitive, thoughtful, serious, contemplative, subtle, introspective, inner-directed, gentle, calm, modest, solitude-seeking, shy, risk-averse, thin-skinned. *Quiet* is also about this person's opposite number: the "man of action" who is ebullient, expansive, sociable, gregarious, excitable, dominant, assertive, active, risk-taking, thick-skinned, outer-directed, lighthearted, bold, and comfortable in the spotlight.

These are broad categories, of course. Few individuals identify fully with only one or the other. But most of us recognize these types immediately, because they play meaningful roles in our culture.

Contemporary personality psychologists may have a conception of introversion and extroversion that differs from the one I use in this book. Adherents of the Big Five taxonomy often view such characteristics as the tendency to have a cerebral nature, a rich inner life, a strong conscience, some degree of anxiety (especially shyness), and a risk-averse nature as belonging to categories quite separate from introversion. To them, these traits may fall under "openness to experience," "conscientiousness," and "neuroticism."

My use of the word *introvert* is deliberately broader, drawing on the insights of Big Five psychology, but also encompassing Jungian thinking on the introvert's inner world of "inexhaustible charm" and subjective experience; Jerome Kagan's research on high reactivity and anxiety (see chapters 4 and 5); Elaine Aron's work on sensory processing sensitivity and its relationship to conscientiousness, intense feeling, inner-directedness, and depth of processing (see chapter 6); and various research on the persistence and concentration that introverts bring to problem-solving, much of it summarized wonderfully in Gerald Matthews's work (see chapter 7).

Indeed, for over three thousand years, Western culture has linked the qualities in the above constellations of adjectives. As the anthropologist C. A. Valentine once wrote:

> Western cultural traditions include a conception of individual variability which appears to be old, widespread, and persistent. In popular form this is the familiar notion of the man of action, practical man, realist, or sociable person as opposed to the thinker, dreamer, idealist, or shy individual. The most widely used labels associated with this tradition are the type designations extrovert and introvert.

Valentine's concept of introversion includes traits that contemporary psychology would classify as openness to experience ("thinker, dreamer"), conscientiousness ("idealist"), and neuroticism ("shy individual").

A long line of poets, scientists, and philosophers have also tended to group these traits together. All the way back in Genesis, the earliest book of the Bible, we had cerebral Jacob (a "quiet man dwelling in tents" who later becomes "Israel," meaning one who wrestles inwardly with God) squaring off in sibling rivalry with his brother, the swashbuckling Esau (a "skillful hunter" and "man of the field"). In classical antiquity, the physicians Hippocrates and Galen famously proposed that our temperaments—and destinies—were a function of our bodily fluids, with extra blood and "yellow bile" making us sanguine or choleric (stable or neurotic extroversion), and an excess of phlegm and "black bile" making us calm or melancholic (stable or neurotic introversion). Aristotle noted that the melancholic temperament was associated with eminence in philosophy, poetry, and the arts (today we might classify this as openness to experience). The seventeenth-century English poet John Milton wrote *Il Penseroso* ("The Thinker") and *L'Allegro* ("The Merry One"), comparing "the happy person" who frolics in the countryside and revels in the city with "the thoughtful person" who walks meditatively through the nighttime woods and studies in a "lonely Towr." (Again, today the description of *Il Penseroso* would apply not only to introversion but also to openness to experience and neuroticism.) The nineteenth-century German philosopher Schopenhauer contrasted "good-spirited" people (energetic, active, and easily bored) with his preferred type, "intelligent people" (sensitive, imaginative, and melancholic). "Mark this well, ye proud men of action!" declared his countryman Heinrich Heine. "Ye are, after all, nothing but unconscious instruments of the men of thought."

Because of this definitional complexity, I originally planned to invent my own terms for these constellations of traits. I decided against this, again for cultural reasons: the words *introvert* and *extrovert* have the advantage of being well known and highly evocative. Every time I uttered them at a dinner party or to a seatmate on an airplane, they elicited a torrent of confessions and reflections. For similar reasons, I've used the layperson's spelling of *extrovert* rather than the *extravert* one finds throughout the research literature.

Acknowledgments

I could not have written *Quiet* without the help of countless friends, family members, and colleagues, including: Richard Pine, otherwise known (to me) as Super-Agent RSP: the smartest, savviest, and menschiest literary agent that any writer could hope to work with. Richard believed unswervingly in *Quiet*, even before I did. Then he kept on believing, all the way through the five years it took me to research and write it. I consider him not only an agent but a partner in my career. I also enjoyed working with the whole team at InkWell Management, including Ethan Bassoff, Lyndsey Blessing, and Charlie Olsen.

At Crown Publishers, it has been my privilege to work with the remarkable Molly Stern and her all-star team. Rachel Klayman has got to be the most brilliant and dedicated editor in the business. She has been there at two in the afternoon and at two in the morning, spotting flaws in my reasoning and clunkers in my prose, and championing this book indefatigably. I also appreciate how generous Mary Choteborsky and Jenna Ciongoli were with their editorial talents. And I was fortunate to work with outside editor Peter Guzzardi, who has terrific instincts and a knack for making criticism sound delightful. My heartfelt thanks to all of you. This book would be a shadow of itself without your efforts.

Special thanks too to Rachel Rokicki and Julie Cepler for the creativity and enthusiasm they brought to the *Quiet* cause. And thanks to Patty Berg, Mark Birkey, Chris Brand, Stephanie Chan, Tina Constable, Laura Duffy, Songhee Kim, Kyle Kolker, Rachel Meier, Annsley Rosner, and everyone else on the team at Crown.

I have also been very lucky to work with Joel Rickett, Kate Barker, and the rest of the crackerjack group at Viking/Penguin U.K.

The marvelous people at TED embraced the ideas in this book and offered me a chance to talk about them at the TED Long Beach conference in 2012. I am grateful to Chris Anderson, Kelly Stoetzel, June Cohen, Tom Rielly, Michael Glass, Nicholas Weinberg, and the entire TED team.

Brian Little, whose work I profiled in chapter 9, has become an extraordinary mentor and friend. I met Brian early in my research process, when I asked for an interview. He gave me not only the interview but also, over the years, my own personal graduate seminar in personality psychology. I am proud to be one of his many disciples and friends.

Elaine Aron, whose research I profiled in chapter 6, inspired me with her life's work and gave generously of her time, knowledge, and life story.

I relied on the support and advice of innumerable friends, including: Marci Alboher, Gina Bianchini, Tara Bracco, Janis Brody, Greg Bylinksy, David Callahan, Helen Churko, Mark Colodny, Estie Dallett, Ben Dattner, Ben Falchuk, Christy Fletcher, Margo Flug, Jennifer Gandin Le, Rhonda Garelick, Michael Glass, Vishwa Goohya, Leeat Granek, Amy Gutman, Hillary Hazan-Glass, Wende Jaeger-Hyman, Mahima Joishy, Emily Klein, Chris Le, Rachel Lehmann-Haupt, Lori Lesser, Margot Magowan, Courtney Martin, Fran and Jerry Marton, Furaha Norton, Elizabeth O'Neill, Wendy Paris, Leanne Paluck Reiss, Marta Renzi, Gina Rudan, Howard Sackstein, Marisol Simard, Daphna Stern, Robin Stern, Tim Stock, Jillian Straus, Sam Sugiura, Tom Sugiura, Jennifer Taub, Kate Tedesco, Ruti Teitel, Seinenu Thein, Jacquette Timmons, Marie Lena Tupot, Sam Walker, Daniel Wolff, and Cali Yost. A special, super-duper thanks to Anna Beltran, Maritza Flores, and Eliza Simpson.

I am especially grateful for the forbearance of some of my oldest and dearest friends: Mark Colodny, Jeff Kaplan, Hitomi Komatsu, Cathy Lankenau-Weeks, Lawrence Mendenhall, Jonathan Sichel, Brande Stellings, Judith van der Reis, Rebecca and Jeremy Wallace-Segall, and Naomi Wolf, who remain close even though we barely had time to talk, let alone visit, during the years I wrote this book and gave birth to my two children.

Thank you, too, to my fellow members of the Invisible Institute, who inspire and astonish me on a regular basis: Gary Bass, Elizabeth Devita-Raeburn, Abby Ellin, Randi Epstein, Sheri Fink, Christine Kenneally, Judith Matloff, Katie Orenstein, Annie Murphy Paul, Pamela Paul, Joshua Prager, Alissa Quart, Paul Raeburn, Kathy Rich, Gretchen Rubin, Lauren Sandler, Deborah Siegel, Rebecca Skloot, Debbie Stier, Stacy Sullivan, Maia Szalavitz, Harriet Washington, and Tom Zoellner.

For inspiration that I would bottle and sell if I could, I thank the owners of the cottage in Amagansett: Alison (Sunny) Warriner and Jeanne Mclemore. The same goes for Evelyn and Michael Polesny, proprietors of the magical Doma Café in Greenwich Village, where I wrote most of this book.

Thanks also to those who helped with various aspects of getting *Quiet* off the ground: Nancy Ancowitz, Mark Colodny, Bill Cunningham, Ben Dattner, Aaron Fedor, Boris Fishman, David Gallo, Christopher Glazek, Suzy Hansen, Jayme Johnson, Jennifer Kahweiler, David Lavin, Ko-Shin Mandell, Andres Richner, JillEllyn Riley, Gretchen Rubin, Gregory Samanez-Larkin, Stephen Schueller, Sree Sreenivasan, Robert Stelmack, Linda Stone, John Thompson, Charles Yao, Helen Wan, Georgia Weinberg, and Naomi Wolf.

I owe a special debt to the people I wrote about or quoted, some of whom have become friends: Michel Anteby, Jay Belsky, Jon Berghoff, Wayne Cascio, Hung Wei Chien, Boykin Curry, Tom DeMarco, Richard Depue, Dr. Janice Dorn, Anders Ericsson, Jason Fried, Francesca Gino, Adam Grant, William Graziano, Stephen Harvill, David Hofmann, Richard Howard, Jadzia Jagiellowicz, Roger Johnson, Jerry Kagan, Guy Kawasaki, Camelia Kuhnen, Tiffany Liao, Richard Lippa, Joanna Lipper, Adam McHugh, Mike Mika, Emily Miller, Jerry Miller, Quinn Mills, Purvi Modi, Joseph Newman, Preston Ni, Carl Schwartz, Dave Smith, Mark Snyder, Jacqueline Strickland, Avril Thorne, David Weiss, Mike Wei, and Shoya Zichy.

There are many, many others who aren't mentioned by name in *Quiet* but who gave generously of their time and wisdom, via interviews and the like, and who dramatically informed my thinking: Marco Acevedo, Anna Allanbrook, Andrew Ayre, Dawn Rivers Baker, Susan Blew, Jonathan Cheek, Jeremy Chua, Dave Coleman, Ben Dattner, Matthew Davis, Scott Derue, Carl Elliott, Brad Feld, Kurt Fischer, Alex Forbes,

Donna Genyk, Carole Grand, Stephen Gerras, Lenny Gucciardi, Anne Harrington, Naomi Karten, James McElroy, Richard McNally, Greg Oldham, Christopher Peterson, Lise Quintana, Lena Roy, Chris Scherpenseel, Hersh Shefrin, Nancy Snidman, Sandy Tinkler, Virginia Vitzthum, E. O. Wilson, David Winter, and Patti Wollman. Thank you, all.

Most of all I thank my family: Lawrence and Gail Horowitz, Barbara Schnipper, and Mitchell Horowitz, whom I wrote about in the dedication; Lois, Murray, and Steve Schnipper, who make the world a warmer place; Steve and Gina Cain, my wonderful West Coast siblings; and the inimitable Heidi Postlewait.

Special thanks and love to Al and Bobbi Cain, who lent me their advice, contacts, and professional counsel as I researched and wrote, and who constantly cause me to hope that one day I will be as devoted and supportive an in-law to some young person as they are to me.

And to my beloved Gonzo (a.k.a. Ken), who may just be the most generous person on earth, and the most dashing. During the years I wrote this book, he edited my drafts, sharpened my ideas, made me tea, made me laugh, brought me chocolate, seeded our garden, turned his world upside down so I had time to write, kept our lives colorful and exciting, and got us the hell out of the Berkshires. He also, of course, gave us Sammy and Elishku, who have filled our house with trucks and our hearts with love.

Notes

INTRODUCTION: THE NORTH AND SOUTH OF TEMPERAMENT

1 **Montgomery, Alabama. December 1, 1955:** For an excellent biography of Rosa Parks, see Douglas Brinkley, *Rosa Parks: A Life* (New York: Penguin, 2000). Most of the material in *Quiet* about Parks is drawn from this work.

   A note about Parks: Some have questioned the singularity of her actions, pointing out that she'd had plenty of civil rights training before boarding that bus. While this is true, there's no evidence, according to Brinkley, that Parks acted in a premeditated manner that evening, or even as an activist; she was simply being herself. More important for *Quiet*'s purposes, her personality did not prevent her from being powerful; on the contrary, it made her a natural at nonviolent resistance.

2 **"north and south of temperament":** Winifred Gallagher (quoting J. D. Higley), "How We Become What We Are," *The Atlantic Monthly*, September 1994. (Higley was talking about boldness and inhibition, not extroversion and introversion per se, but the concepts overlap in many ways.)

3 **governs how likely we are to exercise:** Robert M. Stelmack, "On Personality and Arousal: A Historical Perspective on Eysenck and Zuckerman," in Marvin Zuckerman and Robert M. Stelmack, eds., *On the Psychobiology of Personality: Essays in Honor of Marvin Zuckerman* (San Diego: Elsevier, 2004), 22. See also Caroline Davis et al., "Motivations to Exercise as a Function of Personality Characteristics, Age, and Gender," *Personality and Individual Differences* 19, no. 2 (1995): 165–74.

3 **commit adultery:** Daniel Nettle, *Personality: What Makes You the Way You Are* (New York: Oxford University Press, 2007), p. 100. See also David P. Schmitt, "The Big Five Related to Risky Sexual Behaviour Across 10 World Regions: Differential Personality Associations of Sexual Promiscuity and Relationship Infidelity," *European Journal of Personality* 18, no. 4 (2004): 301–19.

3 **function well without sleep:** William D. S. Killgore et al., "The Trait of Introversion-Extraversion Predicts Vulnerability to Sleep Deprivation," *Journal of Sleep Research* 16, no. 4 (2007): 354–63. See also Daniel Taylor and Robert M. McFatter, "Cognitive Performance After Sleep Deprivation: Does Personality Make a Difference?" *Personality and Individual Differences* 34, no. 7 (2003): 1179–93; and Andrew Smith and Andrea Maben, "Effects of Sleep Deprivation, Lunch, and Personality on Performance, Mood, and Cardiovascular Function," *Physiology and Behavior* 54, no. 5 (1993): 967–72.

3 **learn from our mistakes:** See chapter 7.

3 **place big bets in the stock market:** See chapter 7.

3 **be a good leader:** See chapter 2.

3 **and ask "what if":** See chapters 3 and 7.

3 **exhaustively researched subjects:** As of May 2, 2010, in the PSYCINFO database, there were 9,194 entries on "extraversion," 6,111 on "introversion," and 12,494 on the overlapping subject of "neuroticism." There were fewer entries for the other "Big 5" personality traits: openness to experience, conscientiousness, and agreeableness. Similarly, as of June 14, 2010, a Google scholar search found about 64,700 articles on "extraversion," 30,600 on "extroversion," 55,900 on "introversion," and 53,300 on "neuroticism." The psychologist William Graziano, in an e-mail dated July 31, 2010, refers to introversion/extroversion as "the 300 lb. gorilla of personality, meaning that it is big and cannot be ignored easily."

3 **in the Bible:** See "A Note on Terminology."

3 **some evolutionary psychologists:** See chapter 6.

3 **one third to one half of Americans are introverts:** Rowan Bayne, in *The Myers-Briggs Type Indicator: A Critical Review and Practical Guide* (London: Chapman and Hall, 1995), 47, finds the incidence of introversion at 36 percent, which is in turn determined from Isabel Myers's own study from 1985. A more recent study, published by the Center for Applications of Psychological Type Research Services in 1996, sampled 914,219 people and found that 49.3 percent were extroverts and 50.7 percent were introverts. See "Estimated Frequencies of the Types in the United States Population," a brochure published by the Center for Application of Psychological Type (CAPT) in 1996 and 2003. That the percentage of introverts found by these studies rose from 36 percent to 50.7 percent doesn't necessarily mean that there are now more introverts in the United States, according to CAPT. It may be "simply a reflection of the populations sampled and included." In fact, a wholly separate survey, this one using the Eysenck Personality Inventory and Eysenck Personality Questionnaire rather than the Myers-Briggs test, indicates that extraversion scores have increased over time (from 1966 to 1993) for both men and women: see Jean M. Twenge, "Birth Cohort

Changes in Extraversion: A Cross-Temporal Meta-Analysis, 1966–1993," *Personality and Individual Differences* 30 (2001): 735–48.

4 **United States is among the most extroverted of nations:** This has been noted in two studies: (1) Juri Allik and Robert R. McCrae, "Toward a Geography of Personality Traits: Patterns of Profiles Across 36 Cultures," *Journal of Cross-Cultural Psychology* 35 (2004): 13–28; and (2) Robert R. McCrae and Antonio Terracciano, "Personality Profiles of Cultures: Aggregate Personality Traits," *Journal of Personality and Social Psychology* 89:3 (2005): 407–25.

4 **Talkative people, for example:** William B. Swann Jr. and Peter J. Rentfrow, "Blirtatiousness: Cognitive, Behavioral, and Physiological Consequences of Rapid Responding," *Journal of Personality and Social Psychology* 81, no. 6 (2001): 1160–75.

4 **Velocity of speech counts:** Howard Giles and Richard L. Street Jr., "Communicator Characteristics and Behavior," in M. L. Knapp and G. R. Miller, eds., *Handbook of Interpersonal Communication*, 2nd ed. (Thousand Oaks, CA: Sage, 1994), 103–61. (But note some good news for introverts: slow speech can be perceived as honest and benevolent, according to other studies.)

5 **the voluble are considered smarter:** Delroy L. Paulhus and Kathy L. Morgan, "Perceptions of Intelligence in Leaderless Groups: The Dynamic Effects of Shyness and Acquaintance," *Journal of Personality and Social Psychology* 72, no. 3 (1997): 581–91.

5 **one informal study:** Laurie Helgoe, *Introvert Power: Why Your Inner Life Is Your Hidden Strength* (Naperville, IL: Sourcebooks, 2008), 3–4.

5 **the theory of gravity:** Gale E. Christianson, *Isaac Newton* (Oxford University Press, Lives and Legacies Series, 2005).

5 **the theory of relativity:** Walter Isaacson, *Einstein: His Life and Universe* (New York: Simon & Schuster, 2007), 4, 12, 18, 2, 31, etc.

5 **W. B. Yeats's "The Second Coming":** Michael Fitzgerald, *The Genesis of Artistic Creativity: Asperger's Syndrome and the Arts* (London: Jessica Kingsley, 2005), 69. See also Ira Progoff, *Jung's Psychology and Its Social Meaning* (London: Routledge, 1999), 111–12.

5 **Chopin's nocturnes:** Tad Szulc, *Chopin in Paris: The Life and Times of the Romantic Composer* (New York: Simon & Schuster, 2000), 69.

5 **Proust's *In Search of Lost Time*:** Alain de Botton, *How Proust Can Change Your Life* (New York: Vintage International), 1997.

5 **Peter Pan:** Lisa Chaney, *Hide-and-Seek with Angels: A Life of J. M. Barrie* (New York: St. Martin's Press, 2005), 2.

5 **Orwell's *1984* and *Animal Farm*:** Fitzgerald, *The Genesis of Artistic Creativity*, 89.

5 **Charlie Brown:** David Michaelis, *Schulz and Peanuts: A Biography* (New York: Harper, 2007).

5 **Schindler's List, E.T., and Close Encounters of the Third Kind:** Joseph McBride, *Steven Spielberg: A Biography* (New York: Simon & Schuster, 1997), 57, 68.

5 **Google:** Ken Auletta, *Googled: The End of the World as We Know It* (New York: Penguin, 2009), 32

5 **Harry Potter:** Interview of J. K. Rowling by Shelagh Rogers and Lauren McCormick, Canadian Broadcasting Corp., October 26, 2000.

5 **"Neither $E=mc^2$ nor Paradise Lost":** Winifred Gallagher, *I.D.: How Heredity and Experience Make You Who You Are* (New York: Random House, 1996), 26.

6 **vast majority of teachers believe:** Charles Meisgeier et al., "Implications and Applications of Psychological Type to Educational Reform and Renewal," *Proceedings of the First Biennial International Conference on Education of the Center for Applications of Psychological Type* (Gainesville, FL: Center for Applications of Psychological Type, 1994), 263–71.

10 **Carl Jung had published a bombshell:** Carl G. Jung, *Psychological Types* (Princeton, NJ: Princeton University Press, 1971; originally published in German as *Psychologische Typen* [Zurich: Rascher Verlag, 1921]), see esp. 330–37.

10 **the majority of universities and Fortune 100 companies:** E-mail to the author, dated July 9, 2010, from Leah L. Walling, director, Marketing Communications and Product Marketing, CPP, Inc.

11 **introverts and extroverts differ in the level of outside stimulation . . . Many have a horror of small talk:** See Part Two: "Your Biology, Your Self?"

11 **introvert is not a synonym for hermit:** Introversion is also very different from Asperger's syndrome, the autism spectrum disorder that involves difficulties with social interactions such as reading facial expressions and body language. Introversion and Asperger's both can involve feeling overwhelmed in social settings. But unlike people with Asperger's, introverts often have strong social skills. Compared with the one third to one half of Americans who are introverts, only one in five thousand people has Asperger's. See National Institute of Neurological Disorders and Stroke, Asperger Syndrome Fact Sheet, http://www.ninds.nih.gov/disorders/asperger/detail_asperger.htm.

12 **the distinctly introverted E. M. Forster:** Sunil Kumar, *A Companion to E. M. Forster*, vol. 1 (New Delhi: Atlantic Publishers and Distributors, 2007).

12 **"human love at its height":** E. M. Forster, *Howards End* (London: Edward Arnold, 1910).

12 **Shyness is the fear of social disapproval:** Elaine N. Aron et al., "Adult Shyness: The Interaction of Temperamental Sensitivity and an Adverse Childhood Environment," *Personality and Social Psychology Bulletin* 31 (2005): 181–97.

12 **they sometimes overlap:** Many articles address this question. See, for example, Stephen R. Briggs, "Shyness: Introversion or Neuroticism?" *Journal of Research in Personality* 22, no. 3 (1988): 290–307.

14 **"Such a man would be in the lunatic asylum":** William McGuire and R. F. C. Hall, C. G. *Jung Speaking: Interviews and Encounters* (Princeton, NJ: Princeton University Press, 1977), 304.

14 **Finland is a famously introverted nation:** Aino Sallinen-Kuparinen et al., *Willingness to Communicate, Communication Apprehension, Introversion, and Self-Reported Communication Competence: Finnish and American Comparisons.* Communication Research Reports, 8 (1991): 57.

14 **Many introverts are also "highly sensitive":** See chapter 6.

CHAPTER 1: THE RISE OF THE "MIGHTY LIKEABLE FELLOW"

19–**The date: 1902 . . . held him back as a young man:** Giles Kemp and Ed
20 ward Claflin, *Dale Carnegie: The Man Who Influenced Millions* (New York: St. Martin's Press, 1989). The 1902 date is an estimate based on the rough contours of Carnegie's biography.

20 **"In the days when pianos and bathrooms were luxuries":** Dale Carnegie, *The Quick and Easy Way to Effective Speaking* (New York: Pocket Books, 1962; revised by Dorothy Carnegie from *Public Speaking and Influencing Men in Business,* by Dale Carnegie).

21 **a Culture of Character to a Culture of Personality:** Warren Susman, *Culture as History: The Transformation of American Society in the Twentieth Century* (Washington, DC: Smithsonian Institution Press, 2003), 271–85. See also Ian A. M. Nicholson, "Gordon Allport, Character, and the 'Culture of Personality,' 1897–1937," *History of Psychology* 1, no. 1 (1998): 52–68.

21 **The word *personality* didn't exist:** Susman, *Culture as History,* 277: The modern idea of personality emerged in the early twentieth century and came into its own only in the post–World War I period. By 1930, according to the early personality psychologist Gordon W. Allport, interest in personality had reached "astonishing proportions." See also Sol Cohen, "The Mental Hygiene Movement, the Development of Personality and the School: The Medicalization of American Education," *History of Education Quarterly* 32, no. 2 (1983), 123–49.

22 **In 1790, only 3 percent . . . a third of the country were urbanites:** Alan Berger, *The City: Urban Communities and Their Problems* (Dubuque, IA: Wil-

liam C. Brown Co., 1978). See also Warren Simpson Thompson et al., *Population Trends in the United States* (New York: Gordon and Breach Science Publishers, 1969).

22 **"We cannot all live in cities":** David E. Shi, *The Simple Life: Plain Living and High Thinking in American Culture* (Athens, GA: University of Georgia Press, 1985), 154.

22 **"The reasons why one man gained a promotion":** Roland Marchand, *Advertising the American Dream: Making Way for Modernity, 1920–1940* (Berkeley: University of California Press, 1985), 209.

22 *The Pilgrim's Progress:* John Bunyan, *The Pilgrim's Progress* (New York: Oxford University Press, 2003). See also Elizabeth Haiken, *Venus Envy: A History of Cosmetic Surgery* (Baltimore: Johns Hopkins University Press, 1997), 99.

22 **a modest man who did not . . . "offend by superiority":** Amy Henderson, "Media and the Rise of Celebrity Culture," *Organization of American Historians Magazine of History* 6 (Spring 1992).

22 **A popular 1899 manual:** Orison Swett Marden, *Character: The Grandest Thing in the World* (1899; reprint, Kessinger Publishing, 2003), 13.

22– **But by 1920, popular self-help guides . . . "That is the beginning of a**
23 **reputation for personality":** Susman, *Culture as History*, 271–85.

23 *Success* **magazine and** *The Saturday Evening Post:* Carl Elliott, *Better Than Well: American Medicine Meets the American Dream* (New York: W. W. Norton, 2003), 61.

23 **a mysterious quality called "fascination":** Susman, 279.

23 **"People who pass us on the street":** Hazel Rawson Cades, "A Twelve-to-Twenty Talk," *Women's Home Companion,* September 1925: 71 (cited by Haiken, p. 91).

24 **Americans became obsessed with movie stars:** In 1907 there were five thousand movie theaters in the United States; by 1914 there were 180,000 theaters and counting. The first films appeared in 1894, and though the identities of screen actors were originally kept secret by the film studios (in keeping with the ethos of a more private era), by 1910 the notion of a "movie star" was born. Between 1910 and 1915 the influential filmmaker D. W. Griffith made movies in which he juxtaposed close-ups of the stars with crowd scenes. His message was clear: here was the successful personality, standing out in all its glory against the undifferentiated nobodies of the world. Americans absorbed these messages enthusiastically. The vast majority of biographical profiles published in *The Saturday Evening Post* and *Collier's* at the dawn of the twentieth century were about politicians, businessmen, and professionals. But by the 1920s and 1930s, most profiles were written about entertainers like Gloria Swanson and Charlie Chaplin. (See

Susman and Henderson; see also Charles Musser, *The Emergence of Cinema: The American Screen to 1907* [Berkeley: University of California Press, 1994], 81; and Daniel Czitrom, *Media and the American Mind: From Morse to McLuhan* [Chapel Hill: University of North Carolina Press, 1982, p. 42].)

24 "EATON'S HIGHLAND LINEN": Marchand, *Advertising the American Dream*, 11.

24 "ALL AROUND YOU PEOPLE ARE JUDGING YOU SILENTLY": Jennifer Scanlon, *Inarticulate Longings: The Ladies' Home Journal, Gender, and the Promises of Consumer Culture* (Routledge, 1995), 209.

24 "CRITICAL EYES ARE SIZING YOU UP RIGHT NOW": Marchand, *Advertising the American Dream*, 213.

24 "EVER TRIED SELLING YOURSELF TO YOU?": Marchand, 209.

24 "LET YOUR FACE REFLECT CONFIDENCE, NOT WORRY!": Marchand, *Advertising the American Dream*, 213.

25 "longed to be successful, gay, triumphant": This ad ran in *Cosmopolitan*, August 1921: 24.

25 "How can I make myself more popular?": Rita Barnard, *The Great Depression and the Culture of Abundance: Kenneth Fearing, Nathanael West, and Mass Culture in the 1930s* (Cambridge, UK: Cambridge University Press, 1995), 188. See also Marchand, *Advertising the American Dream*, 210.

25–both genders displayed some reserve . . . sometimes called "frigid": Patri-
26 cia A. McDaniel, *Shrinking Violets and Caspar Milquetoasts: Shyness, Power, and Intimacy in the United States, 1950–1995* (New York: New York University Press, 2003), 33–43.

26 In the 1920s an influential psychologist . . . "Our current civilization . . . seems to place a premium upon the aggressive person": Nicholson, "Gordon Allport, Character, and the Culture of Personality, 1897–1937," 52–68. See also Gordon Allport, "A Test for Ascendance-Submission," *Journal of Abnormal & Social Psychology* 23 (1928): 118–36. Allport, often referred to as a founding figure of personality psychology, published "Personality Traits: Their Classification and Measurement" in 1921, the same year Jung published *Psychological Types*. He began teaching his course "Personality: Its Psychological and Social Aspects" at Harvard University in 1924; it was probably the first course in personality ever taught in the United States.

26 Jung himself . . . "all the current prejudices against this type": C. G. Jung, *Psychological Types* (Princeton, NJ: Princeton University Press, 1990; reprint of 1921 edition), 403–5.

26–The IC, as it became known . . . "the backbone along with it": Haiken,
27 *Venus Envy*, 111–14.

27 Despite the hopeful tone of this piece . . . "A healthy personality for every child": McDaniel, *Shrinking Violets*, 43–44.

27 **Well-meaning parents . . . agreed:** Encyclopedia of Children and Childhood in History and Society: "Shyness," http://www.faqs.org/childhood/Re-So/Shyness.html.

27 **Some discouraged their children . . . learning to socialize:** David Riesman, *The Lonely Crowd* (Garden City, NY: Doubleday Anchor, reprinted by arrangement with Yale University Press, 1953), esp. 79–85 and 91. See also "The People: Freedom—New Style," *Time*, September 27, 1954.

27 **Introverted children . . . "suburban abnormalities":** William H. Whyte, *The Organization Man* (New York: Simon & Schuster, 1956; reprint, Philadelphia: University of Pennsylvania Press, 2002), 382, 384.

28 **Harvard's provost Paul Buck:** Jerome Karabel, *The Chosen: The Hidden History of Admission and Exclusion at Harvard, Yale, and Princeton* (Boston: Houghton Mifflin, 2005), 185, 223.

28 **"We see little use for the "brilliant" introvert' ":** Whyte, *The Organization Man*, 105.

28 **This college dean . . . "it helps if they make a good impression":** Whyte, *The Organization Man*, 212.

28 **"We're selling, just selling, IBM":** Hank Whittemore, "IBM in Westchester—The Low Profile of the True Believers." *New York*, May 22, 1972. The singing ended in the 1950s, according to this article. For the full words to "Selling IBM," see http://www.digibarn.com/collections/songs/ibm-songs.

29 **The rest of the organization men . . . read the Equanil ad:** Louis Menand, "Head Case: Can Psychiatry Be a Science?" *The New Yorker*, March 1, 2010.

29 **The 1960s tranquilizer Serentil:** Elliott, *Better Than Well*, xv.

29 **Extroversion is in our DNA:** Kenneth R. Olson, "Why Do Geographic Differences Exist in the Worldwide Distribution of Extraversion and Openness to Experience? The History of Human Emigration as an Explanation," *Individual Differences Research* 5, no. 4 (2007): 275–88. See also Chuansheng Chen, "Population Migration and the Variation of Dopamine D4 Receptor (DRD4) Allele Frequencies Around the Globe," *Evolution and Human Behavior* 20 (1999): 309–24.

29 **the Romans, for whom the worst possible punishment:** Mihalyi Csikszentmihalyi, *Flow: The Psychology of Optimal Experience* (New York: Harper Perennial, 1990), 165.

30 **Even the Christianity of early American religious revivals:** Long before that silver-tongued Chautauqua speaker turned Dale Carnegie's world upside down, religious revivals were taking place under huge tents all over the country. Chautauqua itself was inspired by these "Great Awakenings," the first in the 1730s and 1740s, and the second in the early decades of the nineteenth century. The Christianity on offer in the Awakenings was new and theatrical; its leaders were sales-oriented, focused on packing followers

under their great tents. Ministers' reputations depended on how exuberant they were in speech and gesture.

The star system dominated Christianity long before the concept of movie stars even existed. The dominant evangelist of the First Great Awakening was a British showman named George Whitefield who drew standing-room-only crowds with his dramatic impersonations of biblical figures and unabashed weeping, shouting, and crying out. But where the First Great Awakening balanced drama with intellect and gave birth to universities like Princeton and Dartmouth, the Second Great Awakening was even more personality-driven; its leaders focused purely on drawing crowds. Believing, as many megachurch pastors do today, that too academic an approach would fail to pack tents, many evangelical leaders gave up on intellectual values altogether and embraced their roles as salesmen and entertainers. "My theology! I didn't know I had any!" exclaimed the nineteenth-century evangelist D. L. Moody.

This kind of oratory affected not only styles of worship, but also people's ideas of who Jesus *was*. A 1925 advertising executive named Bruce Fairchild Barton published a book called *The Man Nobody Knows*. It presented Jesus as a superstar sales guy who "forged twelve men from the bottom ranks of business into an organization that conquered the world." This Jesus was no lamb; this was "the world's greatest business executive" and "The Founder of Modern Business." The notion of Jesus as a role model for business leadership fell on extraordinarily receptive ears. *The Man Nobody Knows* became one of the best-selling nonfiction books of the twentieth century, according to Powell's Books. See Adam S. McHugh, *Introverts in the Church: Finding Our Place in an Extroverted Culture* (Downers Grove, IL: IVP Books, 2009), 23–25. See also Neal Gabler, *Life: The Movie: How Entertainment Conquered Reality* (New York: Vintage Books, 1998), 25–26.

30 **early Americans revered action:** Richard Hofstadter, *Anti-Intellectualism in American Life* (New York: Vintage Books, 1962); see, for example, pp. 51 and 256–57.

30 **The 1828 presidential campaign:** Neal Gabler, *Life: The Movie*, 28.

30 **John Quincy Adams, incidentally:** Steven J. Rubenzer et al., "Assessing the U.S. Presidents Using the Revised NEO Personality Inventory," *Assessment* 7, no. 4 (2000): 403–20.

30 **"Respect for individual human personality":** Harold Stearns, *America and the Young Intellectual* (New York: George H. Duran Co., 1921).

30 **"It is remarkable how much attention":** Henderson, "Media and the Rise of Celebrity Culture."

31 **wandered lonely as a cloud:** William Wordsworth, "I Wandered Lonely as a Cloud," 1802.

31 **repaired in solitude to Walden Pond:** Henry David Thoreau, *Walden*, 1854.

31 **Americans who considered themselves shy:** Bernardo Carducci and Philip G. Zimbardo, "Are You Shy?" *Psychology Today*, November 1, 1995.

31 **"Social anxiety disorder" . . . one in five of us:** M. B. Stein, J. R. Walker, and D. R. Forde, "Setting Diagnostic Thresholds for Social Phobia: Considerations from a Community Survey of Social Anxiety," *American Journal of Psychiatry* 151 (1994): 408–42.

31 **The most recent version of the *Diagnostic and Statistical Manual*:** American Psychiatric Association, *Diagnostic and Statistical Manual of Mental Disorders*, 4th ed. (*DSM-IV*), 2000. See 300.23, "Social Phobia (Social Anxiety Disorder)": "The diagnosis is appropriate only if the avoidance, fear, or anxious anticipation of encountering the social or performance situation interferes significantly with the person's daily routine, occupational functioning, or social life, or if the person is markedly distressed about having the phobia. . . . In feared social or performance situations, individuals with Social Phobia experience concerns about embarrassment and are afraid that others will judge them to be anxious, weak, 'crazy,' or stupid. They may fear public speaking because of concern that others will notice their trembling hands or voice or they may experience extreme anxiety when conversing with others because of fear that they will appear inarticulate. . . . The fear or avoidance must interfere significantly with the person's normal routine, occupational or academic functioning, or social activities or relationships, or the person must experience marked distress about having the phobia. For example, a person who is afraid of speaking in public would not receive a diagnosis of Social Phobia if this activity is not routinely encountered on the job or in the classroom and the person is not particularly distressed about it."

31 **"It's not enough . . . to be able to sit at your computer":** Daniel Goleman, *Working with Emotional Intelligence* (New York: Bantam, 2000), 32.

32 **a staple of airport bookshelves and business best-seller lists:** See, for example, http://www.nationalpost.com/Business+Bestsellers/3927572/story.html.

32 **"all talking is selling and all selling involves talking":** Michael Erard, *Um: Slips, Stumbles, and Verbal Blunders, and What They Mean* (New York: Pantheon, 2007), 156.

32 **more than 12,500 chapters in 113 countries:** http://www.toastmasters.org/MainMenuCategories/WhatisToastmasters.aspx (accessed September 10, 2010).

32 **The promotional video:** http://www.toastmasters.org/DVDclips.aspx (accessed July 29, 2010). Click on "Welcome to Toastmasters! The entire 15 minute story."

CHAPTER 2: THE MYTH OF CHARISMATIC LEADERSHIP

35 **President Clinton . . . 50 million other people:** These names and statistics are according to Tony Robbins's website and other promotional materials as of December 19, 2009.

35 **some $11 billion a year:** Melanie Lindner, "What People Are Still Willing to Pay For," *Forbes*, January 15, 2009. The $11 billion figure is for 2008 and is, according to Marketdata Enterprises, a research firm. This amount was forecast to grow by 6.2 percent annually through 2012.

37 **chairman of seven privately held companies:** This figure is according to Robbins's website.

38 **"hyperthymic" temperament:** Hagop S. Akiskal, "The Evolutionary Significance of Affective Temperaments," *Medscape CME*, published June 12, 2003, updated June 24, 2003.

40 **superhuman physical size:** Steve Salerno made this point in his book *Sham* (New York: Crown Publishers, 2005), 75. He also made the later point about Robbins's remark that he was once so poor that he kept his dishes in the bathtub.

44 **Founded in 1908 . . . "educating leaders who make a difference in the world":** Harvard Business School website, September 11, 2010.

44 **President George W. Bush . . . were HBS grads:** Philip Delves Broughton, *Ahead of the Curve: Two Years at Harvard Business School* (New York: Penguin, 2008), 2. See also www.reuters.com, Factbox: Jeffrey Skilling, June 24, 2010.

48 **will graduate into a business culture:** Stanford Business School professor of applied psychology Thomas Harrell tracked Stanford MBAs who graduated between 1961 and 1965, and published a series of studies about them. He found that high earners and general managers tended to be outgoing and extroverted. See, e.g., Thomas W. Harrell and Bernard Alpert, "Attributes of Successful MBAs: A 20-Year Longitudinal Study," *Human Performance* 2, no. 4 (1989): 301-322.

48 **" 'Here everyone knows that it's important to be an extrovert' ":** Reggie Garrison et al., "Managing Introversion and Extroversion in the Workplace," Wharton Program for Working Professionals (WPWP) (Philadelphia: University of Pennsylvania, Spring 2006).

49 BOSS TO TED AND ALICE: Here I must apologize: I can't recall the company that ran this ad, and haven't been able to locate it.

49 "DEPART FROM YOUR INHIBITIONS": http://www.advertolog.com/amtrak/print-outdoor/depart-from-your-inhibitions-2110505/ (accessed September 11, 2010).

49 **a series of ads for the psychotropic drug Paxil:** Christopher Lane, *How*

Normal Behavior Became a Sickness (New Haven: Yale University Press, 2007), 127, 131.

51 **We perceive talkers as smarter:** Delroy L. Paulhus and Kathy L. Morgan, "Perceptions of Intelligence in Leaderless Groups: The Dynamic Effects of Shyness and Acquaintance," *Journal of Personality and Social Psychology* 72, no. 3 (1997): 581–91. See also Cameron Anderson and Gavin Kilduff, "Why Do Dominant Personalities Attain Influence in Face-to-Face Groups? The Competence Signaling Effects of Trait Dominance," *Journal of Personality and Social Psychology* 96, no. 2 (2009): 491–503.

51 **two strangers met over the phone:** William B. Swann Jr. and Peter J. Rentfrow, "Blirtatiousness: Cognitive, Behavioral, and Physiological Consequences of Rapid Responding," *Journal of Personality and Social Psychology* 81, no. 6 (2001): 1160–75.

51 **We also see talkers as leaders:** Simon Taggar et al., "Leadership Emergence in Autonomous Work Teams: Antecedents and Outcomes," *Personnel Psychology* 52, no. 4 (Winter 1999): 899–926. ("The person that speaks most is likely to be perceived as the leader.")

51 **The more a person talks, the more other group members:** James Surowiecki, *The Wisdom of Crowds* (New York: Doubleday Anchor, 2005), 187.

51 **It also helps to speak fast:** Howard Giles and Richard L. Street Jr., "Communicator Characteristics and Behavior," in M. L. Knapp and G. R. Miller, eds., *Handbook of Interpersonal Communication*, 2nd ed. (Thousand Oaks, CA: Sage, 1994), 103–61.

51 **college students were asked to solve math problems:** Cameron Anderson and Gavin Kilduff, "Why Do Dominant Personalities Attain Influence in Face-to-Face Groups? The Competence-Signaling Effects of Trait Dominance."

52 **A well-known study out of UC Berkeley:** Philip Tetlock, *Expert Political Judgment* (Princeton, NJ: Princeton University Press, 2006).

52 **"the Bus to Abilene":** Kathrin Day Lassila, "A Brief History of Groupthink: Why Two, Three or Many Heads Aren't Always Better Than One," *Yale Alumni Magazine*, January/February 2008.

53 **Schwab . . . Tohmatsu:** Del Jones, "Not All Successful CEOs Are Extroverts," *USA Today*, June 7, 2006.

53 **"some locked themselves into their office":** Peter F. Drucker, *The Leader of the Future 2: New Visions, Strategies, and Practices for the Next Era*, edited by Frances Hesselbein, Marshall Goldsmith, and Richard Beckhard (San Francisco: Jossey-Bass, 2006), xi–xii.

53 **those considered charismatic by their top executives:** Bradley Agle et al., "Does CEO Charisma Matter? An Empirical Analysis of the Relationships

Among Organizational Performance, Environmental Uncertainty, and Top Management Team Perceptions of CEO Charisma," *Academy of Management Journal* 49, no. 1 (2006): 161–74. See also Del Jones, "Not All Successful CEOs Are Extroverts." For an excellent book on this topic, see Rakesh Khurana, *Searching for a Corporate Savior: The Irrational Quest for Charismatic CEOs* (Princeton, NJ: Princeton University Press, 2002).

54 **the influential management theorist Jim Collins:** Jim Collins, *Good to Great: Why Some Companies Make the Leap—and Others Don't* (New York: HarperCollins, 2001). Note that some have questioned whether the companies Collins profiled are as "great" as he claimed. See Bruce Niendorf and Kristine Beck, "*Good to Great*, or Just Good?" *Academy of Management Perspectives* 22, no. 4 (2008): 13–20. See also Bruce Resnick and Timothy Smunt, "Good to Great to . . . ?" *Academy of Management Perspectives* 22, no. 4 (2008): 6–12.

56 **correlation between extroversion and leadership:** Timothy Judge et al., "Personality and Leadership: A Qualitative and Quantitative Review," *Journal of Applied Psychology* 87, no. 4 (2002): 765–80. See also David Brooks, "In Praise of Dullness," *New York Times,* May 18, 2009, citing Steven Kaplan et al., "Which CEO Characteristics and Abilities Matter?" *National Bureau of Economic Research Working Paper No. 14195,* July 2008, a study finding that CEO success is more strongly related to "execution skills" than to "team-related skills." Brooks also cited another study by Murray Barrick, Michael Mount, and Timothy Judge, surveying a century's worth of research into business leadership and finding that extroversion did not correlate well with CEO success, but that conscientiousness did.

56–In the first study . . . fold more shirts: Adam M. Grant et al., "Reversing
57 the Extraverted Leadership Advantage: The Role of Employee Proactivity," *Academy of Management Journal* 54, no. 3 (June 2011).

57 **"Often the leaders end up doing a lot of the talking":** Carmen Nobel, "Introverts: The Best Leaders for Proactive Employees," *Harvard Business School Working Knowledge: A First Look at Faculty Research,* October 4, 2010.

58 **For years before the day in December 1955:** I drew largely on Douglas Brinkley's excellent biography, *Rosa Parks: A Life* (New York: Penguin Books, 2000). Note: Unlike King, Parks did come to believe that violence was sometimes a justifiable weapon of the oppressed.

60 **Moses, for example, was not:** My analysis of Moses is based on my own reading of Exodus, especially 3:11, 4:1, 4:3, 4:10, 4:12–17, 6:12, 6:30, and Numbers 12:3. Others have made similar analyses; see, for example, http://www.theologyweb.com/campus/showthread.php?t=50284. See also Doug Ward, "The Meanings of Moses' Meekness," http://godward.org/Hebrew%20Roots/

meanings_of_moses.htm. Also see Marissa Brostoff, "Rabbis Focus on Professional Development," http://www.forward.com/articles/13971/ (accessed August 13, 2008).

62 **a "classic Connector" named Robert Horchow:** Malcolm Gladwell, *The Tipping Point* (New York: Back Bay Books, 2002; originally published by Little, Brown, March 2000), 42–46.

62 **As of May 28, 2011:** Craigslist fact sheet, available on its website, www .craigslist.com (accessed May 28, 2010). Other information about Craigslist comes from (1) phone interview between Craig Newmark and the author, December 4, 2006, (2) Idelle Davidson, "The Craigslist Phenomenon," *Los Angeles Times*, June 13, 2004, and (3) Philip Weiss, "A Guy Named Craig," *New York* magazine, January 8, 2006.

63 **"Guy Kawasaki an introvert?":** Maria Niles, post on Blogher, a blogging community for women, August 19, 2008. See http://www.blogher.com/ social-media-introverts.

63 **"Wouldn't it be a great irony":** Pete Cashmore, "Irony Alert: Social Media Introverts?" mashable.com, August 2008. See http://mashable.com/ 2008/08/15/irony-alert-social-media-introverts/.

63 **introverts are more likely than extroverts:** Yair Amichai-Hamburger, "Personality and the Internet," in *The Social Net: Understanding Human Behavior in Cyberspace*, edited by Yair Amichai-Hamburger (New York: Oxford University Press, 2005): 27–56. See also Emily S. Orr et al., "The Influence of Shyness on the Use of Facebook in an Undergraduate Sample," *CyberPsychology and Behavior* 12, no. 3 (2009); Levi R. Baker, "Shyness and Online Social Networking Services," *Journal of Social and Personal Relationships* 27, no. 8 (2010). Richard N. Landers and John W. Lounsbury, "An Investigation of Big Five and Narrow Personality Traits in Relation to Internet Usage," *Computers in Human Behavior* 22 (2006): 283–93. See also Luigi Anolli et al., "Personality of People Using Chat: An On-Line Research," *CyberPsychology and Behavior* 8, no. 1 (2005). But note that extroverts tend to have more Facebook friends than do introverts: Pavica Sheldon, "The Relationship Between Unwillingness-to-Communicate and Students' Facebook Use," *Journal of Media Psychology* 20, no. 2, (2008): 67–75. This is unsurprising, as Facebook has come to be a place where people collect large quantities of friends.

64 **an average weekly attendance of 22,000:** Pastor Rick and Kay Warren, Online Newsroom, http://www.rickwarrennews.com/ (accessed September 12, 2010).

66 **Contemporary evangelicalism says:** For background on evangelicalism, I conducted a series of fascinating interviews with, among others, the ef-

fortlessly articulate Lauren Sandler, author of *Righteous: Dispatches from the Evangelical Youth Movement* (New York: Viking, 2006).

67 **"cry from the heart wondering *how* to fit in":** Mark Byron, "Evangelism for Introverts," http://markbyron.typepad.com/main/2005/06/evangalism_for_.html (accessed June 27, 2005).

67 **"not serve on a parish committee":** Jim Moore, "I Want to Serve the Lord— But Not Serve on a Parish Committee," http://www.beliefnet.com/Faiths/ Christianity/Catholic/2000/07/I-Want-To-Serve-The-Lord-But-Not-Serve-On-A-Parish-Committee.aspx

69 **"that fruitful miracle":** Jean Autret, William Burford, and Phillip J. Wolfe, trans. and ed., *Marcel Proust on Reading Ruskin* (New Haven, CT: Yale University Press, 1989).

CHAPTER 3: WHEN COLLABORATION KILLS CREATIVITY

71 **"I am a horse for a single harness":** Albert Einstein, in "Forum and Century," vol. 84, pp. 193–94 (the thirteenth in the Forum series *Living Philosophies*, a collection of personal philosophies of famous people, published in 1931).

71 **"March 5, 1975":** The story of Stephen Wozniak throughout this chapter is drawn largely from his autobiography, *iWoz* (New York: W. W. Norton, 2006). The description of Woz as being the "nerd soul" of Apple comes from http://valleywag.gawker.com/220602/wozniak-jobs-design-role-overstated.

74 **a series of studies on the nature of creativity:** Donald W. MacKinnon, "The Nature and Nurture of Creative Talent" (Walter Van Dyke Bingham Lecture given at Yale University, New Haven, Connecticut, April 11, 1962). See also MacKinnon, "Personality and the Realization of Creative Potential," Presidential Address presented at Western Psychological Association, Portland, Oregon, April 1964.

74 **One of the most interesting findings:** See, for example, (1) Gregory J. Feist, "A Meta-Analysis of Personality in Scientific and Artistic Creativity," *Personality and Social Psychology Review* 2, no. 4 (1998): 290–309; (2) Feist, "Autonomy and Independence," *Encyclopedia of Creativity*, vol. 1 (San Diego, CA: Academic Press, 1999), 157–63; and (3) Mihaly Csikszentmihalyi, *Creativity: Flow and the Psychology of Discovery and Invention* (New York: Harper Perennial, 1996), 65–68. There *are* some studies showing a correlation between extroversion and creativity, but in contrast to the studies by MacKinnon, Csikszentmihalyi, and Feist, which followed people whose careers had proven them to be exceptionally creative "in real life," these tend to be studies of college students measuring subjects' creativity in more

casual ways, for example by analyzing their personal hobbies or by asking them to play creativity games like writing a story about a picture. It's likely that extroverts would do better in high-arousal settings like these. It's also possible, as the psychologist Uwe Wolfradt suggests, that the relationship between introversion and creativity is "discernable at a higher level of creativity only." (Uwe Wolfradt, "Individual Differences in Creativity: Personality, Story Writing, and Hobbies," *European Journal of Personality* 15, no. 4, [July/August 2001]: 297–310.)

74 **Hans Eysenck:** Hans J. Eysenck, *Genius: The Natural History of Creativity* (New York: Cambridge University Press, 1995).

75 **"Innovation—the heart of the knowledge economy":** Malcolm Gladwell, "Why Your Bosses Want to Turn Your New Office into Greenwich Village," *The New Yorker*, December 11, 2000.

75 **"None of us is as smart as all of us":** Warren Bennis, *Organizing Genius: The Secrets of Creative Collaboration* (New York: Basic Books, 1997).

76 **"Michelangelo had assistants":** Clay Shirky, *Here Comes Everybody: The Power of Organizing Without Organizations* (New York: Penguin, 2008).

76 **organize workforces into teams:** Steve Koslowski and Daniel Ilgen, "Enhancing the Effectiveness of Work Groups and Teams," *Psychological Science in the Public Interest* 7, no. 3 (2006): 77–124.

76 **By 2000 an estimated half:** Dennis J. Devine, "Teams in Organizations: Prevalence, Characteristics, and Effectiveness," *Small Group Research* 20 (1999): 678–711.

76 **today virtually all of them do:** Frederick Morgeson et al., "Leadership in Teams: A Functional Approach to Understanding Leadership Structures and Processes," *Journal of Management* 36, no. 1 (2010): 5–39.

76 **91 percent of high-level managers:** Ibid.

76 **The consultant Stephen Harvill told me:** Author interview, October 26, 2010.

76 **over 70 percent of today's employees:** Davis, "The Physical Environment of the Office." See also James C. McElroy and Paula C. Morrow, "Employee Reactions to Office Redesign: A Naturally Occurring Quasi-Field Experiment in a Multi-Generational Setting," *Human Relations* 63, no. 5 (2010): 609–36. See also Davis, "The Physical Environment of the Office": open-plan offices are "the most popular office design" today. See also Joyce Gannon, "Firms Betting Open-Office Design, Amenities Lead to Happier, More Productive Workers," *Post-Gazette* (Pittsburgh), February 9, 2003. See also Stephen Beacham, *Real Estate Weekly*, July 6, 2005. The first company to use an open plan in a high-rise building was Owens Corning, in 1969. Today, many companies use them, including Proctor & Gamble, Ernst & Young, GlaxoSmithKline, Alcoa, and H. J. Heinz. http://www.owens

corning.com/acquainted/about/history/1960.asp. See also Matthew Davis et al., "The Physical Environment of the Office: Contemporary and Emerging Issues," in G. P. Hodgkinson and J. K. Ford, eds., *International Review of Industrial and Organizational Psychology*, vol. 26 (Chichester, UK: Wiley, 2011), 193–235: ". . . there was a 'widespread introduction of open-plan and landscaped offices in North America in the 1960s and 1970s.'" But see Jennifer Ann McCusker, "Individuals and Open Space Office Design: The Relationship Between Personality and Satisfaction in an Open Space Work Environment," dissertation, Organizational Studies, Alliant International University, April 12, 2002 ("the concept of open space design began in the mid 1960s with a group of German management consultants," citing Karen A. Edelman, "Take Down the Walls," *Across the Board* 34, no. 3 [1997]: 32–38).

76 **The amount of space per employee shrank:** Roger Vincent, "Office Walls Are Closing in on Corporate Workers," *Los Angeles Times*, December 15, 2010.

76 **"There has been a shift from 'I' to 'we' work":** Paul B. Brown, "The Case for Design," *Fast Company*, June 2005.

76 **Rival office manufacturer Herman Miller, Inc.:** "New Executive Office-scapes: Moving from Private Offices to Open Environments," Herman Miller Inc., 2003.

76 **In 2006, the Ross School of Business:** Dave Gershman, "Building Is 'Heart and Soul' of the Ross School of Business," mlive.com, January 24, 2009. See also Kyle Swanson, "Business School Offers Preview of New Home, Slated to Open Next Semester," *Michigan Daily*, September 15, 2008.

77 **According to a 2002 nationwide survey:** Christopher Barnes, "What Do Teachers Teach? A Survey of America's Fourth and Eighth Grade Teachers," conducted by the Center for Survey Research and Analysis, University of Connecticut, Civic Report no. 28, September 2002. See also Robert E. Slavin, "Research on Cooperative Learning and Achievement: What We Know, What We Need to Know," *Contemporary Educational Psychology* 21, no. 1 (1996): 43–69 (citing 1993 national survey findings that 79 percent of elementary school teachers and 62 percent of middle school teachers made sustained use of cooperative learning). Note that in "real life," many teachers are simply throwing students into groups but not using "cooperative learning" per se, which involves a highly specific set of procedures, according to an e-mail sent to the author by Roger Johnson of the Cooperative Learning Center at the University of Minnesota.

77 **"Cooperative learning":** Bruce Williams, *Cooperative Learning: A Standard for High Achievement* (Thousand Oaks, CA: Corwin, 2004), 3–4.

78 **Janet Farrall and Leonie Kronborg:** Janet Farrall and Leonie Kronborg,

"Leadership Development for the Gifted and Talented," in *Fusing Talent—Giftedness in Australian Schools*, edited by M. McCann and F. Southern (Adelaide: The Australian Association of Mathematics Teachers, 1996).

79 **"Employees are putting their whole lives up":** Radio interview with Kai Ryssdal, "Are Cubicles Going Extinct?", *Marketplace*, from American Public Media, December 15, 2010.

79 **A significant majority of the earliest computer enthusiasts:** Sarah Holmes and Philip L. Kerr, "The IT Crowd: The Type Distribution in a Group of Information Technology Graduates," *Australian Psychological Type Review* 9, no. 1 (2007): 31–38. See also Yair Amichai-Hamburger et al., "'On the Internet No One Knows I'm an Introvert': Extraversion, Neuroticism, and Internet Interaction," *CyberPsychology and Behavior* 5, no. 2 (2002): 125–28.

79 **"It's a truism in tech":** Dave W. Smith, e-mail to the author, October 20, 2010.

80 **"Why could that boy, whom I had beaten so easily":** See Daniel Coyle, *The Talent Code* (New York: Bantam Dell, 2009), 48.

80 **three groups of expert violinists:** K. Anders Ericsson et al., "The Role of Deliberate Practice in the Acquisition of Expert Performance," *Psychological Review* 100, no. 3 (1993): 363–406.

81 **"Serious study alone":** Neil Charness et al., "The Role of Deliberate Practice in Chess Expertise," *Applied Cognitive Psychology* 19 (2005): 151–65.

81 **College students who tend to study alone:** David Glenn, "New Book Lays Failure to Learn on Colleges' Doorsteps," *The Chronicle of Higher Education*, January 18, 2001.

81 **Even elite athletes in team sports:** Starkes and Ericsson, "Expert Performance in Sports: Advances in Research on Sports Expertise," *Human Kinetics* (2003): 67–71.

81 **In many fields, Ericsson told me:** Interview with the author, April 13, 2010.

81 **ten thousand hours of Deliberate Practice:** By the age of eighteen, the best violinists in the Berlin Music Academy study had spent an average of over 7,000 hours practicing alone, about 2,000 hours more than the good violinists, and 4,000 hours more than the music teachers.

82 **"intense curiosity or focused interest seems odd to their peers":** Csikszentmihalyi, *Creativity*, 177.

83 **"because practicing music or studying math":** Ibid., 65.

83 **Madeleine L'Engle:** Ibid., 253–54.

83 **"My dear Mr. Babbage":** Charles Darwin, *The Correspondence of Charles Darwin Volume 2: 1837–1843* (Cambridge, England: Cambridge University Press, 1987), 67.

83 **the Coding War Games:** These are described in Tom DeMarco and Timothy

Lister, *Peopleware: Productive Projects and Teams* (New York: Dorset House, 1987).

84 **A mountain of recent data on open-plan offices:** See, for example, the following: (1) Vinesh Oommen et al., "Should Health Service Managers Embrace Open Plan Work Environments? A Review," *Asia Pacific Journal of Health Management* 3, no. 2 (2008). (2) Aoife Brennan et al., "Traditional Versus Open Office Design: A Longitudinal Field Study," *Environment and Behavior* 34 (2002): 279. (3) James C McElroy and Paula Morrow, "Employee Reactions to Office Redesign: A Naturally Occurring Quasi-Field Experiment in a Multi-Generational Setting," *Human Relations* 63 (2010): 609. (4) Einar De Croon et al., "The Effect of Office Concepts on Worker Health and Performance: A Systematic Review of the Literature," *Ergonomics*, 48, no. 2 (2005): 119–34. (5) J. Pejtersen et al., "Indoor Climate, Psychosocial Work Environment and Symptoms in Open-Plan Offices," *Indoor Air* 16, no. 5 (2006): 392–401. (6) Herman Miller Research Summary, 2007, "It's All About Me: The Benefits of Personal Control at Work." (7) Paul Bell et al., *Environmental Psychology* (Lawrence Erlbaum, 2005), 162. (8) Davis, "The Physical Environment of the Office."

85 **people learn better after a quiet stroll:** Marc G. Berman et al., "The Cognitive Benefits of Interacting with Nature," *Psychological Science* 19, no. 12 (2008): 1207–12. See also Stephen Kaplan and Marc Berman, "Directed Attention as a Common Resource for Executive Functioning and Self-Regulation," *Perspectives on Psychological Science* 5, no. 1 (2010): 43–57.

85 **Another study, of 38,000 knowledge workers:** Davis et al., "The Physical Environment of the Office."

85 **Even multitasking . . . a myth:** John Medina, *Brain Rules* (Seattle, WA: Pear Press, 2008), 87.

85 **Backbone Entertainment:** Mike Mika, interview with the author, July 12, 2006.

85 **Reebok International:** Kimberly Blanton, "Design It Yourself: Pleasing Offices Laid Out by the Workers Who Use Them Can Be a Big Advantage When Companies Compete for Talent," *Boston Globe*, March 1, 2005.

85 **For ten years, beginning in 2000:** TEDx Midwest Talk, October 15, 2010. Also, e-mail to the author, November 5, 2010.

86 **Kafka, for example:** Anthony Storr, *Solitude: A Return to the Self* (New York: Free Press, 2005), 103.

86 **considerably more cheerful Theodor Geisel:** Judith Morgan and Neil Morgan, *Dr. Seuss and Mr. Geisel: A Biography* (New York: DaCapo, 1996).

86 **legendary advertising man Alex Osborn:** Alex Osborn, *Your Creative Power* (W. Lafayette, IN: Purdue University Press, 1948).

88 **group brainstorming doesn't actually work:** Marvin D. Dunnette et al.,

"The Effect of Group Participation on Brainstorming Effectiveness for Two Industrial Samples," *Journal of Applied Psychology* 47, no. 1 (1963): 30–37.

88 **some forty years of research:** See, for example, Paul A. Mongeau and Mary Claire Morr, "Reconsidering Brainstorming," *Group Facilitation* 1, no. 1 (1999): 14. See also Karan Girotra et al., "Idea Generation and the Quality of the Best Idea," *Management Science* 56, no. 4 (April 2010): 591–605. (The highest level innovation comes from a hybrid process in which people brainstorm on their own before sharing ideas with colleagues.)

88 **"business people must be insane":** Adrian Furnham, "The Brainstorming Myth," *Business Strategy Review* 11, no. 4 (2000): 21–28.

89 **Groups brainstorming electronically:** Paul Mongeau and Mary Claire Morr, "Reconsidering Brainstorming."

89 **The same is true of academic research:** Charlan Nemeth and Jack Goncalo, "Creative Collaborations from Afar: The Benefits of Independent Authors," *Creativity Research Journal* 17, no. 1 (2005): 1–8.

89 **usually believe that their group performed much better:** Keith Sawyer, *Group Genius: The Creative Power of Collaboration* (New York: Basic Books, 2007), 66.

90 **the fear of public humiliation:** Susan K. Opt and Donald A. Loffredo, "Rethinking Communication Apprehension: A Myers-Briggs Perspective," *Journal of Psychology* 134, no. 5 (2000): 556–70.

90 **two NCAA basketball teams:** James C. Moore and Jody A. Brylinsky, "Spectator Effect on Team Performance in College Basketball," *Journal of Sport Behavior* 16, no. 2 (1993): 77.

90 **behavioral economist Dan Ariely:** Dan Ariely, "What's the Value of a Big Bonus?" *New York Times*, November 19, 2008.

91 **Gregory Berns:** The Solomon Asch and Gregory Berns experiments are described in Gregory Berns, *Iconoclast: A Neuroscientist Reveals How to Think Differently* (Boston, MA: Harvard Business Press, 2008), 59–81. See also Sandra Blakeslee, "What Other People Say May Change What You See," *New York Times*, June 28, 2005. And see Gregory S. Berns et al., "Neurobiological Correlates of Social Conformity and Independence During Mental Rotation," *Biological Psychiatry* 58 (2005): 245–53.

92 **heightened activation in the amygdala:** In fact, in some iterations of the experiment, where the volunteers played with a group of computers rather than with a group of people, their amygdalae stayed quiet even when they disagreed with the computers. This suggests that people who don't conform suffer not so much the fear of being wrong as the anxiety of being excluded from the group.

93 **face-to-face interactions create trust:** Belinda Luscombe, "Why E-Mail May Be Hurting Off-Line Relationships," *Time*, June 22, 2010.

93   **population density is correlated with innovation:** Jonah Lehrer, "How the City Hurts Your Brain," *Boston Globe*, January 2, 2009.

94   **creating "flexible" open plans:** Davis et al., "The Physical Environment of the Office."

94   **At Pixar Animation Studios:** Bill Capodagli, "Magic in the Workplace: How Pixar and Disney Unleash the Creative Talent of Their Workforce," *Effectif*, September/October 2010: 43–45.

94   **Similarly, at Microsoft:** Michelle Conlin, "Microsoft's Meet-My-Mood Offices," *Bloomberg Businessweek*, September 10, 2007.

CHAPTER 4: IS TEMPERAMENT DESTINY?

A **general note on this chapter**: Chapter 4 discusses the psychologist Jerome Kagan's work on high reactivity, which some contemporary psychologists would consider to lie at the intersection of introversion and another trait known as "neuroticism." For the sake of readability, I have not elucidated that distinction in the text.

99   **For one of those studies, launched in 1989:** This study is discussed at length in Jerome Kagan and Nancy Snidman, *The Long Shadow of Temperament* (Cambridge, MA: Harvard University Press, 2004).

100   **"Carl Jung's descriptions of the introvert and extrovert":** Ibid., 218.

100   **reserved Tom and extroverted Ralph:** Jerome Kagan, *Galen's Prophecy* (New York: Basic Books, 1998), 158–61.

101   **Some say that temperament is the foundation:** See http://www.selfgrowth.com/articles/Warfield3.html.

101   **potent organ:** Kagan and Snidman, *The Long Shadow of Temperament*, 10.

102   **When the Frisbee looks like it's headed straight for your nose:** This image comes from an online video with Joseph Ledoux, a scientist at NYU who studies the neural basis of emotions, especially fear and anxiety. See "Fearful Brain in an Anxious World," *Science & the City*, http://www.nyas.org/Podcasts/Atom.axd (accessed November 20, 2008).

103   **"alert attention":** Elaine N. Aron, *Psychotherapy and the Highly Sensitive Person* (New York: Routledge, 2010), 14.

103   **They literally use more eye movements:** Various studies have documented these tendencies in high-reactive children. See, for example, Jerome Kagan, "Reflection-Impulsivity and Reading Ability in Primary Grade Children," *Child Development* 363, no. 3 (1965): 609–28. See also Ellen Siegelman, "Reflective and Impulsive Observing Behavior," *Child Development* 40, no. 4 (1969): 1213–22. These studies use the term "reflective" rather than "high-reactive," but it's a safe bet that they're talking about the same group of children. Siegelman describes them as "preferring low-risk situations generally but choosing harder, more solitary intellectual

tasks ... less motorically active, and more cautious" (p. 1214). (Similar studies have been done on adults; see chapters 6 and 7.)

103 **High-reactive kids also tend to think and feel deeply:** Elaine Aron, *The Highly Sensitive Child: Helping Our Children Thrive When the World Overwhelms Them* (New York: Broadway Books), 2002.

103 **If a high-reactive toddler breaks another child's toy:** See the studies by Grazyna Kochanska referred to in chapter 6.

103 **how a group of kids should share a coveted toy:** Winifred Gallagher (quoting Kagan), "How We Become What We Are." *The Atlantic Monthly,* September 1994.

104 **blue eyes, allergies, and hay fever ... thin body and narrow face:** Kagan, *Galen's Prophecy,* 160–61.

104 **Take Disney movies:** Ibid., 161.

104 **extroversion and introversion are physiologically:** David G. Winter, *Personality: Analysis and Interpretation of Lives* (New York: McGraw-Hill, 1996), 511–16.

105 **40 to 50 percent heritable:** Thomas J. Bouchard Jr. and Matt McGue, "Genetic and Environmental Influences on Human Psychological Differences," *Journal of Neurobiology* 54 (2003): 4–5.

106 **Nazi eugenics and white supremacism:** This has been written about in various places including, for example, Peter D. Kramer, *Listening to Prozac* (New York: Penguin, 1993), 150.

106 **"I have been dragged, kicking and screaming":** Gallagher (quoting Kagan), "How We Become What We Are."

106 **The publication of his early findings:** Kramer, *Listening to Prozac*, 154.

106 **Kagan ushers me inside:** I conducted a series of interviews with Jerome Kagan between 2006 and 2010.

106 **describes himself as having been an anxious:** Jerome Kagan, *An Argument for Mind* (New Haven, CT: Yale University Press, 2006), 4, 7.

107 **public speaking is the number-one fear:** Victoria Cunningham, Morty Lefkoe, and Lee Sechrest, "Eliminating Fears: An Intervention that Permanently Eliminates the Fear of Public Speaking," *Clinical Psychology and Psychotherapy* 13 (2006): 183–93.

107 **Public speaking phobia has many causes:** Gregory Berns, *Iconoclast: A Neuroscientist Reveals How to Think Differently* (Boston, MA: Harvard Business Press, 2008), 59–81.

108 **introverts are significantly more likely:** Susan K. Opt and Donald A. Loffredo, "Rethinking Communication Apprehension: A Myers-Briggs Perspective," *Journal of Psychology* 134, no. 5 (2000): 556–70. See also Michael J. Beatty, James C. McCroskey, and Alan D. Heisel, "Communication Apprehension as Temperamental Expression: A Communibiological

Paradigm," *Communication Monographs* 65 (1998): 197–219. See also Peter D. Macintyre and Kimly A. Thivierge, "The Effects of Speaker Personality on Anticipated Reactions to Public Speaking," *Communication Research Reports* 12, no. 2 (1995): 125–33.

108 **in a group of people, on average half of the variability:** David G. Winter, *Personality*, 512.

109 **temperature or humidity:** Natasha Mitchell, "Jerome Kagan: The Father of Temperament," radio interview with Mitchell on ABC *Radio International*, August 26, 2006 (accessed at http://www.abc.net.au/rn/allinthe mind/stories/2006/1722388.htm).

109 **"climb a few fences . . . danger and excitement":** Gallagher (quoting Lykken), "How We Become What We Are."

109 **"The university is filled with introverts":** Interview with the author, June 15, 2006.

110 **if raised by attentive families in safe environments . . . "twigs on the same genetic branch":** Winifred Gallagher, *I.D.: How Heredity and Experience Make You Who You Are* (New York: Random House, 1996), 29, 46–50. See also Kagan and Snidman, *The Long Shadow of Temperament*, 5.

110 **kids acquire their sense of right and wrong:** Grazyna Kochanska and R. A. Thompson, "The Emergence and Development of Conscience in Toddlerhood and Early Childhood," in *Parenting and Children's Internalization of Values*, edited by J. E. Grusec and L. Kucynski (New York: John Wiley and Sons), 61. See also Grazyna Kochanska, "Toward a Synthesis of Parental Socialization and Child Temperament in Early Development of Conscience," *Child Development* 64 no. 2 (1993): 325–47; Grazyna Kochanska and Nazan Aksan, "Children's Conscience and Self-Regulation," *Journal of Personality* 74, no. 6 (2006): 1587–1617; Grazyna Kochanska et al., "Guilt and Effortful Control: Two Mechanisms That Prevent Disruptive Developmental Trajectories," *Journal of Personality and Social Psychology* 97, no. 2 (2009): 322–33.

111 **tragedy of a bold and exuberant temperament:** Gallagher, *I.D.*, 46–50.

111 **dubbed "the orchid hypothesis":** David Dobbs, "The Science of Success," *The Atlantic* magazine, 2009. See also Jay Belsky et al., "Vulnerability Genes or Plasticity Genes?" *Molecular Psychiatry*, 2009: 1–9; Michael Pluess and Jay Belsky, "Differential Susceptibility to Rearing Experience: The Case of Childcare," *The Journal of Child Psychology and Psychiatry* 50, no. 4 (2009): 396–404; Pluess and Belsky, "Differential Susceptibility to Rearing Experience: Parenting and Quality Child Care," *Developmental Psychology* 46, no. 2 (2010): 379–90; Jay Belsky and Michael Pluess, "Beyond Diathesis Stress: Differential Susceptibility to Environmental Influences," *Psychological Bulletin* 135, no. 6 (2009): 885–908; Bruce J. Ellis and W. Thomas Boyce, "Bio-

logical Sensitivity to Context," *Current Directions in Psychological Science* 17, no. 3 (2008): 183–87.

111 **with depression, anxiety, and shyness:** Aron, *Psychotherapy and the Highly Sensitive Person*, 3. See also A. Engfer, "Antecedents and Consequences of Shyness in Boys and Girls: A 6-year Longitudinal Study," in *Social Withdrawal, Inhibition, and Shyness in Childhood*, edited by K. H. Rubin and J. B. Asendorpf (Hillsdale, NJ: Lawrence Erlbaum, 1993), 49–79; W. T. Boyce et al., "Psychobiologic Reactivity to Stress and Childhood Respiratory Illnesses: Results of Two Prospective Studies," *Psychosomatic Medicine* 57 (1995): 411–22; L. Gannon et al., "The Mediating Effects of Psychophysiological Reactivity and Recovery on the Relationship Between Environmental Stress and Illness," *Journal of Psychosomatic Research* 33 (1989): 165–75.

111 **Indeed, about a quarter of Kagan's high-reactive kids:** E-mail from Kagan to the author, June 22, 2010.

111 **good parenting, child care, and a stable home environment:** See, for example, Belsky et al., "Vulnerability Genes or Plasticity Genes?", 5. See also Pluess and Belsky, "Differential Susceptibility to Rearing Experience: The Case of Childcare," 397.

112 **kind, conscientious:** Aron, *The Highly Sensitive Child*.

112 **They don't necessarily turn into class presidents:** Author interview with Jay Belsky, April 28, 2010.

112 **world of rhesus monkeys:** Stephen J. Suomi, "Early Determinants of Behaviour: Evidence from Primate Studies," *British Medical Bulletin* 53, no. 1 (1997): 170–84 ("high-reactive infants cross-fostered to nurturant females actually appeared to be behaviourally precocious. . . . These individuals became especially adept at recruiting and retaining other group members as allies in response to agonistic encounters and, perhaps as a consequence, they subsequently rose to and maintained top positions in the group's dominance hierarchy. . . . Clearly, high-reactivity need not always be associated with adverse short- and long-term outcomes," p. 180). See also this video on the *Atlantic Monthly* website: (http://www.theatlantic.com/magazine/archive/2009/12/the-science-of-success/7761/), in which Suomi tells us that "the monkeys who had that same short allele and grew up with good mothers had no problems whatsoever. They turned out as well or better than monkeys who had the other version of this gene." (Note also that the link between the short allele of the SERT gene and depression in humans is well discussed but somewhat controversial.)

112 **thought to be associated with high reactivity and introversion:** Seth J. Gillihan et al., "Association Between Serotonin Transporter Genotype and

Extraversion," *Psychiatric Genetics* 17, no. 6 (2007): 351–54. See also M. R. Munafo et al., "Genetic Polymorphisms and Personality in Healthy Adults: A Systematic Review and Meta-Analysis," *Molecular Psychiatry* 8 (2003): 471–84. And see Cecilie L. Licht et al., "Association Between Sensory Processing Sensitivity and the 5-HTTLPR Short/Short Genotype."

112 **has speculated that these high-reactive monkeys:** Dobbs, "The Science of Success."

112– **adolescent girls with the short allele of the SERT gene . . . *less* anxiety**
13 **on calm days:** Belsky et al., "Vulnerability Genes or Plasticity Genes?"

113 **this difference remains at age five:** Elaine Aron, *Psychotherapy and the Highly Sensitive Person*, 240–41.

113 **even more resistant than other kids:** Boyce, "Psychobiologic Reactivity to Stress and Childhood Respiratory Illnesses: Results of Two Prospective Studies." See also W. Thomas Boyce and Bruce J. Ellis, "Biological Sensitivity to Context: I. Evolutionary-Developmental Theory of the Origins and Functions of Stress Reactivity," *Development and Psychopathology* 27 (2005): 283.

113 **The short allele of the SERT gene:** See Judith R. Homberg and Klaus-Peter Lesch, "Looking on the Bright Side of Serotonin Transporter Gene Variation," *Biological Psychiatry*, 2010.

113 **"sailors are so busy—and wisely—looking under the water line":** Belsky et al., "Vulnerability Genes or Plasticity Genes?"

113 **"The time and effort they invest":** Author interview with Jay Belsky, April 28, 2010.

CHAPTER 5: BEYOND TEMPERAMENT

115 **"Enjoyment appears at the boundary":** Mihaly Csikszentmihalyi, *Flow: The Psychology of Optimal Experience* (New York: Harper Perennial, 1990), 52.

115 **windowless room with Dr. Carl Schwartz:** I conducted a series of interviews with Dr. Schwartz between 2006 and 2010.

117 *the footprint of a high- or low-reactive temperament:* Carl Schwartz et al., "Inhibited and Uninhibited Infants 'Grown Up': Adult Amygdalar Response to Novelty," *Science* 300, no. 5627 (2003): 1952–53.

118 **If you were a high-reactive baby:** For a good overview of the relationship between the amygdala and the prefrontal cortex, see Joseph Ledoux, *The Emotional Brain: The Mysterious Underpinnings of Emotional Life* (New York: Simon & Schuster, 1996), chapters 6 and 8. See also Gregory Berns, *Iconoclast: A Neuroscientist Reveals How to Think Differently* (Boston, MA: Harvard Business Press, 2008), 59–81.

118 **self-talk to reassess upsetting situations:** Kevin N. Ochsner et al., "Rethinking Feelings: An fMRI Study of the Cognitive Regulation of Emotion," *Journal of Cognitive Neuroscience* 14, no. 8 (2002): 1215–29.

118 **scientists conditioned a rat:** Ledoux, *The Emotional Brain*, 248–49.

122 **Hans Eysenck:** David C. Funder, *The Personality Puzzle* (New York: W. W. Norton, 2010), 280–83.

123 **high arousal levels in the brain:** E-mail from Jerome Kagan to the author, June 23, 2010.

123 **many different kinds of arousal:** E-mail from Carl Schwartz to the author, August 16, 2010. Also note that introverts seem not to be in a baseline state of high arousal so much as susceptible to tipping over into that state.

123 **excited fans at a soccer game:** E-mail from Jerome Kagan to the author, June 23, 2010.

123 **a host of evidence that introverts *are* more sensitive:** This has been written about in many places. See, for example, Robert Stelmack, "On Personality and Arousal: A Historical Perspective on Eysenck and Zuckerman," in *On the Psychobiology of Personality: Essays in Honor of Marvin Zuckerman*, edited by Marvin Zuckerman and Robert Stelmack (Pergamon, 2005), 17–28. See also Gerald Matthews et al., *Personality Traits* (Cambridge, UK: Cambridge University Press, 2003), 169–70, 186–89, 329–42. See also Randy J. Larsen and David M. Buss, *Personality Psychology: Domains of Knowledge About Human Nature* (New York: McGraw Hill, 2005), 202–6.

124 **lemon juice:** Funder, *The Personality Puzzle*, 281.

124 **noise level preferred by the extroverts:** Russell G. Geen, "Preferred Stimulation Levels in Introverts and Extroverts: Effects on Arousal and Performance," *Journal of Personality and Social Psychology* 46, no. 6 (1984): 1303–12.

125 **They can hunt for homes:** This idea comes from Winifred Gallagher, *House Thinking: A Room-by-Room Look at How We Live* (New York: Harper Collins, 2006).

125 **introverts function better than extroverts when sleep deprived:** William Kilgore et al., "The Trait of Introversion-Extraversion Predicts Vulnerability to Sleep Deprivation," *Journal of Sleep Research* 16, no. 4 (2007): 354–63.

125 **Drowsy extroverts behind the wheel:** Matthews, *Personality Traits*, 337.

126 **Overarousal interferes with attention:** Gerald Matthews and Lisa Dorn, "Cognitive and Attentional Processes in Personality and Intelligence," in *International Handbook of Personality and Intelligence*, edited by Donald H. Saklofske and Moshe Zeidner (New York: Plenum Press, 1995): 367–96. Or, as the psychologist Brian Little puts it, "extraverts often find that they

are able to handle cramming for speeches or briefings in a way that would be disastrous for introverts."

127 **a cycle of dread, fear, and shame:** Berns, *Iconoclast*, 59–81.

CHAPTER 6: "FRANKLIN WAS A POLITICIAN, BUT ELEANOR SPOKE OUT OF CONSCIENCE"

130 **"A shy man no doubt dreads the notice":** Charles Darwin, *The Expressions of the Emotions in Man and Animals* (Charleston, SC: BiblioBazaar, 2007), 259.

130 **Easter Sunday, 1939. The Lincoln Memorial:** My description of the concert is based on film footage of the event.

130 **And it wouldn't have, without Eleanor Roosevelt . . . to sing at the Lincoln Memorial:** Allida M. Black, *Casting Her Own Shadow: Eleanor Roosevelt and the Shaping of Postwar Liberalism* (New York: Columbia University Press, 1996), 41–44.

131 **"This was something unique":** *The American Experience: Eleanor Roosevelt* (Public Broadcasting System, Ambrica Productions, 2000). See transcript: http://www.pbs.org/wgbh/amex/eleanor/filmmore/transcript/transcript1 .html.

131 **They met when he was twenty:** Blanche Wiesen Cook, *Eleanor Roosevelt, Volume One: 1884–1933* (New York: Viking Penguin, 1992), esp. 125–236. See also *The American Experience: Eleanor Roosevelt*.

133 **her first scientific publication in 1997:** Elaine N. Aron and Arthur Aron, "Sensory-Processing Sensitivity and Its Relation to Introversion and Emotionality," *Journal of Personality and Social Psychology* 3, no. 2 (1997): 345–68.

135– **When she was a girl . . . She decided to find out:** The biographical infor-
36 mation about Aron comes from (1) interview with the author, August 21, 2008; (2) Elaine N. Aron, *The Highly Sensitive Person: How to Thrive When the World Overwhelms You* (New York: Broadway Books, 1996); (3) Elaine N. Aron, *The Highly Sensitive Person in Love: Understanding and Managing Relationships When the World Overwhelms You* (New York: Broadway Books, 2000).

136 **First Aron interviewed thirty-nine people . . . lightbulb burning a touch too brightly:** Aron and Aron, "Sensory-Processing Sensitivity." See also E. N. Aron, "Revisiting Jung's Concept of Innate Sensitiveness," *Journal of Analytical Psychology* 49 (2004): 337–67. See also Aron, *The Highly Sensitive Person*.

136 **They feel exceptionally strong emotions:** In laboratory studies, looking at pictures designed to create strong positive or negative emotions, they reported feeling more emotionally aroused than nonsensitive people. See

B. Acevedo, A. Aron, and E. Aron, "Sensory Processing Sensitivity and Neural Responses to Strangers' Emotional States," in A. Aron (Chair), *High Sensitivity, a Personality/Temperament Trait: Lifting the Shadow of Psychopathology*, symposium presented at the Annual Meeting of the American Psychological Association, San Diego, California, 2010. See also Jadzia Jagiellowicz, Arthur Aron, Elaine Aron, and Turhan Canli, "Faster and More Intense: Emotion Processing and Attentional Mechanisms in Individuals with Sensory Processing Sensitivity," in Aron, *High Sensitivity*.

136 **scientists at Stony Brook University:** Jadzia Jagiellowicz et al., "Sensory Processing Sensitivity and Neural Responses to Changes in Visual Scenes," *Social Cognitive and Affective Neuroscience*, 2010, doi.10.1093/scan/nsq001.

137 **echoes Jerome Kagan's findings:** Jerome Kagan, "Reflection-Impulsivity and Reading Ability in Primary Grade Children," *Child Development* 363, no. 3 (1965): 609–28. See also Ellen Siegelman, "Reflective and Impulsive Observing Behavior," *Child Development* 40, no. 4 (1969): 1213–22.

137 **"If you're thinking in more complicated ways":** Interview with the author, May 8, 2010.

137 **highly empathic:** Aron and Aron, "Sensory-Processing Sensitivity." See also Aron, "Revisiting Jung's Concept of Innate Sensitiveness." See also Aron, *The Highly Sensitive Person*. And see the following fMRI studies: Acevedo, "Sensory Processing Sensitivity and Neural Responses to Strangers' Emotional States." And see Jadzia Jagiellowicz, "Faster and More Intense: Emotion Processing and Attentional Mechanisms in Individuals with Sensory Processing Sensitivity." Note that many personality psychologists who subscribe to the "Big 5" theory of personality associate empathy not with sensitivity (a construct that is gaining attention, but is relatively less well known than the Big 5), but with a trait known as "Agreeableness" and even extroversion. Aron's work does not challenge these associations, but expands them. One of the most valuable aspects of Aron's work is how radically, and fruitfully, she reinterprets personality psychology.

138 **tentatively associated with sensitivity:** Seth J. Gillihan et al., "Association Between Serotonin Transporter Genotype and Extraversion," *Psychiatric Genetics* 17, no. 6 (2007): 351–54. See also M. R. Munafo et al., "Genetic Polymorphisms and Personality in Healthy Adults: A Systematic Review and Meta-Analysis," *Molecular Psychiatry* 8 (2003): 471–84.

138 **show them pictures of scared faces:** David C. Funder, *The Personality Puzzle* (New York: W. W. Norton, 2010), citing A. R. Hariri et al., "Serotonin Transporter Genetic Variation and the Response of the Human Amygdala," *Science* 297 (2002): 400–403.

138 **faces of people experiencing strong feelings:** Acevedo, "Sensory Process-

ing Sensitivity and Neural Responses to Strangers' Emotional States." See also Jadzia Jagiellowicz, "Faster and More Intense: Emotion Processing and Attentional Mechanisms in Individuals with Sensory Processing Sensitivity."

138– **In 1921, FDR contracted polio . . . how suffering Americans felt:**
40   Cook, *Eleanor Roosevelt, Volume One*, 125–236. See also *The American Experience: Eleanor Roosevelt*.

140– **A kind woman hands a toy to a toddler . . . "prosocial relationships**
41   **with parents, teachers, and friends":** Grazyna Kochanska et al., "Guilt in Young Children: Development, Determinants, and Relations with a Broader System of Standards," *Child Development* 73, no. 2 (March/April 2002): 461–82. See also Grazyna Kochanska and Nazan Aksan, "Children's Conscience and Self-Regulation," *Journal of Personality* 74, no. 6 (2006): 1587–1617. See also Grazyna Kochanska et al., "Guilt and Effortful Control: Two Mechanisms That Prevent Disruptive Developmental Trajectories," *Journal of Personality and Social Psychology* 97, no. 2 (2009): 322–33.

141   **a 2010 University of Michigan study:** S. H. Konrath et al., "Changes in Dispositional Empathy in American College Students Over Time: A Meta-Analysis," *Personality and Social Psychology Review*, August 2010, e-publication ahead of print (accessed at http://www.ncbi.nlm.nih.gov/ pubmed/20688954).

141   **related to the prevalence of social media:** Pamela Paul, "From Students, Less Kindness for Strangers?" *New York Times*, June 25, 2010.

141   **when her peers were teased:** Elaine Aron, *The Highly Sensitive Child* (New York: Random House, 2002), 18, 282–83.

141   **the novelist Eric Malpass:** Eric Malpass, *The Long Long Dances* (London: Corgi, 1978).

142   **High-reactive introverts sweat more:** V. De Pascalis, "On the Psychophysiology of Extraversion," in *On the Psychobiology of Personality: Essays in Honor of Marvin Zuckerman*, edited by Marvin Zuckerman and Robert M. Stelmack (San Diego: Elsevier, 2004), 22. See also Randy J. Larsen and David M. Buss, *Personality Psychology: Domains of Knowledge About Human Nature* (New York: McGraw-Hill, 2005),199.

142   **sociopaths lie at the extreme end:** Van K. Tharp et al., "Autonomic Activity During Anticipation of an Averse Tone in Noninstitutionalized Sociopaths," *Psychophysiology* 17, no. 2 (1980): 123–28. See also Joseph Newman et al., "Validating a Distinction Between Primary and Secondary Psychopathy with Measures of Gray's BIS and BAS Constructs," *Journal of Abnormal Psychology* 114 (2005): 319–23.

142 **sociopaths have damaged amygdalae:** Yaling Yang et al., "Localization of Deformations Within the Amygdala in Individuals with Psychopathy," *Archives of General Psychiatry* 66, no. 9 (2009), 986–94.

142 **Lie detectors . . . are partially skin conductance tests:** They also measure breathing, pulse rate, and blood pressure.

143 **supercool pulse rate during liftoff:** Winifred Gallagher, *I.D.: How Heredity and Experience Make You Who You Are* (New York: Random House, 1996), 24.

143 **Corine Dijk:** Corine Dijk and Peter J. De Jong, "The Remedial Value of Blushing in the Context of Transgressions and Mishaps," *Emotion* 9, no. 2 (2009): 287–91.

144 **"A blush comes online in two or three seconds":** Benedict Carey, "Hold Your Head Up: A Blush Just Shows You Care," *New York Times*, June 2, 2009: D5.

144 **"Because it is impossible to control":** Ibid.

144 **Keltner has tracked the roots of human embarrassment . . . than to mind too little:** Dacher Keltner, *Born to Be Good: The Science of a Meaningful Life* (New York: W. W. Norton, 2009), 74–96.

145 **"The type that is 'sensitive' or 'reactive.' . . . 'opportunity only knocks once'":** Elaine Aron, "Revisiting Jung's Concept of Innate Sensitiveness," 337–67.

145 **twenty-seven attributes associated:** Author interview with Elaine Aron, August 21, 2008.

145 **other 30 percent are extroverts:** Aron, *Psychotherapy and the Highly Sensitive Person*, 5.

146 *More than a hundred* **species . . . what's going on around them:** Max Wolf et al., "Evolutionary Emergence of Responsive and Unresponsive Personalities," *Proceedings of the National Academy of Sciences* 105, no. 41 (2008): 15825–30. See also Aron, *Psychotherapy and the Highly Sensitive Person*, 2.

146 **animals had parties:** David Sloan Wilson, *Evolution for Everyone: How Darwin's Theory Can Change the Way We Think About Our Lives* (New York: Bantam Dell, 2007), 110.

146 **trade-off theory of evolution:** Daniel Nettle "The Evolution of Personality Variation in Humans and Other Anim s," *American Psychologist* 61, no. 6 (2006): 622–31.

147 **When Wilson dropped metal traps:** Wilson, *Evolution for Everyone*, 100–114.

147 **Trinidadian guppies:** Nettle, "The Evolution of Personality Variation in Humans and Other Animals," 624. See also Shyril O'Steen et al., "Rapid Evolution of Escape Ability in Trinidadian Guppies," *Evolution* 56, no. 4 (2002): 776–84. Note that another study found that bold fish do better

with predators (but these were cichlids in fish tanks, not pike in streams): Brian R. Smith and Daniel T. Blumstein, "Behavioral Types as Predictors of Survival in Trinidadian Guppies," *Behavioral Ecology* 21, no. 5 (2010): 65–73.

148 **nomads who inherited:** Dan Eisenberg et al., "Dopamine Receptor Genetic Polymorphisms and Body Composition in Undernourished Pastoralists: An Exploration of Nutrition Indices Among Nomadic and Recently Settled Ariaal Men of Northern Kenya," *BMC Evolutionary Biology* 8, no. 173 (2008), doi:10.1186/1471-2148-8-173. See also: http://machineslikeus .com/news/adhd-advantage-nomadic-tribesmen.

148 **extroverts have more sex partners . . . commit more crimes.** Nettle, "The Evolution of Personality Variation in Humans and Other Animals," 625. See also Daniel Nettle, *Personality: What Makes You the Way You Are* (New York: Oxford University Press, 2007).

148 **As Jung speculated almost a century ago:** Carl Jung, *Psychological Types*, vol. 6 of *The Collected Works of C. G. Jung* (Princeton, NJ: Princeton University Press, 1971), 559.

148 **whose traits promote group survival:** See, for example, Nicholas Wade, "The Evolution of the God Gene," *New York Times*, November 15, 2009.

148 **"Suppose a herd of antelope":** Elaine Aron, "Book Review: Unto Others: The Evolution and Psychology of Unselfish Behavior," January 2007, *Comfort Zone Online*: http://www.hsperson.com/pages/3Feb07.htm.

149 **"hawk" and "dove" members:** Elaine Aron, "A Future Headline: 'HSPs, the Key to Human Survival?'" August 2007, Comfort Zone Online: http:// www.hsperson.com/pages/1Aug07.htm.

149 **Great tit birds:** Nettle, "The Evolution of Personality Variation in Humans and Other Animals," 624–25. See also Sloan Wilson, *Evolution for Everyone*, 110.

149 **"If you send an introvert into a reception":** David Remnick, "The Wilderness Campaign," *The New Yorker*, September 13, 2004.

150 **"Most people in politics draw energy":** John Heilemann, "The Comeback Kid," *New York* magazine, May 21, 2006.

151 **"It's about the survival of the planet":** Benjamin Svetkey, "Changing the Climate," *Entertainment Weekly*, July 14, 2006.

154 **"warrior kings" and "priestly advisers":** Aron, "Revisiting Jung's Concept of Innate Sensitiveness."

CHAPTER 7: WHY DID WALL STREET CRASH AND WARREN
BUFFETT PROSPER?

155 **Just after 7:30 a.m.:** Alan's story and the description of Dorn and her
house are based on a series of telephone and e-mail interviews with the
author, conducted between 2008 and 2010.

157 **Financial history is full of examples:** There are also many examples from
military history. "Hurrah, boys, we've got them!" General Custer famously
shouted at the battle of Little Bighorn in 1876—just before his entire unit
of two hundred men was wiped out by three thousand Sioux and Cheyenne.
General MacArthur advanced in the face of repeated Chinese threats of
attack during the Korean War, costing almost 2 million lives with little strategic gain. Stalin refused to believe that the Germans would invade Russia
in 1941, even after *ninety* warnings of an impending attack. See Dominic D.
P. Johnson, *Overconfidence and War: The Havoc and Glory of Positive Illusions*
(Cambridge, MA: Harvard University Press, 2004).

157 **The AOL–Time Warner merger:** Nina Monk, *Fools Rush In: Steve Case,
Jerry Levin, and the Unmaking of AOL Time-Warner* (New York: HarperCollins, 2005).

158 **They protect themselves better from the downside:** The psychology professor Richard Howard, in an interview with the author on November 17,
2008, notes that introverts tend to down-regulate positive emotions and
extroverts tend to up-regulate them.

158 **our limbic system:** Note that these days many scientists dislike the phrase
"limbic system." This is because no one really knows which parts of the
brain this term refers to. The brain areas included in this system have
changed over the years, and today many use the term to mean brain areas
that have something to do with emotion. Still, it's a useful shorthand.

159 **"No, no, no! Don't do that":** See, for example, Ahmad R. Hariri, Susan
Y. Bookheimer, and John C. Mazziotta, "Modulating Emotional Responses:
Effects of a Neocortical Network on the Limbic Systems," *NeuroReport* 11
(1999): 43–48.

159 **what *makes* an extrovert an extrovert:** Richard E. Lucas and Ed Diener,
"Cross-Cultural Evidence for the Fundamental Features of Extraversion,"
Journal of Personality and Social Psychology 79, no. 3 (2000): 452–68. See also
Michael D. Robinson et al., "Extraversion and Reward-Related Processing:
Probing Incentive Motivation in Affective Priming Tasks," *Emotion* 10, no. 5
(2010): 615–26.

159 **greater economic, political, and hedonistic ambitions:** Joshua Wilt and
William Revelle, "Extraversion," in *Handbook of Individual Differences in
Social Behavior*, edited by Mark R. Leary and Rich H. Hoyle (New York:
Guilford Press, 2009), 39.

159 **The key seems to be positive emotion:** See Lucas and Diener, "Cross-Cultural Evidence for the Fundamental Features of Extraversion." See also Daniel Nettle, *Personality: What Makes You the Way You Are* (New York: Oxford University Press, 2007).

160 **The basis of buzz:** Richard Depue and Paul Collins, "Neurobiology of the Structure of Personality: Dopamine, Facilitation of Incentive Motivation, and Extraversion," *Behavioral and Brain Sciences* 22, no. 3 (1999): 491–569. See also Nettle, *Personality: What Makes You the Way You Are.*

160 **Dopamine is the "reward chemical":** Depue and Collins, "Neurobiology of the Structure of Personality: Dopamine, Facilitation of Incentive Motivation, and Extraversion." See also Nettle, *Personality: What Makes You the Way You Are.* See also Susan Lang, "Psychologist Finds Dopamine Linked to a Personality Trait and Happiness," *Cornell Chronicle* 28, no. 10 (1996).

160 **early findings have been intriguing:** Some of the findings in this line of research have been contradictory or have not been replicated, but together they pose an important avenue of inquiry.

160 **In one experiment, Richard Depue:** Depue and Collins, "Neurobiology of the Structure of Personality: Dopamine, Facilitation of Incentive Motivation, and Extraversion."

160 **extroverts who win gambling games:** Michael X. Cohen et al., "Individual Differences in Extraversion and Dopamine Genetics Predict Neural Reward Responses," *Cognitive Brain Research* 25 (2005): 851–61.

160 **other research has shown that the medial orbitofrontal cortex:** Colin G. DeYoung et al., "Testing Predictions from Personality Neuroscience: Brain Structure and the Big Five," *Psychological Science* 21, no. 6 (2010): 820–28.

161 **introverts "have a smaller response" . . . "break a leg to get there":** Nettle, *Personality: What Makes You the Way You Are.*

161 **"This is great!":** Michael J. Beatty et al., "Communication Apprehension as Temperamental Expression: A Communibiological Paradigm," *Communication Monographs* 65 (1988): reporting that people with high communication apprehension "value moderate . . . success less than do those low in the trait."

161 **"Everyone assumes that it's good to accentuate positive emotions":** Richard Howard interview with the author, November 17, 2008. Howard also pointed to this interesting take by Roy F. Baumeister et al., "How Emotions Facilitate and Impair Self-Regulation," in *Handbook of Emotion Regulation*, edited by James J. Gross (New York: Guilford Press, 2009), 422: "positive emotion can sweep aside the normal restraints that promote civilized behavior."

161 **Another disadvantage of buzz:** Note that this sort of risk-taking be-

havior is in what Daniel Nettle (*Personality: What Makes You the Way You Are*, 83) calls "the shared territory" of extroversion and another personality trait, conscientiousness. In some cases conscientiousness is the better predictor.

161– **extroverts are more likely than introverts to be killed while driving . . .**
62 **remarry:** Nettle, *Personality: What Makes You the Way You Are*. See also Timo Lajunen, "Personality and Accident Liability: Are Extroversion, Neuroticism and Psychoticism Related to Traffic and Occupational Fatalities?" *Personality and Individual Differences* 31, no. 8 (2001): 1365–73.

162 **extroverts are more prone than introverts to overconfidence:** Peter Schaefer, "Overconfidence and the Big Five," *Journal of Research in Personality* 38, no. 5 (2004): 473–80.

162 **better off with more women:** See, for example, Sheelah Kolhatkar, "What if Women Ran Wall Street?" *New York Magazine*, March 21, 2010.

162 **a strong predictor of financial risk-taking:** Camelia M. Kuhnen and Joan Y. Chiao, "Genetic Determinants of Financial Risk Taking," *PLoS ONE* 4(2): e4362. doi:10.1371/journal.pone.0004362 (2009). See also Anna Dreber et al., "The 7R Polymorphism in the Dopamine Receptor D4 Gene (DRD4) Is Associated with Financial Risk Taking in Men." *Evolution and Human Behavior* 30, no. 2 (2009): 85–92.

162 **When faced with a low probability of winning:** J. P. Roiser et al., "The Effect of Polymorphism at the Serotonin Transporter Gene on Decision-making, Memory and Executive Function in Ecstasy Users and Controls," *Psychopharmacology* 188 (2006): 213–27.

162 **Another study, of sixty-four traders:** Mark Fenton O'Creevy et al., *Traders: Risks, Decisions, and Management in Financial Markets* (Oxford, UK: Oxford University Press, 2005), 142–43.

163 **delaying gratification, a crucial life skill:** Jonah Lehrer, "Don't," *The New Yorker*, May 18, 2009. See also Jacob B. Hirsh et al., "Positive Mood Effects on Delay Discounting," *Emotion* 10, no. 5 (2010): 717–21. See also David Brooks, *The Social Animal* (New York: Random House, 2011), 124.

163 **scientists gave participants the choice:** Samuel McClure et al., "Separate Neural Systems Value Immediate and Delayed Monetary Rewards," *Science* 306 (2004): 503–7.

163 **A similar study suggests:** Hirsch, "Positive Mood Effects on Delay Discounting."

163 **Yet it was just this kind of risk-reward miscalculation:** Wall Street's judgment was clouded by a strange brew of (1) lemming-like behavior, (2) the opportunity to earn large transaction fees, (3) the fear of losing market share to competitors, and (4) the inability to properly balance opportunity against risk.

164 **Too much power was concentrated in the hands of aggressive risk-takers:**
Interview with the author, March 5, 2009.

164 **"For twenty years, the DNA":** Fareed Zakaria, "There Is a Silver Lining,"
Newsweek, October 11, 2008.

164 **Vincent Kaminski:** Steven Pearlstein, "The Art of Managing Risk," *The
Washington Post*, November 8, 2007. See also Alexei Barrionuevo, "Vin-
cent Kaminski: Sounding the Alarm But Unable to Prevail," in "10 Enron
Players: Where They Landed After the Fall," *The New York Times*, Janu-
ary 29, 2006. And see Kurt Eichenwald, *Conspiracy of Fools: A True Story*
(New York: Broadway, 2005), 250.

165 **Imagine that you've been invited to Newman's lab:** C. M. Patterson
and Joseph Newman, "Reflectivity and Learning from Aversive Events:
Toward a Psychological Mechanism for the Syndromes of Disinhibition,"
Psychological Review 100 (1993): 716–36. Carriers of the s-variant of the
5HTTLPR polymorphism (which is associated with introversion and
sensitivity) have also been show to be faster to learn to avoid penalizing
stimuli in passive avoidance tasks. See E. C. Finger et al., "The Impact of
Tryptophan Depletion and 5-HTTLPR Genotype on Passive Avoidance
and Response Reversal Instrumental Learning Tasks," *Neuropsychopharma-
cology* 32 (2007): 206–15.

166 **introverts are "geared to inspect":** John Brebner and Chris Cooper,
"Stimulus or Response-Induced Excitation: A Comparison of the Behavior of Introverts and Extroverts," *Journal of Research in Personality* 12, no. 3
(1978): 306–11.

166 **more likely you are to learn:** Indeed, it's been shown that one of the crucial ways that we learn is to analyze our mistakes. See Jonah Lehrer, *How
We Decide* (New York: Houghton Mifflin Harcourt, 2009), 51.

166– **If you *force* extroverts to pause . . . how to behave around warning sig-
67 nals in the future:** Interview with the author, November 13, 2008. Another way to understand why some people worry about risks and others
ignore them is to go back to the idea of brain networks. In this chapter I
focused on the dopamine-driven reward system and its role in delivering
life's goodies. But there's a mirror-image brain network, often called the
loss avoidance system, whose job is to call our attention to risk. If the
reward network chases shiny fruit, the loss avoidance system worries about
bad apples.

The loss avoidance system, like the reward network, is a double-edged
sword. It can make people anxious, unpleasantly anxious, so anxious
that they sit out bull markets while everyone else gets rich. But it also
causes them to take fewer stupid risks. This system is mediated in part
by a neurotransmitter called serotonin—and when people are given drugs

like Prozac (known as selective serotonin reuptake inhibitors) that affect the loss avoidance system, they become more blasé about danger. They also become more gregarious. These features coincide uncannily, points out the neurofinance expert Dr. Richard Peterson, with the behavior of irrationally exuberant investors. "The characteristics of decreased threat perception and increased social affiliation [resulting from drugs like Prozac] mirror the decreased risk perception and herding of excessively bullish investors," he writes. "It is as if bubble investors are experiencing a partial deactivation of their brains' loss avoidance systems."

167 **relative performance of introverts and extroverts:** Dalip Kumar and Asha Kapila, "Problem Solving as a Function of Extraversion and Masculinity," *Personality and Individual Differences* 8, no. 1 (1987): 129–32.

167 **Extroverts get better grades:** Adrian Furnham et al., "Personality, Cognitive Ability, and Beliefs About Intelligence as Predictors of Academic Performance," *Learning and Individual Differences* 14 (2003): 49–66. See also Isabel Briggs Myers and Mary H. McCaulley, *MBTI Manual: A Guide to the Development and Use of the Myers-Briggs Type Indicator* (Palo Alto, CA: Consulting Psychologists Press, 1985), 116; see also the Myers 1980 study referred to in Allan B. Hill, "Developmental Student Achievement: The Personality Factor," *Journal of Psychological Type* 9, no. 6 (2006): 79–87.

167 **141 college students' knowledge:** Eric Rolfhus and Philip Ackerman, "Assessing Individual Differences in Knowledge: Knowledge, Intelligence, and Related Traits," *Journal of Educational Psychology* 91, no. 3 (1999): 511–26.

167 **disproportionate numbers of graduate degrees:** G. P. Macdaid, M. H. McCaulley, and R. I. Kainz, *Atlas of Type Tables* (Gainesville, FL: Center for Applications of Psychological Type, 1986), pp. 483–85. See also Hill, "Developmental Student Achievement."

167 **outperform extroverts on the Watson-Glaser:** Joanna Moutafi, Adrian Furnham, and John Crump, "Demographic and Personality Predictors of Intelligence: A Study Using the NEO Personality Inventory and the Myers-Briggs Type Indicator," *European Journal of Personality* 17, no. 1 (2003): 79–84.

168 **Introverts are not smarter than extroverts:** Author interview with Gerald Matthews, November 24, 2008. See also D. H. Saklofske and D. D. Kostura, "Extraversion-Introversion and Intelligence," *Personality and Individual Differences* 11, no. 6 (1990): 547–51.

168 **those performed under time or social pressure:** Gerald Matthews and Lisa Dorn, "Cognitive and Attentional Processes in Personality and Intel-

ligence," in *International Handbook of Personality and Intelligence*, edited by Donald H. Saklofske and Moshe Zeidner (New York: Plenum Press, 1995), 367–96. See also Gerald Matthews et al., *Personality Traits* (Cambridge, UK: Cambridge University Press, 2003), ch. 12.

168 **also direct their attention differently . . . are asking "what if":** Debra L. Johnson et al., "Cerebral Blood Flow and Personality: A Positron Emission Tomography Study," *The American Journal of Psychiatry* 156 (1999): 252–57. See also Lee Tilford Davis and Peder E. Johnson, "An Assessment of Conscious Content as Related to Introversion-Extroversion," *Imagination, Cognition and Personality* 3, no. 2 (1983).

168 **a difficult jigsaw puzzle to solve:** Colin Cooper and Richard Taylor, "Personality and Performance on a Frustrating Cognitive Task," *Perceptual and Motor Skills* 88, no. 3 (1999): 1384.

168 **a complicated series of printed mazes:** Rick Howard and Maeve McKillen, "Extraversion and Performance in the Perceptual Maze Test," *Personality and Individual Differences* 11, no. 4 (1990): 391–96. See also John Weinman, "Noncognitive Determinants of Perceptual Problem-Solving Strategies," *Personality and Individual Differences* 8, no. 1 (1987): 53–58.

169 **Raven Standard Progressive Matrices:** Vidhu Mohan and Dalip Kumar, "Qualitative Analysis of the Performance of Introverts and Extroverts on Standard Progressive Matrices," *British Journal of Psychology* 67, no. 3 (1976): 391–97.

169 **personality traits of effective call-center employees:** Interview with the author, February 13, 2007.

170 **if you were staffing an investment bank:** Interview with the author, July 7, 2010.

170 **men who are shown erotic pictures:** Camelia Kuhnen et al., "Nucleus Accumbens Activation Mediates the Influence of Reward Cues on Financial Risk Taking," *NeuroReport* 19, no. 5 (2008): 509–13.

171 **all introverts are constantly . . . vigilant about threats:** Indeed, many contemporary personality psychologists would say that threat-vigilance is more characteristic of a trait known as "neuroticism" than of introversion per se.

171 **threat-vigilance is more characteristic of a trait:** But harm avoidance is correlated with both introversion and neuroticism (both traits are associated with Jerry Kagan's "high reactivity" and Elaine Aron's "high sensitivity"). See Mary E. Stewart et al., "Personality Correlates of Happiness and Sadness: EPQ-R and TPQ Compared," *Personality and Individual Differences* 38, no. 5 (2005): 1085–96.

171 **"If you want to determine":** can be found at http://www.psy.miami.edu/

faculty/ccarver/sclBISBAS.html. I first came across this scale in Jonathan Haidt's excellent book, *The Happiness Hypothesis: Finding Modern Truth in Ancient Wisdom* (New York: Basic Books, 2005), 34.

172 **"become independent of the social environment":** Mihalyi Csikszentmihalyi, *Flow: The Psychology of Optimal Experience* (New York: Harper Perennial, 1990), 16.

172 **"Psychological theories usually assume":** Mihalyi Csikszentmilhalyi, *The Evolving Self: A Psychology for the Third Millennium* (New York: Harper Perennial, 1994), xii.

173 **you probably find that your energy is boundless:** The same goes for happiness. Research suggests that buzz and other positive emotions seem to come a little easier to extroverts, and that extroverts as a group are happier. But when psychologists compare happy extroverts with happy introverts, they find that the two groups share many of the same characteristics—self-esteem; freedom from anxiety; satisfaction with their life work—and that those features predict happiness more strongly than extroversion itself does. See Peter Hills and Michael Argyle, "Happiness, Introversion-Extraversion and Happy Introverts," *Personality and Individual Differences* 30 (2001): 595–608.

173 **"Release Your Inner Extrovert":** *BusinessWeek* online column, November 26, 2008.

173 **Chuck Prince:** For an account of Chuck Prince's persona, see, for example, Mara Der Hovanesian, "Rewiring Chuck Prince," *Bloomberg BusinessWeek*, February 20, 2006.

174 **Seth Klarman:** For information on Klarman, see, for example, Charles Klein, "Klarman Tops Griffin as Investors Hunt for 'Margin of Safety,'" *Bloomberg BusinessWeek*, June 11, 2010. See also Geraldine Fabrikant, "Manager Frets Over Market but Still Outdoes It," *New York Times*, May 13, 2007.

175 **Michael Lewis:** Michael Lewis, *The Big Short: Inside the Doomsday Machine* (New York: W. W. Norton, 2010).

176 **Warren Buffett:** Warren Buffett's story, as related in this chapter, comes from an excellent biography: Alice Schroeder, *The Snowball: Warren Buffett and the Business of Life* (New York: Bantam Books, 2008).

177 **"inner scorecard":** Some psychologists would relate Warren Buffett's self-direction not necessarily to introversion but to a different phenomenon called "internal locus of control."

CHAPTER 8: SOFT POWER

181 **Mike Wei:** The interviews with Mike Wei and others from Cupertino, related throughout this chapter, were conducted with the author at various stages between 2006 and 2010.

182 **article called "The New White Flight":** Suein Hwang, "The New White Flight," *Wall Street Journal*, November 19, 2005.

182– **53 were National Merit Scholarship . . . 27 percent higher than the**
83 **nationwide average:** Monta Vista High School website, as of May 31, 2010.

184 **Talking is simply not a focus:** Richard C. Levin, "Top of the Class: The Rise of Asia's Universities," *Foreign Affairs*, May/June 2010.

185 **the San Jose Mercury News ran an article:** Sarah Lubman, "East West Teaching Traditions Collide," *San Jose Mercury News*, February 23, 1998.

186 **"colleges can learn to listen to their sound of silence":** Heejung Kim, "We Talk, Therefore We Think? A Cultural Analysis of the Effect of Talking on Thinking," *Journal of Personality and Social Psychology* 83, no. 4 (2002): 828–42.

186 **The *Journal of Research in Personality*:** Robert R. McCrae, "Human Nature and Culture: A Trait Perspective," *Journal of Research in Personality* 38 (2004): 3–14.

186 **Americans are some of the most extroverted:** See, for example, David G. Winter, *Personality: Analysis and Interpretation of Lives* (New York: McGraw-Hill, 1996), 459.

187 **One study comparing eight- to ten-year-old children:** Xinyin Chen et al., "Social Reputation and Peer Relationships in Chinese and Canadian Children: A Cross-Cultural Study," *Child Development* 63, no. 6 (1992): 1336–43. See also W. Ray Crozier, *Shyness: Development, Consolidation and Change* (Routledge, 2001), 147.

187 **Chinese high school students tell researchers:** Michael Harris Bond, *Beyond the Chinese Face: Insights from Psychology* (New York: Oxford University Press, 1991), 62.

187 **Another study asked Asian-Americans:** Kim, "We Talk, Therefore We Think?"

187 **Asian attitudes to the spoken word:** See, for example, Heejung Kim and Hazel Markus, "Freedom of Speech and Freedom of Silence: An Analysis of Talking as a Cultural Practice," in *Engaging Cultural Differences in Liberal Democracies*, edited by Richard K. Shweder et al. (New York: Russell Sage Foundation, 2002), 432–52.

187 **proverbs from the East:** Some of these come from the epigraph of the article by Heejung Kim and Hazel Markus, cited above.

188 **grueling Ming dynasty–era *jinshi* exam:** Nicholas Kristof, "The Model Students," *New York Times*, May 14, 2006.

189 **pictures of men in dominance poses:** Jonathan Freeman et al., "Culture Shapes a Mesolimbic Response to Signals of Dominance and Subordination that Associates with Behavior," *NeuroImage* 47 (2009): 353–59.

190 **"It is only those from an explicit tradition":** Harris Bond, *Beyond the Chinese Face*, 53.

190 *taijin kyofusho:* Carl Elliott, *Better Than Well: American Medicine Meets the American Dream* (New York: W. W. Norton, 2003), 71.

190 **Tibetan Buddhist monks find inner peace:** Marc Kaufman, "Meditation Gives Brain a Charge, Study Finds," *Washington Post*, January 3, 2005.

190 **"Their civility has been well documented":** Lydia Millet, "The Humblest of Victims," *New York Times*, August 7, 2005.

190 **Westernization of the past several decades:** See, for example, Xinyin Chen et al., "Social Functioning and Adjustment in Chinese Children: The Imprint of Historical Time," *Child Development* 76, no. 1 (2005): 182–95.

193 **One study comparing European-American:** C. S. Huntsinger and P. E. Jose, "A Longitudinal Investigation of Personality and Social Adjustment Among Chinese American and European American Adolescents," *Child Development* 77, no. 5 (2006): 1309–24. Indeed, the same thing seems to be happening to Chinese kids *in China* as the country Westernizes, according to a series of longitudinal studies measuring changes in social attitudes. While shyness was associated with social and academic achievement for elementary school children as recently as 1990, by 2002 it predicted peer rejection and even depression. See Chen, "Social Functioning and Adjustment in Chinese Children."

194 **The journalist Nicholas Lemann:** "Jews in Second Place," *Slate*, June 25, 1996.

196 **"A . . . E . . . U . . . O . . . I":** These vowels were presented out of the usual sequence at Preston Ni's seminar.

197 **Gandhi was, according to his autobiography:** The story of Gandhi related in this chapter comes primarily from *Gandhi: An Autobiography: The Story of My Experiments with Truth* (Boston: Beacon Press, 1957), esp. 6, 20, 40–41, 59, 60–62, 90–91.

200 **The TIMSS exam:** I originally learned about this from Malcom Gladwell, *Outliers: The Story of Success* (New York: Little Brown and Company, 2008).

200 **In 1995, for example, the first year the TIMSS was given:** "Pursuing Excellence: A Study of U.S. Eighth-Grade Mathematics and Science Teaching, Learning Curriculum, and Achievement in International Context, Initial Findings from the Third International Mathematics and Science Study," U.S. Department of Education, National Center for Education Statistics, Pursuing Excellence, NCES 97-198 (Washington, DC: U.S. Government Printing Office, 1996).

200 **In 2007, when researchers measured:** TIMSS Executive Summary. The nations whose students fill out more of the questionnaire also tend to have students who do well on the TIMSS test: Erling E. Boe et al., "Student Task Persistence in the Third International Mathematics and Science Study: A Major Source of Achievement Differences at the National, Classroom and Student Levels" (Research Rep. No. 2002-TIMSS1) (Philadelphia: University of Pennsylvania, Graduate School of Education, Center for Research and Evaluation in Social Policy). Note that this study was based on 1995 data.

201 **cross-cultural psychologist Priscilla Blinco:** Priscilla Blinco, "Task Persistence in Japanese Elementary Schools," in *Windows on Japanese Education*, edited by Edward R. Beauchamp (Westport, CT: Greenwood Press, 1991). Malcolm Gladwell wrote about this study in his book *Outliers*.

CHAPTER 9: WHEN SHOULD YOU ACT MORE EXTROVERTED THAN YOU REALLY ARE?

205 **Meet Professor Brian Little:** The stories about Brian Little throughout this chapter come from numerous telephone and e-mail interviews with the author between 2006 and 2010.

206 **Hippocrates, Milton, Schopenhauer, Jung:** Please see A Note on the Words *Introvert* and *Extrovert* for more on this point.

206 **Walter Mischel:** For an overview of the person-situation debate, see, for example, David C. Funder, *The Personality Puzzle* (New York: W. W. Norton, 2010), 118–44. See also Walter Mischel and Yuichi Shoda, "Reconciling Processing Dynamics and Personality Dispositions," *Annual Review of Psychology* 49 (1998): 229–58. In further support of the premise that there truly is such a thing as a fixed personality: We know now that people who score as introverts on personality tests tend to have different physiologies and probably inherit some different genes from those who measure as extroverts. We also know that personality traits predict an impressive variety of important life outcomes. If you're an extrovert, you're more likely to have a wide circle of friends, have risky sex, get into accidents, and excel at people-oriented work like sales, human resources, and teaching. (This doesn't mean that you *will* do these things—only that you're more *likely* than your typical introvert to do them.) If you're an introvert, you're more likely to excel in high school, in college, and in the land of advanced degrees, to have smaller social networks, to stay married to your original partner, and to pursue autonomous work like art, research, math, and engineering. Extroversion and introversion even predict the psychological challenges you might face: depression and anxiety for introverts

(think Woody Allen); hostility, narcissism, and overconfidence for extroverts (think Captain Ahab in *Moby-Dick*, drunk with rage against a white whale).

In addition, there are studies showing that the personality of a seventy-year-old can be predicted with remarkable accuracy from early adulthood on. In other words, despite the remarkable variety of situations that we experience in a lifetime, our core traits remain constant. It's not that our personalities don't evolve; Kagan's research on the malleability of high-reactive people has singlehandedly disproved this notion. But we tend to stick to predictable patterns. If you were the tenth most introverted person in your high school class, your behavior may fluctuate over time, but you probably still find yourself ranked around tenth at your fiftieth reunion. At that class reunion, you'll also notice that many of your classmates will be more introverted than you remember them being in high school: quieter, more self-contained, and less in need of excitement. Also more emotionally stable, agreeable, and conscientious. All of these traits grow more pronounced with age. Psychologists call this process "intrinsic maturation," and they've found these same patterns of personality development in countries as diverse as Germany, the UK, Spain, the Czech Republic, and Turkey. They've also found them in chimps and monkeys.

This makes evolutionary sense. High levels of extroversion probably help with mating, which is why most of us are at our most sociable during our teenage and young adult years. But when it comes to keeping marriages stable and raising children, having a restless desire to hit every party in town may be less useful than the urge to stay home and love the one you're with. Also, a certain degree of introspection may help us age with equanimity. If the task of the first half of life is to put yourself out there, the task of the second half is to make sense of where you've been.

207 **social life is performance:** See, for example, Carl Elliott, *Better Than Well: American Medicine Meets the American Dream* (New York: W. W. Norton, 2003), 47.

207 **Jack Welch advised in a *BusinessWeek*:** Jack Welch, "Release Your Inner Extrovert," *BusinessWeek* online, November 26, 2008.

209 **Free Trait Theory:** For an overview of Free Trait Theory, see, for example, Brian R. Little, "Free Traits, Personal Projects, and Ideo-Tapes: Three Tiers for Personality Psychology," *Psychological Inquiry* 7, no. 4 (1996): 340–44.

210 **"To thine own self be true":** Actually, this advice comes not so much from Shakespeare as from his character Polonius in *Hamlet*.

212 **research psychologist named Richard Lippa:** Richard Lippa, "Expressive Control, Expressive Consistency, and the Correspondence Between Ex-

pressive Behavior and Personality," *Journal of Behavior and Personality* 36, no. 3 (1976): 438–61. Indeed, psychologists have found that some people who claim not to be shy in a written questionnaire are quite adept at concealing those aspects of shyness that they can control consciously, such as talking to members of the opposite sex and speaking for long periods of time. But they often "leak" their shyness unwittingly, with tense body postures and facial expressions.

212 **psychologists call "self-monitoring":** Mark Snyder, "Self-Monitoring of Expressive Behavior," *Journal of Personality and Social Psychology* 30, no. 4 (1974): 526–37.

213 **experience less stress while doing so:** Joyce E. Bono and Meredith A. Vey, "Personality and Emotional Performance: Extraversion, Neuroticism, and Self-Monitoring," *Journal of Occupational Health Psychology*" 12, no. 2 (2007): 177–92.

219 **"Restorative niche" is Professor Little's term:** See, for example, Brian Little, "Free Traits and Personal Contexts: Expanding a Social Ecological Model of Well-Being," in *Person-Environment Psychology: New Directions and Perspectives*, edited by W. Bruce Walsh et al. (Mahwah, NJ: Lawrence Erlbaum Associates, 2000).

220 **"a Free Trait Agreement":** See, for example, Brian Little and Maryann F. Joseph, "Personal Projects and Free Traits: Mutable Selves and Well Beings," in *Personal Project Pursuit: Goals, Action, and Human Flourishing*, edited by Brian R. Little et al. (Mahwah, NJ: Lawrence Erlbaum Associates, 2007), 395.

223 **"Emotional labor":** Howard S. Friedman, "The Role of Emotional Expression in Coronary Heart Disease," in *In Search of the Coronary-Prone: Beyond Type A*, edited by A. W. Siegman et al. (Hillsdale, NJ: Lawrence Erlbaum Associates, 1989), 149–68.

223 **people who suppress negative emotions:** Melinda Wenner, "Smile! It Could Make You Happier: Making an Emotional Face—or Suppressing One—Influences Your Feelings," *Scientific American Mind*, October 14, 2009, http://www.scientificamerican.com/article.cfm?id=smile-it-could-make-you-happier.

CHAPTER 10: THE COMMUNICATION GAP

226 **people who value intimacy highly:** Randy J. Larsen and David M. Buss, *Personality Psychology: Domains of Knowledge About Human Nature* (New York: McGraw-Hill, 2005), 353.

226 **"Extroverts seem to need people as a forum":** E-mail from William Graziano to the author, July 31, 2010.

227 **In a study of 132 college students:** Jens B. Aspendorf and Susanne Wilpers, "Personality Effects on Social Relationships," *Journal of Personality and Social Psychology* 74, no. 6 (1998): 1531–44.

227 **so-called Big Five traits:** Agreeableness is defined later in this chapter. "Openness to Experience" measures curiosity, openness to new ideas, and appreciation for art, invention, and unusual experiences; "Conscientious" people are disciplined, dutiful, efficient, and organized; "Emotional Stability" measures freedom from negative emotions.

227 **sit them down in front of a computer screen:** Benjamin M. Wilkowski et al., "Agreeableness and the Prolonged Spatial Processing of Antisocial and Prosocial Information," *Journal of Research in Personality* 40, no. 6 (2006): 1152–68. See also Daniel Nettle, *Personality: What Makes You the Way You Are* (New York: Oxford University Press, 2007), chapter on agreeableness.

227 **equally likely to be agreeable:** Under the "Big Five" definitions of personality, extroversion and agreeableness are by definition orthogonal. See, for example, Colin G. DeYoung et al., "Testing Predictions from Personality Neuroscience: Brain Structure and the Big Five," *Psychological Science* 21, no. 6 (2010): 820–28: "Agreeableness appears to identify the collection of traits related to altruism: one's concern for the needs, desires, and rights of others (as opposed to one's enjoyment of others, which appears to be related primarily to Extraversion)."

230 **latter are "confrontive copers":** See, for example: (1) Donald A. Loffredo and Susan K. Opt, "Argumentation and Myers-Briggs Personality Type Preferences," paper presented at the National Communication Association Convention, Atlanta, GA; (2) Rick Howard and Maeve McKillen, "Extraversion and Performance in the Perceptual Maze Test," *Personality and Individual Differences* 11, no. 4 (1990): 391–96; (3) Robert L. Geist and David G. Gilbert, "Correlates of Expressed and Felt Emotion During Marital Conflict: Satisfaction, Personality, Process and Outcome," *Personality and Individual Differences* 21, no. 1 (1996): 49–60; (4) E. Michael Nussbaum, "How Introverts Versus Extroverts Approach Small-Group Argumentative Discussions," *The Elementary School Journal* 102, no. 3 (2002): 183–97.

230 **An illuminating study by the psychologist William Graziano:** William Graziano et al., "Extraversion, Social Cognition, and the Salience of Aversiveness in Social Encounters," *Journal of Personality and Social Psychology* 49, no. 4 (1985): 971–80.

231 **robots interacted with stroke patients:** See Jerome Groopman, "Robots That Care," *The New Yorker*, November 2, 2009. See also Adriana Tapus and Maja Mataric, "User Personality Matching with Hands-Off Robot for

Post-Stroke Rehabilitation Therapy," in *Experimental Robotics*, vol. 39 of *Springer Tracts in Advance Robotics* (Berlin: Springer, 2008), 165–75.

231 **University of Michigan business school study:** Shirli Kopelman and Ashleigh Shelby Rosette, "Cultural Variation in Response to Strategic Emotions in Negotiations," *Group Decision and Negotiation* 17, no. 1 (2008): 65–77.

232 **In her book *Anger*:** Carol Tavris, *Anger: The Misunderstood Emotion* (New York: Touchstone, 1982).

233 **catharsis hypothesis is a myth:** Russell Geen et al., "The Facilitation of Aggression by Aggression: Evidence against the Catharsis Hypothesis," *Journal of Personality and Social Psychology* 31, no. 4 (1975): 721–26. See also Tavris, *Anger*.

233 **people who use Botox:** Carl Zimmer, "Why Darwin Would Have Loved Botox," *Discover*, October 15, 2009. See also Joshua Ian Davis et al., "The Effects of BOTOX Injections on Emotional Experience," *Emotion* 10, no. 3 (2010): 433–40.

236 **thirty-two pairs of introverts and extroverts:** Matthew D. Lieberman and Robert Rosenthal, "Why Introverts Can't Always Tell Who Likes Them: Multitasking and Nonverbal Decoding," *Journal of Personality and Social Psychology* 80, no. 2 (2006): 294–310.

237 **It requires a kind of mental multitasking:** Gerald Matthews and Lisa Dorn, "Cognitive and Attentional Processes in Personality and Intelligence," in *International Handbook of Personality and Intelligence*, edited by Donald H. Saklofske and Moshe Zeidner (New York: Plenum, 1995), 367–96.

237 **interpreting what the other person is saying:** Lieberman and Rosenthal, "Why Introverts Can't Always Tell Who Likes Them."

238 **experiment by the developmental psychologist Avril Thorne:** Avril Thorne, "The Press of Personality: A Study of Conversations Between Introverts and Extraverts," *Journal of Personality and Social Psychology* 53, no. 4 (1987): 718–26.

CHAPTER 11: ON COBBLERS AND GENERALS

Some of the advice in this chapter is based on interviews I conducted with many caring teachers, school administrators, and child psychologists, and on the following wonderful books:

Elaine Aron, *The Highly Sensitive Child: Helping Our Children Thrive When the World Overwhelms Them* (New York: Broadway Books), 2002.

Bernardo J. Carducci, *Shyness: A Bold New Approach* (New York: Harper Paperbacks, 2000).

Natalie Madorsky Elman and Eileen Kennedy-Moore, *The Unwritten Rules of Friendship* (Boston: Little Brown, 2003).

Jerome Kagan and Nancy Snidman, *The Long Shadow of Temperament* (Cambridge, MA: Harvard University Press, 2004).

Barbara G. Markway and Gregory P. Markway, *Nurturing the Shy Child* (New York: St. Martin's Press, 2005).

Kenneth H. Rubin, *The Friendship Factor* (New York: Penguin, 2002).

Ward K. Swallow, *The Shy Child: Helping Children Triumph Over Shyness* (New York: Time Warner, 2000).

241 **Mark Twain once told a story:** This comes from Donald Mackinnon, who believed (but was not 100 percent certain) that Mark Twain told this story. See Donald W. MacKinnon, "The Nature and Nurture of Creative Talent," (Walter Van Dyke Bingham Lecture given at Yale University, New Haven, CT, April 11, 1962).

241 **this cautionary tale . . . by Dr. Jerry Miller:** I conducted several in-person and e-mail interviews with Dr. Miller between 2006 and 2010.

246 **Emily Miller:** I conducted several interviews with Emily Miller between 2006 and 2010.

247 **Elaine Aron:** Elaine N. Aron, *Psychotherapy and the Highly Sensitive Person* (New York: Routledge, 2010), 18–19.

249 **Dr. Kenneth Rubin:** Rubin, *The Friendship Factor*.

253 **"very little is made available to that learner":** Jill D. Burruss and Lisa Kaenzig, "Introversion: The Often Forgotten Factor Impacting the Gifted," *Virginia Association for the Gifted Newsletter* 21, no. 1 (1999).

255 **Experts believe that negative public speaking:** Gregory Berns, *Iconoclast: A Neuroscientist Reveals How to Think Differently* (Boston, MA: Harvard Business Press, 2008), 77.

255 **Extroverts tend to like movement:** Isabel Myers et al., *MBTI Manual: A Guide to the Development and Use of the Myers-Briggs Type Indicator*, 3rd ed., 2nd printing (Palo Alto, CA: Consulting Psychologists Press, 1998), 261–62. See also Allen L. Hammer, ed., *MBTI Applications: A Decade of Research on the Myers-Briggs Type Indicator* (Palo Alto, CA: Consulting Psychologists Press, 1996).

255 **prerequisite to talent development:** See chapter 3, especially on the work of Anders Ericsson.

256 **"they are usually very comfortable talking with one or two of their classmates":** E-mail from Roger Johnson to the author, June 14, 2010.

256 **Don't seat quiet kids in "high interaction" areas:** James McCroskey, "Quiet Children in the Classroom: On Helping Not Hurting," *Communication Education* 29 (1980).

258 **being popular isn't necessary:** Rubin, *The Friendship Factor*: "Research findings do not suggest that popularity is the golden route to all manner of good things. There simply is not much evidence that it guarantees social or academic success in adolescence, young adulthood, or later life. . . . If your child finds one other child to befriend, and the pair clearly have fun together and enjoy each other's company and are supportive companions, good for him. Stop worrying. Not every child needs to be part of a big, happy gang. Not every child needs many friends; for some, one or two will do."

259 **intense engagement in and commitment to an activity:** I. McGregor and Brian Little, "Personal Projects, Happiness, and Meaning: On Doing Well and Being Yourself," *Journal of Personality and Social Psychology* 74, no. 2 (1998): 494–512.

263 **the psychologist Dan McAdams:** Jack J. Bauer, Dan P. McAdams, and Jennifer L. Pals, "Narrative Identity and Eudaimonic Well-Being," *Journal of Happiness Studies* 9 (2008): 81–104.

A NOTE ON THE WORDS *INTROVERT* AND *EXTROVERT*

270 **the anthropologist C. A. Valentine:** C. A. Valentine, "Men of Anger and Men of Shame: Lakalai Ethnopsychology and Its Implications for Sociological Theory," *Ethnology* no. 2 (1963): 441–77. I first learned about this article from David Winter's excellent textbook, *Personality: Analysis and Interpretation of Lives* (New York: McGraw-Hill, 1996).

270 **Aristotle:** *Aristoteles, Problematica Physica* XXX, 1 (Bekker 953A 10 ff.), as translated in Jonathan Barnes, *The Complete Works of Aristotle, the Revised Oxford Translation II* (Princeton, N.J.: Bollingen, 1984).

271 **John Milton:** Cited in David G. Winter, *Personality: Analysis and Interpretation of Lives* (New York: McGraw-Hill, 1996), 380–84.

271 **Schopenhauer:** Arthur Schopenhauer, "Personality, or What a Man Is," in *The Wisdom of Life and Other Essays* (New York and London: Dunne, 1901), 12–35 (original work published 1851); cited in Winter, *Personality*, 384–86.

Index

He just wanted a decent book to read ...

Not too much to ask, is it? It was in 1935 when Allen Lane, Managing Director of Bodley Head Publishers, stood on a platform at Exeter railway station looking for something good to read on his journey back to London. His choice was limited to popular magazines and poor-quality paperbacks – the same choice faced every day by the vast majority of readers, few of whom could afford hardbacks. Lane's disappointment and subsequent anger at the range of books generally available led him to found a company – and change the world.

'We believed in the existence in this country of a vast reading public for intelligent books at a low price, and staked everything on it'
Sir Allen Lane, 1902–1970, founder of Penguin Books

The quality paperback had arrived – and not just in bookshops. Lane was adamant that his Penguins should appear in chain stores and tobacconists, and should cost no more than a packet of cigarettes.

Reading habits (and cigarette prices) have changed since 1935, but Penguin still believes in publishing the best books for everybody to enjoy. We still believe that good design costs no more than bad design, and we still believe that quality books published passionately and responsibly make the world a better place.

So wherever you see the little bird – whether it's on a piece of prize-winning literary fiction or a celebrity autobiography, political tour de force or historical masterpiece, a serial-killer thriller, reference book, world classic or a piece of pure escapism – you can bet that it represents the very best that the genre has to offer.

Whatever you like to read – trust Penguin.